W9-DEC-503

Professor Hamilton and his colleagues in the English Department of the University of Queensland have presented a challenging and eminently readable collection of critical essays which make a significant contribution to the understanding and appreciation of this vital and popular aspect of Australian literature.

Studies
in the
Recent Australian
Novel

10672

WITHDRAWN

PR
9609.2
.S74

Studies
in the
Recent Australian
Novel

Edited by K. G. Hamilton

From the Australian Studies
Centre, University of Queensland

BIP 88
BCL 3

University of Queensland Press

GOSHEN COLLEGE LIBRARY
GOSHEN, INDIANA

WITHDRAWN

© University of Queensland Press, St Lucia, Queensland, 1978

This book is copyright. Apart from any fair dealing for the purposes of private study, research, criticism, or review, as permitted under the Copyright Act, no part may be reproduced by any process without written permission. Enquiries should be made to the publishers.

Typeset, printed and bound by Academy Press Pty Ltd, Brisbane

Distributed in the United Kingdom, Europe, the Middle East, Africa, and the Caribbean by Prentice-Hall International, International Book Distributors Ltd, 66 Wood Lane End, Hemel Hempstead, Herts., England

National Library of Australia
Cataloguing-in-Publication data

Studies in the recent Australia novel.

ISBN 0 7022 1247 4

1. Australian fiction—History and criticism—
Addresses, essays, lectures. I. Hamilton,
Kenneth Gordon, 1921—, ed.

A823.03

Contents

Foreword

This book had its origins in a common interest in the Australian novel among members of the staff of the English Department of the University of Queensland. It was planned to present a number of individual viewpoints but, unlike most volumes of this type, to subject these viewpoints to intensive scrutiny by the whole group before their final presentation in the book. Each chapter as it stands is finally the responsibility of the individual author, but in accepting this responsibility the writer has had the advantage, throughout the whole period of composition, of the sometimes trenchant criticism of his or her fellow contributors.

The book is not intended as a history of the post-war novel. It is rather a series of "essays", in the basic sense of attempts on, or approaches to such a history through some of its major aspects. The choice of aspects to be attempted was largely determined by what seemed most fruitful; but it also reflects to an extent the personal interests, even eccentricities, of the contributors, and this must be taken into account in any endeavour to understand the rationale of the volume.

The decision was taken to make individual novels rather than novelists the basis of the work, and to emphasize more recent work—from, say, 1965 onwards—using for preference the most recent publication of any particular novelist. A series of eight chapters was planned, each devoted to a single novel. In the event, however, this plan came to need some modification.

Xavier Herbert's massive *Poor Fellow My Country*, published just as the book was being planned, was an obvious choice, as was Patrick White's *The Eye of the Storm*. Thomas Keneally was accepted as a strong candidate for inclusion, but the choice of a particular novel was less obvious. *The Chant of Jimmie Blacksmith* was chosen mainly because of the belief that it was the best of his more recent work, but partly also because of its Australian setting. Randolph Stow was a slightly less clear choice; but only because he had not published since 1965, and it was decided that his importance was such that we should go outside our original guidelines. The choice of the slightly earlier *Tourmaline*, rather than Stow's latest novel, *The Merry-Go-Round in the Sea*, was largely a matter of the personal preference of the contributor concerned.

Beyond this, decisions became much more difficult. There seemed to remain, after these four, a large number of novels among which the choice of only a further four would be quite arbitrary. It was decided, therefore, to depart from the original plan in a way that would allow for the inclusion of more than four novels in the remaining four chapters, to this extent reducing, though not altogether eliminating, the element of abitrariness—indeed it might be felt that a new element of arbitrariness has been introduced in the linking of novels within these chapters.

Martin Boyd and Christina Stead were two novelists whose standing throughout the period since the 1930s was such that they could not well be ignored. Little seemed to link them except their contemporaneousness, and the fact that both had done most of their work as expatriates. However, when it was decided to pass over their latest novels and go back instead to *A Difficult Young Man*, the basic work of Boyd's "Langton" series, and *The People with the Dogs*, one of the less well known of Stead's American novels, some interesting grounds for comparison did appear. Some justification for this particular choice of novels is attempted in the relevant chapter.

George Johnston and Hal Porter appealed as giving an opportunity to look at a particular phenomenon of the Australian novel—the autobiographical element, whether it be fiction under the guise of autobiography, or autobiography under the guise of fiction—while at the same time looking at two writers obviously deserving of attention. In each case a trilogy was available—itself another common occurrence —and the choice fell on *Clean Straw for Nothing* and *The Paper Chase*.

A final chapter covering some of the experimental work in the novel form in the seventies seemed reasonable. This left a number of novels to be linked together in a chapter whose *raison d'être* I must leave the chapter itself to define; though it is just possible that the reader will find this as much in the personality of the author of the chapter as in any qualities of the novels themselves—something which, of course, may apply to an extent to other chapters as well.

By these devices then the original plan for eight novels has been increased to sixteen. None the less, there will still be novels that readers will feel have been overlooked, and I would stress that inclusion, or omission, does not always necessarily carry connotations of relative worth. Thea Astley is one name which there was general agreement might well have been included, but even with the very loose groupings adopted, no satisfactory means of including her work was apparent.

To provide a context for the essays that follow, a historical sketch of the Australian novel during the period roughly 1930–76 has been attempted. Mainly dealing with facts, concerning both the Australian novel and, to a limited extent, its literary and social milieu, this sketch should be helpful to those not fully familiar with the field. It is, however, intended as something less than a history.

K.G.H.
St Lucia,
May 1977

A Prefatory Sketch

If one were asked to name a holy trinity of Australian novels published before 1930, then the answer would certainly be Marcus Clarke's *His Natural Life* (1874), Joseph Furphy's *Such Is Life* (1903), and Henry Handel Richardson's trilogy, *The Fortunes of Richard Mahony* (1917, 1925, and 1929). These at least would have to be saved from the everlasting bonfire.

Different as they are, these three novels have something in common—something, moreover, which is the basis of their lasting importance. Clarke shows us conditions and events battering a man who can do little more than resist with a stubborn integrity; Furphy's characters both change circumstances and are changed by them; Richardson's Mahony becomes the reader's chief concern, not merely because he is the chief character but because the complexity of his temperament preoccupies the reader. With Clarke and Furphy the background is important: without the peculiarly local settings, the Tasmanian convict system and the Riverina, *His Natural Life* and *Such Is Life* could not exist. With Richardson, despite the pictures of the diggings, of Melbourne life, of small country towns, the background is less important. But equally for all three, even with different settings, the essential theme would still be available. This is significant, for man is more important than things—or rather man in his relationship to things is more important, at least to man, than things themselves—and it is because of their realization of this that these three works have lived, lasting evidence of the early maturity of the Australian novel.

No similar trinity is to be found in the years between 1930 and the end of World War II; for a comparable figure the literature had to wait until Patrick White's later novels offered their rich choices. This period lacks peaks; but its significance is considerable. It has at least sixteeen novelists whose names would demand mention in even a cursory sketch of our fiction. Six of these had published before 1930—Miles Franklin, Henry Handel Richardson, Katharine Susannah Prichard, Vance Palmer, Martin Boyd, and M. Barnard Eldershaw. And, except for Richardson, they were to write some of their best novels in this period. (Even William Gosse Hay, first appearing in 1901, issued an expiratory effort in 1937). Ten others who first published novels in this period are, in order of appearance, Frank Dalby Davison, Eleanor Dark, Leonard Mann, Helen Simpson, Brian Penton, Christina Stead, Kylie Tennant, Kenneth (Seaforth) Mackenzie, Xavier Herbert, and Patrick White. An impressive group of writers; indeed, from our position in the seventies we may question whether a comparable group of first novels in the fifteen years to, say, 1985, is likely to emerge. They are not the first to bring the Australian novel to prominence, but they consolidate its position—and, with the work of White, add the distinction of international recognition.

Leaving aside the few significant names and, at the opposite end of the scale, a spate of urban novels by three distinctly minor writers—Ada Cambridge, Jessie Couvreur, and Rosa Praed—the novelists of the period from 1830 to 1930 looked mostly at the oddities of their environment, present or past—flora and fauna, aboriginality, convictism, bushranging, pioneering, pastoral life. They described the externals they saw or the externals they remembered or read about. They looked very little at their own lives. The trend of the fifteen years after 1930 is different. Only three of the ten new novelists, for instance, wrote historical novels—Dark, Simpson, and Penton—an indication of maturity, one may think; for proliferation of historical fiction in a period suggests uncertainty in the consciousness of national identity. The accounts of externals, too, are different. The last century tended to deal with such things because they were new and surprising; this period portrays them because they are familiar. Nor are they introduced for their own sake: they serve a functional purpose in the fictional structure. What had been true of the Australian novel only at its highest levels becomes more nearly its general rule.

These novelists then differ from all but the best who preceded them. They differ also from one another. Even contentious, if defensible, potted comments serve to underline their variety—the empathetic sympathy of Davison, the earlier tortuosity and later panoramic sweep of Dark, the psychological stresses of Mann, the deceptive ease of Simpson's lucid and even brilliant style, the implacable brutalities of Penton, the inexhaustible cumulative detail of Stead, the ironic humorous sympathy and political awareness of Tennant, the richly multitudinous farrago of Herbert, the delicate probings of Mackenzie, the complex symbolism and intricate nuances of White. But along with such differences they have a common interest in people, in the individual human being; and even more in the web of social relationships that enmesh them. They are social novelists, and for this reason they seem to belong to a "modern" period. Some passages from Ada Cambridge may have a tart subtlety in analysis of character and motive that is not bettered by these novelists of the thirties; but the patina of older customs —dress, manners, speech, and outlook—is so thick in Cambridge that the gap between even her later work and that of these writers twenty or thirty years afterwards seems unbridgeable. Nobody wrote or would wish to write in her fashion a generation after her. However, it should be said that this aspect of "modernism" entails a difference in theme, and more particularly of a choice of stress within that theme; it does not entail at this time any noticeable modernity in structure or stylistic methods. Apart from Stead and White, these novelists seem unaware of what happened in English fiction in the 1920s.

The extent to which they depict the Australian world and life of their time varies from member to member of the group. But there are two omissions that may seem either unexpected or remarkable or both. The reasons for the omissions are hypothetical. The writers may have felt constrained by their interest in the individual human personality, an interest felt by all. Some, or perhaps most, of them may have felt or recognized there were some themes lying beyond their normal provenance or perhaps capacity. Or that the themes may have required, so to speak, a period for emotional assimilation before any use could be made of them in fiction. These two themes were, of course, the Great Depression and World War II, which in their world-wide impact spared no nation. Except for Tennant, and Barnard Eldershaw's later *Tomorrow and Tomorrow* (1947), any of the group using the Depression uses it almost incidentally: it is there, it affects certain characters, but the stress is not on the economic and humanly disastrous consequences or the nationally traumatic changes in outlook. Even Tennant, with political sympathies strongly felt, uses it mostly as a sort of backdrop, a varied landscape through which her vivid oddities find their way. In scope and vision and intensity there is nothing to compare, for instance, with John Steinbeck's *The Grapes of Wrath* (1939). As for World War II, the only novel from the group to deal directly with it was written outside this period— Mackenzie's *Dead Men Rising* (1951)—and the setting lay in Australia in a camp for Japanese prisoners of war. It is interesting that the omissions are rectified (if that is the right word) in the poetry and short stories of the period. And, in any case, the position may only be made to seem apparent by a perhaps arbitrary choice of significant writers. There *were* novels on the theme of the war—by, for example, Lawson Glassop, Russell Braddon, and T.A.G. Hungerford.

The period has one last importance. This does not directly derive from the novelists, though their work can be adduced as pointing to a need, to an earlier and continuing lack of national awareness of our writing. It was during this period that Australian literature attracted an increasing amount of critical attention in this country. It witnessed, for instance, the appearance of the first history of the literature in H.M. Green's trail-blazing little volume in 1930, *An Outline of Australian Literature*. There had been partial studies before, but nothing that could be called a history of Australian literature to the date of publication. This was followed by other books dealing with various aspects—regional with H.A. Kellow's *Queensland Poets* (1930), temporal with Arthur

Jose's *Romantic Nineties* (1933), cultural in P.R. Stephensen's *Foundations of Culture in Australia* (1936), selective with M. Barnard Eldershaw's *Essays in Australian Fiction* (1938), T. Inglis Moore's *Six Australian Poets* (1942), and H.M. Green's *Fourteen Minutes* (1944). But the really momentous publication was Morris Miller's *Australian Literature* (1940). With whatever faults, pointed out with some relish by reviewers, it still remains an essential reference work, and its mere bulk of detail is a treasure house: it is, so to speak, reassuring and heart-warming to learn that our literature is full of endlessly interesting—not to say odd— writers and relationships.

Together with these appeared critical and personal biographies of writers: A.G. Stephens (1933), Randolph Hughes (1934), and H. M. Green (1939) each produced his individual assessment of Christopher Brennan's life and work; E.E. Pescott (1938) wrote a life of Furphy, to be followed by the collaborative work of Miles Franklin and Kate Baker (1944); Stephensen (1940) and Palmer (1941) each dealt with A.G. Stephens; and Shaw Neilson had his tributes in the essays edited by J.K. Moir (1942) and the memoir by James Devaney (1944).

Literary periodicals had begun early last century, and with varying success and length of life. The same fate exercised its erratic sway in this period over the destinies of such magazines as *Desiderata* (1929-39), *Manuscripts* (1931-35), the *Australian Mercury* (1935), *Southerly* (1939-), *Angry Penguins* (1940-46), *Meanjin* (1940-), and *Barjai* (1943-47).

The importance of literature was recognized in other ways. The Commonwealth government provided money in 1940 to establish a series of Literary Fund lectures on Australian literature, which were given annually in the various states. S.J. Baker in 1945 issued the first version of what was to be for some years the definitive account of the English language in Australia. Perhaps most indicative of all, J.A. Ferguson published (1941) the first volume of his monumental *Bibliography of Australia*, which covered the period 1784-1830. Three more volumes (in 1945, 1951, and 1955) brought up to 1850 his elaborated listing of books published in Australia and of books dealing with Australia published elsewhere.

(Three later volumes covered the period 1850–1900, but only selectively.)

The thirties and early forties, then, may be said to have established, both by its fiction and by its scholarly attentions, that Australian literature has its significance. The serious study of it, in fact, dates from somewhere in the period. From then on it has been and continues to be, for better or worse, an academic as well as a popular subject of attention.

The second half of the forties produced very few new novelists—most of the relatively small number of novels published in these years immediately after the war were by well-established, older novelists. Of the new novelists only Robert Close (*Love Me Sailor*, 1945), Morris West (*Moon in My Pocket* by "Julian Morris", 1945), Jon Cleary (*You Can't See Round Corners*, 1947), and Frank Hardy (*Power Without Glory*, 1950) are worth mentioning and still worth reading. None could be regarded as extending the frontiers of the Australian novel, though they all attracted popular attention: Morris West made the international best-seller lists; Hardy and Cleary subsequently saw their books produced on Australian television; Close and Hardy earned court appearances for their work.

These years saw the arts before the Bench and before the delighted public gaze as the butt of some characteristic anti-intellectual contempt on several occasions. In 1944 the "Ern Malley" hoax (and its attendant obscenity trial) and the legal squabble over William Dobell's right to the Archibald Prize each, according to some commentators, put the cause of their moderately progressive movements back years. In 1948 Sumner Locke-Elliott's play *Rusty Bugles* was banned by the New South Wales chief secretary for its "indecent language"; for a similar offence in *Love Me Sailor*, Robert Close was imprisoned in Victoria. In 1951 Frank Hardy had to defend his *Power Without Glory* against a charge of libel.

In addition to this sort of internal nervousness there were other international signs that the recently won peace was a precarious one. There were the beginnings of atomic bomb tests, the Berlin blockade, the establishment of a rocket range in Australia (at Woomera), the McCarthy committee in the United States, and the outbreak of war in Korea. Within

Australia other developments were beginning which shaped society for the next quarter of a century. Between 1945 and 1949 the new immigration campaign (based on a nervous "populate or perish" thesis) brought half a million immigrants to Australia; the national economy flourished; the spread of suburbia (to accommodate the products of the postwar baby boom) began in earnest, and in 1948 the first Holden car was produced. In 1949 the Labor Party departed from the federal government for the next twenty-three years.

While the work of the new novelists did little to indicate new things for Australian fiction, the situation in poetry was strikingly different. Important first volumes by James McAuley and Judith Wright in 1946, Francis Webb in 1948, and David Campbell in 1949 established the most significant directions in Australian poetry for a decade or more to come. Each was, more or less, conservative, but each too demonstrated an interest in re-examining, in a way that a number of novelists have done subsequently, the notion of discovery of identity through myths and metaphors of national discovery and settlement. These first volumes were part of a burst of poetic activity at the end of the war which also included books by Douglas Stewart (1946, 1947), William Hart-Smith (1946, 1948), Rosemary Dobson (1948), R.D. FitzGerald (1949), Kenneth Slessor (1944), and Val Vallis (1947) as well as posthumous collections of Neilson, Daley, Harpur, and a volume by the eighty-year-old Mary Gilmore.

While it is not in the emergence of major new novelists that one finds any significant developments in Australian literature immediately after the war, there are a couple of other notable landmarks. There is, for instance, evidence of a survival of earlier literature and earlier literary values. This retrospective mood is apparent in the appearance of the posthumous poetry just mentioned, in Alec H. Chisholm's 1950 edition of C.J. Dennis (following his 1946 biography), in the publication of Furphy's novel *The Buln Buln and the Brolga* (1948) and in Richardson's posthumous *Myself When Young* (1948).

The scholarly output of these years presents no real highlights, but several introductory and general surveys by Colin Roderick and John K. Ewers undoubtedly reflected widening interest in the native literary product. The various posthumous publications just mentioned and much of the scholarship indicate a growing awareness, not always widely held in Australia, of the need to preserve the work of earlier writers. This mood is manifested in the most significant scholarly volumes of the period (as well as in the continuation of Ferguson's *Bibliography*, already mentioned); Bernard Smith's stimulating and influential essay about Australian art, *Place, Taste and Tradition* (1945), Vance Palmer's recognition of a major movement in the most neglected of the literary genres in Australia, *Louis Esson and the Australian Theatre* (1948), and the Percival Serle's monumental (in two senses) *Dictionary of Australian Biography* (1949). To these should be added Palmer's collection of *Old Australian Bush Ballads* (1951).

But, for years which at first glance appear to have been lean ones for the Australian novel, the actual achievement was remarkably solid. Most importantly there were major novels by three of the best modern Australian writers. Christina Stead, nearing the end of her most prolific years, produced *For Love Alone* (1944), *Letty Fox, Her Luck* (1946), and *A Little Tea, A Little Chat* (1948). While the latter two works contain little to extend her reputation, *For Love Alone* is undoubtedly one of her greatest novels— alongside *The Man Who Loved Children* (1940). It also links various elements in Australian literature, with its fine realistic social observation, its socio-economic awareness, its psychological insight, and its mythic extensions. Indeed the underlying myth, that of Odysseus, or the wanderer/voyager figure, is one that appears in the other two major novels of the period, Martin Boyd's *Lucinda Brayford* (1946) and Patrick White's *The Aunt's Story* (1948). It is also remarkable that all three novels are concerned with heroines who leave Australia and who, though concerned with their relationship to their birthplace, do not (at least within the narrative) return to it. Of these three novelists, White and Stead had published their first novel about ten years earlier and Boyd about twenty years earlier, but with these books of the mid-forties they undeniably "arrived" as major forces in Australian fiction.

Most of the other notable novelists who published in these years had more or less secure reputations: many indeed, in terms of interests, style, technique, and reputation, look back to a previous era. The two important trilogies that were begun in this period each has this quality. They were Katharine Susannah Prichard's "Goldfields" trilogy, *The Roaring Nineties* (1946), *Golden Miles* (1948), and *Winged Seeds* (1950); and Vance Palmer's "Donovan" trilogy, *Golconda* (1948), *Seedtime* (1957), and *The Big Fellow* (1959). Each, too, is political but in strikingly different ways: with Prichard, politics informs and directs the point of view; for Palmer it is the subject-matter, the fascinatingly related personal and political fortunes of the union organizer who becomes state premier.

Other survivors of the twenties and earlier included Miles Franklin and also Norman Lindsay, who completed, with *Halfway to Anywhere* (1947), the boisterous Ballarat boyhood trilogy begun with *Redheap* (1930) and *Saturdee* (1933). Indeed, the interest shown in the trilogy by novelists writing in this period is remarkable. In addition to those begun by Palmer and Prichard and concluded by Lindsay, there appeared also the middle volume of Eleanor Dark's historical trilogy, *The Timeless Land* (1941), *Storm of Time* (1948), and *No Barrier* (1953). Hal Porter and George Johnston, both of whom later produced autobiographical trilogies, published their first books in the 1940s. Of these two writers, Johnston was the more prolific, but his early works are of a stature and genre distinctly different from those for which he is well known, and of the several books appearing by 1950 only *High Valley* (1949), written in collaboration with his wife, Charmian Clift, is of much interest. The much more productive collaboration between Marjorie Barnard and Flora Eldershaw came to an end in 1947 with the last M. Barnard Eldershaw novel, *Tomorrow and Tomorrow*, a view, among other things, of the history of Sydney in the 1930s as seen by a young man writing in the closing years of the century. The previous year also witnessed the appearance (the book was written about forty years earlier) of the last novel to which Miles Franklin affixed her own name, *My Career Goes Bung*. Like so many authors of the period, these two notables are best remembered for their work in the historical novel genre such as *A House is Built* (1929), *All That Swagger* (1936) and the "Brent of Bin Bin" novels.

The 1950s began as a lean period for Australian fiction —and for Australian literature generally. Indeed, the decade was half over before the tide turned, although when it did the change was dramatic. Our major novelists were either not publishing (as in the case of Patrick White) or were working totally outside the Australian cultural and publishing context (as in the case of Christina Stead, whose *People with the Dogs* appeared in New York in 1952). Even Boyd, with two novels during the period to his credit—*The Cardboard Crown* (1952) and *A Difficult Young Man* (1955) —was outside the mainstream of what was happening in Australian fiction. His return to this country, with the intention of staying, had been short-lived, and he returned permanently to Europe in 1951. Both *The Cardboard Crown* and *A Difficult Young Man* are concerned with the rival claims and tensions of the old world and the new, and form the first two volumes of what has become known as the "Langton" series, a tetralogy not completed till 1962. For all of their at times infuriating preciousness, these novels speak deeply of such things as cultural heritage and spiritual harmony. They enjoyed considerable popularity in the south of England, but their readership and impact in Australia were not large. Indeed, Boyd's themes and style were curiously old-fashioned, even at the time he was writing. *A Difficult Young Man* ends in 1911, leaving one with the impression that Boyd preferred writing of a bygone age, with its assurance and ease, because the contemporary world was too terrible to contemplate. Certainly the contemporary world, and some of the most unpleasant aspects of it, was frequently the subject of novels by other Australian writers of the time. Frank Hardy's *Power Without Glory* (1950), with its exposé of the roughness and toughness of the political machine, stands at the head of a line of novels about the exploitation of the working class and the importance of political commitment.

Indeed, the relationship between what was happening in

Australian politics (and world politics, for that matter) and what was happening in the Australian novel and in Australian literature generally is of vital, if unclear, importance during the 1951–55 period. The victory of Menzies in 1949, at the height of the cold war, polarized political opinion in Australia. The attempts to outlaw the Communist Party, the participation in the Korean War, the Petrov "conspiracy", were brilliant electoral ploys which left the Labour Party and the socialist opposition generally disunited and dispirited, though aware that they were participants in a major struggle. There were a number of literary manifestations of this political polarization. The Australasian Book Society, founded in 1952, was designed to publish democratic literature, especially novels and stories, in a co-operative, self-help way. It had close links with the left of the Labour Party and with the Communist Party, and published novels by Judah Waten, *The Unbending* (1954), Eric Lambert, Ralph de Boissiere, and F.B. Vickers. At the same time the Realist Writers group in Melbourne (Frank Hardy was a prominent and revered member) produced their journal, *The Realist Writer* (1952–54), which was hard-line in both politics and literature. One of the editors, Stephen Murray-Smith, broke from the journal's Moscow orientation in 1954 to found *Overland* ("Temper, democratic; bias, offensively Australian"), and the right-wing Congress for Cultural Freedom responded in 1956 with *Quadrant*.

A more subtle manifestation of the politicization of Australian literature during this time comes from a consideration of the themes of a representative range of novels. Dymphna Cusack and Florence James's *Come in Spinner* (1951) was the forerunner of a number of novels about the corrupting influence of American soldiers in Sydney during the war. Gambling, drinking, prostitution are its recurrent concerns, as they are in Xavier Herbert's *Soldiers' Women*, not published till 1961 though written during this time. In *Southern Steel* (1953) Cusack writes of Newcastle during the war, of the American soldiers, and of the Sweetapple family, split between working for the war effort through the corporation that owns the steelworks and through the Communist Party, with its plans to nationalize all industry. Such political themes, using the novel as a part of political strategy, are perhaps the major hallmark of Australian fiction during this time. And though one does not object to ideology in fiction (it is present in all novels), the Australian social realists of the early fifties tended to allow ideology to swamp their art or, to put it a less kind way, attempted to cover up the paucity of their art with a veneer of ideology. Waten's *The Unbending*, one of the best of the Australasian Book Society novels, is concerned with a Jewish migrant family in Australia at the time of World War I. They are forced to take a stand on such issues as conscription and the radical role of the IWW (International Workers of the World) as well as come to terms with an entrenched community, suspicious of foreigners and Jews. Several elements in the book (for instance, the relationship between Hannah and her husband, the migrant couple) suggest material for another novel, for Waten is not completely successful in welding his "documentary" work to his character studies. Indeed, the former is often more interesting than the latter, suggesting perhaps that had the social realists stuck to their basic purpose of expressing the aims of the working class, they could have produced works of more even quality. As it is, Waten's picture of Australian class and racial prejudices veers off in the direction of D.H. Lawrence's concept of family politics and ends, like so many Lawrence novels, on a not very convincing note of hope.

Dal Stivens was never closely associated with the left-wing school of Australian novelists, but his *Jimmy Brockett* (1951), perhaps partly inspired by *Power Without Glory* (though it has American antecedents as well), fits well into their ideological framework. It is a mildly humorous study of a Sydney commercial and political boss in the 1920s, ruthlessly bent on building his empire of wealth and power. Two other novelists from the period are worth mentioning, for they lie somewhat outside this general picture. Kenneth Mackenzie had published two novels in the late thirties, before *Dead Men Rising* (1951) and *The Refuge* (1954). *Dead Men Rising* is a fictionalized account of the break-out from the Cowra prisoner-of-war camp by the Japanese in 1944. It suffers principally from centring its concerns on the guards, who are much less energetic and impassioned than the prisoners themselves. Among Australian novelists only Hal Porter, in some stories, and in *The Actors* (1968) or *The Paper Chase* (1966), has been able to write convincingly of Japanese ways. *The Refuge* is a more successful work, a variant on the emigrant theme, in which a refugee from European totalitarianism meets an Australian counterpart in the person of her lover, a Sydney journalist. Mackenzie's novels (he also published several volumes of verse) give the impression of talent which is never fulfilled. He does continue the trend towards realism, however, though his accounts of city life lack the ideological coherence and patterning of the socialist writers. Perhaps the potential of his art combined with their ideology could have produced the major novel the period lacks.

Tom Ronan's novels *Vision Splendid* (1954) and *Moleskin Midas* (1956) stand out as two of the few novels from the earlier fifties (apart from *The Tree of Man* and the first appearance of several Miles Franklin works written years before) which are concerned with life outside of the cities or towns. *Vision*, which won first prize in the Commonwealth Jubilee literary competition in 1951, traces the fortunes of Charles Toppingham in the Northern Territory during the twenties and thirties. No doubt partly inspired by *Capricornia* (it is interesting that both the sesquicentenary prize of 1938 and the jubilee prize of 1951 should go to novels about life in the Northern Territory), it is a racy, adventurous account of cattle musters, droughts, and drinking sprees and may have been at least partly concerned with "putting down" Herbert's account of racial and class inequality in the Territory. Ronan's "vision splendid" is largely one of blue skies and unlimited potential for those prepared to do a full day's work.

The five years 1950–54 were not a major period for local fiction in terms of the novels actually published. It was, however, a time of intense literary activity, and it is not altogether surprising that the next five years should have been a watershed in the recent development of Australian literature, as it was also in Australian history. The factors that produced this watershed in politics, culture, and literature were in each case international, national, and personal. This was a period in which international recognition came to Australia in many apparently unrelated fields, and Australia, as if attempting to prove the now-famous theory of the "cultural cringe"—a term coined at the time by A.A. Phillips in an essay in *Meanjin* (4/1950)—responded with the customary mixture of assertiveness and uncertainty. In politics the Australian prime minister, R.G. Menzies, had appeared as a statesman on the world stage in the Suez crisis, and the image of Australia as a world diplomatic power was briefly offered to an unsuspecting world. In the same year (1956) world attention was focused even more directly on Australia with the staging of the first Olympic Games to be held outside of Europe and North America. National fervour was aroused by the sight of Australian sportsmen winning the heats (though less frequently the finals) of a large number of events. Nevertheless, feature articles on Australia and its way of life appeared in most countries at this time. Coinciding with these events was the almost simultaneous awakening of interest in Patrick White and Sidney Nolan in London and the consequent attention paid to other Australian novelists, dramatists, and painters in the years that followed.

Within Australia the optimism, material growth, and political complacency and conservatism culminated in another Menzies victory in the election of 1958, which was based on the slogan "Australia Unlimited". This slogan was also the theme of numerous newspaper and magazine documentaries of this period and in subsequent years. This was now the "Lucky Country" that Donald Horne was to write about a few years later (1964). Another phenomenon, whose effect on the Australian novel has been debated often, was introduced (in Sydney) at the end of 1955—television. It is also arguable that other non-literary events of the early fifties had consequences for the Australian novel in this period. The unsuccessful referendum to have communism made illegal, the Petrov "spy" case, and the Labor Party "split" all had the result of discrediting the Left and the social–realist writers associated with it, or of inhibiting them, or of simply causing them to be too busy reorganizing in these years to have much time to write. For one reason or another, the late fifties saw the end of the social-realist hegemony over Australian fiction. As in politics (with Menzies) and painting (with Nolan) so in literature the personal achievement of Patrick White was the pre-eminent symbol of a new order. Many reviewers in fact commented on the significance of the almost simultaneous release in Australia of White's *Voss* and Vance Palmer's *Seedtime* (1957). It would be hard to imagine a more apposite pair of novels to highlight the watershed. The death of Vance Palmer in 1959 represented in many ways the end of an era for which he had been a leading spokesman, practitioner, and critic.

In other ways, too, this period seems, and was seen at the time to be, one of climactic importance for Australian literature. In 1955 there were quite startling new achievements in each of the three major genres: Patrick White's *The Tree of Man*, A.D. Hope's long awaited first volume (*The Wandering Islands*) and Ray Lawler's *Summer of the Seventeenth Doll*. The *Doll* was joint winner of the Playwrights' Advisory Board Prize, a considerable public and critical success, and was subsequently exported. With this play and three others, Richard Beynon's *The Shifting Heart* (1957), Peter Kenna's *The Slaughter of St. Teresa's Day* (1959), and Alan Seymour's *The One Day of the Year* (1960), the claims and concerns of an Australian vernacular drama were firmly established. All were remarkably popular though each offended some nationalistic or sectarian sensibilities by a robust approach to shibboleths and social interests. The combination of social concern and colloquial humour was not to be a feature of the novel for another ten years. However, like novels and paintings, Australian plays were proving to be a popular commodity in London. In 1957 four of the twenty five finalists in the *Observer* play competition were Australian, and the winner was Beynon's *The Shifting Heart*. The other notable achievement in drama was the establishment, in 1958, of the National Institute of Dramatic Art (NIDA), which gave formal academic recognition to the professional aspects of theatre.

These years are also notable for the struggle for academic recognition of Australian literature as a whole. This struggle centred on the campaign for a Chair of Australian Literature at the University of Sydney, actually established in 1961. The question "Is there any Australian literature worth studying?" was answered in the affirmative by numerous articles and public talks. By way of further confirmation, several journals, concerned with the subject in varying degrees, were begun: *Quadrant, Westerly, Hemisphere* (all 1956), *Australian Letters* (1957), *Nation, The Observer* (both 1958), *Australian Book Review*, and *Critic* (both 1961). Perhaps more important was the publication, all within five years, of the two standard literary histories, C.H. Hadgraft, *Australian Literature* (1960) and H.M. Green, *A History of Australian Literature* (1961); the standard literary bibliography, Miller and Macartney, *Australian Literature* (1956); and the national bibliography, *Australian National Bibliography*, (1961–). Russel Ward's *The Australian Legend*, A.A. Phillips's *The Australian Tradition* (both 1958), Bernard Smith's *European Vision and the South Pacific* (1960), and a number of retrospective poetry anthologies and collections of ballads and folksongs all reflected scholarly concern with the origins of our literary, cultural, and social traditions.

While there were a number of exciting new writers in this period, some of the most notable achievements were often by authors returning to publishing after a period of apparent inactivity. Xavier Herbert's *Seven Emus* (1959) came twenty-one years after *Capricornia*; White's two remarkable novels *The Tree of Man* (1955) and *Voss* (1957) were preceded by seven years of silence; Hal Porter's poems *The Hexagon* (1956) and his novel *A Handful of Pennies* (1958) were his first books for fourteen years. In poetry there were new volumes, after long pauses, from James McAuley and David Campbell.

There were nevertheless a number of new novelists of considerable promise and some achievement. The most important of these was Randolph Stow, whose *A Haunted Land* (1956), *The Bystander* (1957), and *To the Islands* (1958) demonstrated a great talent for the subtle combination of literary extravagance, psychological intensity, and a symbolic use of landscape surpassed only by the much older and more experienced White. The relationship of character and landscape, exploited by Stow with great ingenuity in each of these novels, culminates in the final words of Heriot in the third of them, "My soul is a strange country" and clearly puts Stow in the "country of the mind" school. This phrase of course derives from *Voss*, which, with *The Tree of Man*, shows White at his best in exploring the utmost of man's relationship, not to individual or to social man, but to himself and the universe through his peculiar experience of the Australian environment. Herbert's *Seven Emus*, concerned with Aboriginal traditions and the white man's ignorance and disrespect of them, might have been a more germane cousin of these novels by White and Stow had it not been distracted by its unsuccessful syntactical experimentation. As it is, it remains an interesting pointer to the way in which Herbert was to develop his particular version of this theme of "the country of the mind" much later in *Poor Fellow My Country*.

Most of the other new novelists of this period were conscious literary craftsmen. The most important, or at least the most promising, of them were three writers who each, like White and Stow, were already employing a style of considerable virtuosity in the interests of exploring individual minds of more than average sensitivity caught in social environments and personal relationships of more than average oppressiveness. They were Elizabeth Harrower (*Down in the City*, 1957), Christopher Koch (*The Boys in the Island*, 1958; revised edition, 1974), and Thea Astley (*Girl with a Monkey*, 1958). None has unequivocally fulfilled all of that early promise, though Astley has published, at fairly regular intervals, six more novels of increasing assurance. Koch's book, a fine study of the passage from adolescence to maturity which rates comparison with Australia's two other major contributions to this twentieth-century genre, Kenneth Mackenzie's *The Young Desire It* (1937) and Christina Stead's *For Love Alone*, was followed by only one more novel, the less successful *Across the Sea Wall* (1965). Harrower's subsequent output, *The Long Prospect* (1958) and *The Catherine Wheel* (1960), struggled with the problem that was increasingly Patrick White's also: the relationship between the sensitive outsider and the splenetically observed insiders. *The Catherine Wheel*, with its London setting, solves this problem in a most successful manner, but the lesson is not so effectively applied in her fourth (and last?) novel, *The Watch Tower* (1966).

There were two other quite different directions discernible in the Australian novel in the late 1950s. On the one hand there was the rise of the best-selling novels of John O'Grady ("Nino Culotta"), Morris West, and Nevil Shute. O'Grady's *They're a Weird Mob* (1957) obviously appealed to a popular taste eager for self-indulgent manifestations of the national character, a taste which had been satisfied less complacently in the vernacular drama already discussed, and which was one of the subjects of Ward's *Australian Legend* of the following year. At the same time, despite the apparent slackening of social–realist energy, there were still notable books from Kylie Tennant, Miles Franklin, Vance Palmer, Frank Hardy, and Ron Tullipan. Apart from the last of these, whose *Follow the Sun* was a first novel, the others all have a retrospective interest. The best of Tennant's novels in this period, *The Honey Flow* (1956), has the same blend of the picaresque, the sentimental, the sardonic, and an apologetic feminism as her Depression novels. In terms of her œuvre and in terms of the Australian novel it is not an advance but a repeat. Much the same can be said for the final novels of both Palmer, whose *The Big Fellow* (1959) was the last of a trilogy begun in 1948, and Franklin, whose *Gentleman at Gyang Gyang* (1956) was written nearly forty years earlier. Hardy's *Four-Legged Lottery* (1958) has the social indignation at a public evil which characterized *Power Without Glory* but not its rhetorical control or structural focus.

Throughout the fifties and the early sixties a rise in interest in Aboriginal themes and characters was discernible. There are, for example, such collections of legends as Alan Marshall's *People of Dreamtime*; Roland Robinson's *Legend and Dreaming*, and Rex Ingamell's *Aranda Boy*, all published in 1952. Among other novels in this group are D'Arcy Niland's *The Shiralee* (1955), Gavin Casey's *Snowball* (1958), Donald Stuart's *Yandy* (1959), Kylie Tennant's *Speak You So Gently* (1959), Nene Gare's *The Fringe Dwellers* (1961), Nan Chauncy's *Tangara* (1960), dealing with the Aborigines of Tasmania, and Leonard Mann's

Venus Half-Caste (1963). These may perhaps be seen as leading up to Colin Johnson's *Wild Cat Falling* (1965). The only novel by a writer of Aboriginal blood, this treats the problems of a displaced part-Aboriginal youth in Perth. It was a work of more promise than achievement, but because of its subject, seen from inside, it occupies an important place.

Patrick White's *Riders in the Chariot* and Xavier Herbert's *Soldiers' Women*, both appearing in 1961, were not only notable achievements by two of the most distinguished novelists but also signalled new directions for them and for the Australian novel. White had earlier shown his talent for satirical social observation in his counterpointing of the spiritual searches and transcendence of his leading characters against the clogging forces of social conformity, but in *Riders* he focused his social satire on contemporary Australian suburbia, wielding the lash too bitterly and heavily for some readers. In his later works he continued to attack suburbia but was to show some sympathy with its victims. Herbert's *Soldiers' Women* showed him turning from the outback (the far north) setting of *Capricornia* to Sydney and combining a savage social observation with an inquiry into man's chances of rising above the animal level. Love, as against spiritual transcendence in White, is Herbert's means of testing man's capacities and failures.

Both novelists in their different ways showed a spirited attempt to revive and transfigure social realism, by going beyond social documentation both thematically and technically. Both *Riders* and *Soldiers' Women* are highly patterned novels. The patterning shows itself in a complex structure of imagery and symbol through which (as well as through action) man's social life is explored and measured, and which lifts the novels above literal realism though they keep a grip on social detail. It could be argued that both novels are too highly patterned—perhaps in the case of White as a reaction away from the limitations of realism—but they were important in extending the range of the Australian novel. Both represented a claim for the spiritual capacities of man as a main concern of the novel and at the same time a claim of poetic language and artistic pattern as necessary for any deeply revealing picture of social life. White had already been influential in this direction through *The Aunt's Story*, *The Tree of Man*, and *Voss*, but the greater concentration on suburbia was new and was an interest that White was to develop and refine. *Soldiers' Women* was not favourably received on first publication, but though it may not have been an influence it was crucial in Herbert's own development towards the enormously ambitious *Poor Fellow My Country*.

Appearing in the same year (1961) as *Riders in the Chariot* and *Soldiers' Women* is another important novel, Hal Porter's *The Tilted Cross*. A poetic evocation of Australia's past and a re-interpretation of its life and myths, it is comparable to *Voss* (though without its metaphysical ambitions) and looks forward to Keneally's first main novel, *Bring Larks and Heroes*—like it, set in the convict era.

The other notable novels of the period 1961–65 fit within the two broad (and not always separable) categories of social realism and the exploration of the spiritual life, of which *The Fortunes of Richard Mahony* (1930) represented for many years a lone peak (though it also exemplified a combination of the two streams). Thea Astley brings to her social observation a sensitive style and deflating wit as well as a sympathetic understanding of the emotionally vulnerable, as in the young adolescent of *The Slow Natives* (1956). David Martin's *The Young Wife* (1962) is probably the best novel about European (non-British) migrants in Australia; he writes of them with realistic and psychological power, revealing their emotional turmoil and not simply their practical problems. Judah Waten in *Time of Conflict* (1961) treats the economically underprivileged during the Depression years with a similar fidelity to social experience but including the politicial element in the form of a character who turns to communism. The novels of Martin and Waten are set in Melbourne. Martin's *The Hero of Too* (1965) is a witty satire on Australian myth (focusing on the noble bushranger) and looks forward to similar comic deflations by Peter Mathers and Barry Oakley. George Turner in his Treelake series, *A Stranger and Afraid* (1961), *The Cupboard Under the Stairs* (1962), *Waste of Shame* (1965), and *The Lame Dog Man* (1967), deals with the pressures of social life on the individual in country towns and is today a neglected novelist.

The year 1963 saw the appearance of two notable autobiographies, Hal Porter's *The Watcher on the Cast-Iron Balcony* and Xavier Herbert's *Disturbing Element*. Up to this time autobiography was a form almost totally neglected by Australian novelists. Both autobiographies evoke the past in their attempts at self understanding, but in Porter the past becomes almost a subject in itself (as in many of his short stories); also, Porter was more interested in autobiography as a literary form (as shown also in his later continuations, *The Paper Chase*, 1966, and *The Extra*, 1975) than Herbert, who concentrated more on vividness of event than on loving, subtle evocation. The main influence of these works (and of Donald Horne's *The Education of Young Donald*, 1967) is perhaps to be seen in a crop of autobiographical novels of the early 1970s by younger writers. Some also appeared in the 1960s, either by way of influence or because the time was ripe in their personal development or the development of Australian fiction. Stow's latest novel *The Merry-Go-Round in the Sea* (1965), draws on his early life in Geraldton, on country stations, and in Perth and turns away from the interior, mystical explorations of *To the Islands* and *Tourmaline* (1963) to concentrate on the experiences of childhood and adolescence, though Stow's poetic talent shows no lessening. Of Keneally's two early novels preparatory to the final establishing of his reputation, *The Fear* (1965) is a gripping, if uneven novel of the experiences of a young boy; and the earlier *The Place at Whitton* (1964), a gothic thriller of memorable episodes, draws autobiographically on at least the scenes of Keneally's years in a seminary. George Johnston's *My Brother Jack* (1964) skilfully evokes through recollections of childhood and family life a vivid picture of Melbourne during World War I and after. In Johnston's two later works which complete a trilogy, *Clean Straw for Nothing* (1969) and *A Cartload of Clay* (1971), the autobiographical element and the personal search were to dominate the social picture (which was widened to include expatriate life). With Johnston we see the main and perhaps the only direct influence in the 1960s of Porter's first volume of accomplished autobiography.

Two important new literary journals appeared in 1963—*Australian Literary Studies* and *Southern Review*. Around the same time, evidence of international interest in Australian writing was provided by special numbers on Australian literature in the *London Magazine* (1962), the *Texas Quarterly* (1962), the *Literary Review* (1963), and the *Literary Criterion* (1964). Of somewhat similar interest are *The Commonwealth Pen* (edited by A.L. McLeod, 1961); J.P. Matthew's *Tradition in Exile* (1962), which explores relationships between nineteenth-century Australian and Canadian poetry; *The Pattern of Australian Culture* (edited by A.L. Macleod, 1963); and S.B. Liljegren's *Aspects of Australian in Contemporary Literature* (1962). Also at this time there was the influence of a spate of major work in Australian history—volume 1 of Manning Clark's *A History of Australia* (1962); Marjorie Barnard's *A History of Australia* (1962); Margaret Kiddle's *Men of Yesterday* (1961); J. C. Beaglehole's edition of *Joseph Bank's Endeavour Journal* (1962); Douglas Pike's *Australia: The Quiet Continent* (1962); Geoffrey Blainey's *The Rush that Never Ended* (1963), and Geoffrey Serle's *The Golden Age* (1963).

Although it produced no individual giants, the second half of the 1960s was an important time for the Australian novel. It was a time of comings and goings; three long careers were terminated and a number of new novelists appeared. It was a time of promise: the novel as a genre was buoyant (despite television), the society was becoming more self-conscious, and this was manifest in the novel by a new streak of satire. Finally, in the emergence of Thomas Keneally, Australia found its most important novelist to appear since the prematurely silent Randolph Stow.

Of the established writers, few if any produced their best work in these years. After turning for a time in the early 1960s to the drama, Patrick White returned to the novel to continue his exploration of mystical value, in apparently nondescript lives in *The Solid Mandala* (1966) and in an extraordinary life in *The Vivisector* (1970), but neither of these has all the sweep and command of his previous four novels. Christina Stead broke a long silence with *Cotter's England* (1966), but again this does not develop the power that one finds in her novels of two decades earlier, such as *For Love Alone* and *The Man Who Loved Children*. The long career of Martin Boyd came to an end with *The Tea Time of Love* (1969), one of a number of recent novels— albeit if in this instance somewhat tongue in cheek—which explore the exotic romanticism of Europe, thus reversing a dominant trait of the nineteenth century novel which explored the exotic romanticism of Australia. Shirley Hazzard, another expatriate novelist, similarly writes anti-sentimentally, yet with sensitivity, of love in post-war Italy in *The Evening of the Holiday* (1966)—all her novels are set either in Italy or America. It is interesting that two of the fictional autobiographies appearing at this time imply that geographical distancing is necessary for perspective. These are George Johnston's *Clean Straw for Nothing* and David Martin's *Where a Man Belongs* (1969). Another important fictional autobiography (which does not, however, exploit geographical dislocation in this way) is Hal Porter's *The Paper Chase* (1966).

Apart from Boyd's, two other notable careers came to an end in the late sixties. Katharine Susannah Prichard's *Subtle Flame* (1967) was her final novel, more than fifty years after she published *The Pioneers*. Frank Dalby Davison's swansong was *The White Thorntree* (1968), a book that demonstrated that it is possible to write interminable sagas about urban Australian life as well as about parched bucolic dynasties.

Thomas Keneally is the one novelist whose stature increases significantly through work published in these years. His first two novels had been quickly and casually written, but in *Bring Larks and Heroes* (1967) he cultivated the method of imaginatively filling out a historical situation with the ironical, almost sardonic, exploration of human vulnerability that has forged his most powerful fiction since then. Subsequent novels, *Three Cheers for the Paraclete* (1968), and *The Survivor* (1969) were slighter, and although there was an interesting fable *A Dutiful Daughter* (1970), it was not until he resumed the historical formula in the seventies that he again produced his best work.

Another feature of the half-decade is a general interest in the novel, evidenced in part by the influx of writers better known in other genres. While writers often publish in a number of different modes, one notices a preference for the novel form by dramatists like Alan Seymour with his novel-of-the-play *The One Day of the Year* (1967) and *The Coming Self-Destruction of the USA* (1969); or David Ireland with his *The Chantic Bird* (1968); or Barry Oakley with *Wild Ass of a Man* (1967); or the short-story writer Peter Cowan with *Seed* (1966); and the all-rounder Geoffrey Dutton with *Andy* (1968) and *Tamara* (1970). Of these at least Ireland has continued to find the form viable.

Outlets for publishing expanded somewhat in the sixties, and one landmark was the founding of Sun Books in 1965. There had been earlier cheap editions of Australian fiction, the Angus and Robertson Australian Pocket Library being the best example, but Sun Books produced, in addition to reprints, paperbacks that were often the only edition of a new work. Thus novels like Jan Smith's *An Ornament of Grace* (1966), or Donald Horne's *The Permit* (1965) found their way into print solely in the Sun Books edition. Other publishers, including particularly the University of Queensland Press with its Paperback Prose series, have continued this emphasis on paperback publication to minimize production costs on short-run experimental fiction. The support of the Australia Council for publishing, especially the setting and printing subsidy, has in recent years encouraged such presses as Outback and Wild and Woolley, which have done much to foster more experimental, "alternative" writing.

Despite some flurries of political consciousness in literary circles, the political novel have never been particularly important in Australia; however, an increase in self-consciousness in the society of the sixties is reflected in the fiction by the end of the decade. With the withdrawal of Menzies from politics, the founding in 1964 of a national newspaper, *The Australian*, and conscription for the Vietnam war, not to mention a succession of prime ministers who were either drowned or sacked or who sacked themselves, Australian public affairs took on an interest which they had not previously commanded. This awareness, which is manifested in a rash of socio–cultural analyses such as Horne's *The Lucky Country* and his text of *Southern Exposure* (1967), George Johnston's text of *The Australians* (1966), Humphrey McQueen's *A New Britannia* (1970), or Ronald Conway's *The Great Australian Stupor* (1971), also appears in fictional analyses of various aspects of Australianness. The late sixties and seventies saw the publication of Davison's massive Kinsey report on Sydney's northern suburbs, of Keneally's and Mather's probings of the underlying violence in an allegedly phlegmatic and laconic national character, and of the upturning of the conventional society of Melbourne by the outrageous anti-heroes of Oakley's *Let's Hear it for Prendergast* (1970), of Mather's *Trap* (1966), and of David Williamson's play, *The Coming of Stork* (1970).

This strand of satire, which may owe something to the success of Barry Humphries' stage and cartoon characters of the early sixties, is pronounced through the decade. It includes some works already mentioned—David Martin's spoof on the not-so-virile bushranger in *The Hero of Too,* Donald Horne's attack on bureaucracy in *The Permit*, and Peter Mather's on racism in *Trap*. It is a strand that is picked up and broadened in the drama of David Williamson, Fred Hibberd, and Alexander Buzo in the seventies, as well as in such novels as David Ireland's *The Unknown Industrial Prisoner* (1971), Henry Williams's *My Love Has a Black Speed Stripe* (1973), and Mathers's *The Wort Papers* (1972); and it is one characterized, particularly in the novels of Ireland and Mathers, by a comic experimentation which reflects society's disconnections by its departure from any linear plot development in favour of a largely disconnected narrative line.

The strength of the novel in the seventies has also been demonstrated in part by the continued interest of writers already established in other forms. Michael Wilding, making his mark in short stories, Sumner Locke Eliott, long known as a playwright, and well-known young poets David Malouf and Rodney Hall, all turned out novels. Wilding's *Living*

Together (1974) is genuinely light entertainment, but his recent *Short Story Embassy* (1975) and *Scenic Drive* (1976) combine comedy with a serious concern for the stylistic and structural problems confronting the contemporary novelist; Locke–Elliott's *The Man Who Got Away* (1973) and *Going* (1975) demonstrated the dramatist's Coward-like ease with dialogue; Malouf's *Johnno* (1975) and Hall's *A Place Among People* (1975) revealed their sensibilities within the ampler, often nostalgic, content. Among other poets turning to fiction are Robert Adamson and Bruce Hanford, whose *Zimmer's Essay* (1973) gives a picture of prison life from the inside. On the other hand, Hal Porter returned to the short story in *Fredo Fuss Love Life* (1973). Something of a crop of novels about growing up in Australia sprang up in the early 1970s —Lauri Clancy's *A Collapsible Man* (1975) and Gerald Murname's *Tamarisk Row* (1973) both have Catholic boyhood autobiographical backgrounds; and there are also such novels by Desmond O'Grady and D.R. Burns. Among a group of novels with a specifically Queensland background are Malouf's *Johnno*, already mentioned and set in Brisbane of the war years, Ronald McKie's *The Mango Tree* (1974), and Thea Astley's *A Kindness Cup* (1974), a mythic novel about a small Queensland town and one of a projected series. Rather similar, apart from its setting in Macedon, Victoria, is Geoff Wyatt's *Tidal Forest* (1973). Suzanne Holly Jones, whose *Harry's Child* (1964) caused her to be regarded as something of a child prodigy, at last appeared again with *Crying in the Garden* (1973).

David Ireland, already noted for his experimentation, continued to display versatility and has indeed been prolific —*The Unknown Industrial Prisoner*, *The Flesheaters* (1972), *Burn* (1974), and *The Glass Canoe* (1976) are all concerned with exploring aspects of society (especially its dispossessed and impoverished classes) which other recent novelists have tended to ignore. In doing this, Ireland has maintained his interest in experimentation with form, and he must now be regarded as one of the major and most lively innovators in our fiction. Frank Moorhouse's *The Americans, Baby* (1972) and *The Electrical Experience* (1974) are also vigorously experimental.

Some of those writers who had long proved their standing in prose fiction have continued to produce. Thomas Keneally, after *The Chant of Jimmie Blacksmith*, gave us *Blood Red, Sister Rose* in 1974, *Gossip from the Forest* in 1975, and *A Season in Purgatory* in 1976. Patrick White produced in 1973 *The Eye of the Storm*, which some believe to be the most ambitious and successful of his many major contributions to world literature, as well as *The Cockatoos* (1974), a collection of novellas, and *A Fringe of Leaves* (1976). Thea Astley's *A Kindness Cup* has already been mentioned, and she also published *The Acolyte* (1972), possibly her best work to date. Christina Stead, once more living in Australia, came up with *The Little Hotel*, a rather slight work published in 1974 though apparently written as early as 1948, and then in 1976, with *Miss Herbert: The Suburban Wife*, a "depressingly good" study of complacent self-deception. Frank Hardy's *But the Dead Are Many* (1975) was a more elaborate, more literary, and more carefully distanced statement of his abiding political concerns. Then Xavier Herbert re-emerged in the same year with his mightiest undertaking, *Poor Fellow My Country*, breaking all records for length, provoking attention for comprehensiveness as much as for Australianness, challenging reader, reviewer, and scholar to assess the extent of its riches.

Perhaps we could return now to the question posed earlier —whether the fifteen years from 1970 onwards seems likely to produce a crop of new novelists equal to that of the thirties and early forties. From a viewpoint roughly half-way through the period, the answer seems at best that it is highly unlikely. Of the younger writers, Keneally and Ireland stand out, but both began publishing in the sixties. The two really major novels of the seventies thus far—*The Eye of the Storm* and *Poor Fellow My Country*—were both the work of men who first published more than thirty-five years ago. On the other hand, the new writers of the decade have tended to experiment with forms which, interesting as they certainly can be, often are slight and sometimes perhaps to be considered as only on the fringe of the novel. The twenty-first century could see it differently, but it may be that the period we have been considering—the forty-five or so years from the early thirties

—will prove to be, if not the golden age of the Australian novel, then the nearest likely approach to it.

An Australian Tragedy

Xavier Herbert's *Poor Fellow My Country*

LAURIE HERGENHAN

Poor Fellow My Country from the distance, to those who know it only by sight or hearsay, may appear to stand forbiddingly and oddly alone among recent Australian novels, not simply because of its vast size but because it appears to hearken back to the world of the 1930s with its nationalistic dreams inspired by the land. Yet in its general aims Herbert's novel does have resemblances to novels of the last twenty years. Thomas Keneally, writing in 1968, the year after the publication of *Bring Larks and Heroes*, about it and other novels he saw as similar—*Voss, To the Islands,* and *The Tilted Cross*—commented on the influence of "the vision of Australians as a race that lacks a spiritual home-land", as a vision that "occurs frequently in our modern writing", and of how differing writers were "all responding to the peculiar *alien* quality of their country" by trying to "fill its void" with spiritual journeys in which its "demons" were exorcised with the blood of central characters.[1] *Poor Fellow My Country* is concerned to explore such a void, to inquire and to show how it came about and what it consists of.

Keneally added that such novels are "a necessary but passing phase in the development of our literature", but they represent a particular form of what has been a concern of the Australian novel since Furphy or before: a desire to show that the white man belongs in Australia, that he has succeeded in making it habitable for himself in one way or another. Hence, for instance, our pioneering sagas. In *Voss* and *To the Islands* the emphasis is on showing how in the local, in the sense of the Australian, scene the eternal struggles of the human spirit have taken place, or perhaps more accurately, can take place. It follows that in them the Australian context, its particular "void", is finally viewed as subsidiary to a wider human one; in fact this is part of the way of coming to terms with it, if not of filling it, for it is seen as a universal challenge.

If *Poor Fellow My Country* shares this spiritual concern, at times anguished and obsessive, it is less apparent than in the other novels, for greater emphasis is placed on the social emptiness they also depict in their own ways. In them the social element is there mainly to highlight the spiritual drama; *Poor Fellow My Country* stresses more their inseparability and gives them equal weight.

Keneally drew attention to another group of novels represented by Tony Morphett's *Dynasty*—to which could be added Peter Mathers's *Trap* and the novels of David Ireland —in which the emphasis is on society. These works are the heirs of social realism in Australia. According to Keneally, Morphett's characters are meant to "sum up, in the Australian context, the European experience of the twentieth century"—a tall order—and he instances the influence of fascism. Such novels rest in "a rugged belief in the importance of Australian society and a willingness to attack what is called 'a big theme' in local terms". (Keneally himself has shown a loss of this belief in turning towards European themes in European settings.) In *Poor Fellow My Country* Herbert does take Australian society with deadly seriousness, as can be seen partly in his altering of another emphasis: European experience is seen as inevitably contributing to Australian society, yet as definitely peripheral to what has happened in Australia, the be-all and end-all of the novel. In this determined placing of Australia at the centre, Herbert is attempting a culminating, embracing view of the potentialities and defects of its society. Whether this is a narrowly nationalistic element, a turning of the clock back, must enter into consideration of the novel.

In placing *Poor Fellow My Country* in some kind of context, the question of the presentation of the land and of landscape is important. Early in *Voss*, the titular character admonishes the locals for knowing nothing of their country, which, his prescience tells him, is "of great subtlety". Laura soon echoes him: "Everyone is still afraid, or most of us, of this country, and will not say it. We are not yet possessed of understanding." When towards the end of the novel she comments that "knowledge was never a matter of geography ... it overflows all maps that exist", she is stressing that the kind of spiritual knowledge *Voss* values rises above boundaries of national experience, and that while it may come partly through the natural world, it is independent of any particular or national landscape.

Poor Fellow My Country would again appear to be turning the clock back by returning to the detailed picturing of a distinctively Australian landscape, notably the outback. For Herbert, knowledge is "a matter of geography" in the sense that the kind he is seeking depends on national particulars, even if it transcends them. *Poor Fellow My Country* stresses that "earth is spirit" in Judith Wright's phrase,[2] this spirit being inseparable from the particulars of a land and its flora and fauna, while for White and Stow spirit "overflows" them. Herbert's landscape is thus "prophetic" (to use Keneally's term) or capable of revealing or defining spirit in a different way from that of their novels. *Poor Fellow My Country* represents another culmination in the Australian novel by attempting the most thoroughgoing depiction of Australian landscape (the far north).

The all-out ambitions of *Poor Fellow My Country* represent a climactic development of Herbert's own work more than an attempt to develop tendencies in the Australian novel. This may also be seen in the great emphasis on the Aborigines. They are at once a subject in themselves and a means of linking the three elements of the quest for a "spiritual homeland", a critique of Australian society, and a celebration of the land. In attempting to suggest the scope and nature of the novel I shall concentrate on outlining these elements.

The question of what the novel is "about" is a formidable one because of what is involved in its bulk: a cluster of complex concerns developed through an extraordinarily large cast of characters, range of locales, and number of stories woven together to form "one story". The novel presents its individual vision of the human Australian emptiness, of its white inhabitants as directionless aliens because they have no ethos or relatedness to the natural environment and no sense of community, which should help to define and nourish the personal life. Out of this emptiness comes either an apathetic disregard or a destructiveness, confirming rather than easing the alienation. The famous Australian sardonic humour shows that deep down Australians are a "bitter people . . . bitter for the want of a land to love", says a main character, Jeremy Delacy, though love of the land is no simple, isolated matter in the novel. We see more of what has been lost as well as how it was lost, a tragic interaction, than we saw in *Capricornia*. Ideals that are both theoretic (for example the notion of a "True Commonwealth") and applied (the ethos of the Aborigines, and to a lesser extent, of the Jews) are held up against warped and sad realities. The Aborigines could have pointed a way of avoiding alienation through acknowledgement, not imitation, of their relatedness to the land and what they derive from it.

Early in the novel Jeremy contrasts the Aborigines' "belonging" with the spiritual poverty of most whites:

"As to the magical power of the tree, I accept that."
"How d'you mean?"
"As part of an environment I don't want to feel alien in . . . my own native land. According to the blackfellow there's magic in everything . . . every rock, tree, waterhole . . . even in the things he makes . . . his spears, dilly-bags. In fact, if you take the trouble, you yourself can find wonder in everything. We do in scientific things . . . what we see through a microscope, what takes place in chemical reaction. As geologists we'd find it in the rocks through rationalism. As zoologists in the pools, botanists in the trees. The blackfellow's reverence for things strikes me as much more intelligent than the blank disregard of the mass of our own people . . . who'd still be simple-minded enough to believe in the divinity of Christ and the sancity of the Virgin Mary, the Holy Ghost, and all the rest of it." [P. 25][3]

This kind of world-view of the Aborigines is to be dramatized in the novel by the investing of their environment and their actions with the magical significance of legend. The magical, accompanied by the realistic picture and explanation, is shown to go beyond mere superstition: the beliefs are a way of giving meaning to life, of providing glimpses of "the wonder of existence", the main positive of the novel. This attunement is shown in great detail, usually as characters make their many journeys, so that the reader's imagination and sympathies can be wooed towards that of the "negative-capability" of the author's own view. No other novelist has sustained such a convincing and vivid sense of the Aborigines' belonging and captured the enchantment (not a cliché in this context) of a haunted land, so sphinx-like to the whites. For example, a landscape detail such as the northern morning glories finds its place in the enveloping scheme:

In lingo the Morning Glories were called *Gringelli*, which also meant stars. The legend told of how the Bandicoot Sisters, Iyuwuk, were fleeing from that old reprobate Wanjin, the Dingo, who declared that he wanted them for wives, but secretly intended to eat them, as everything he could get his sharp teeth into. It was Wet Season. Wanjin manoeuvred the sisters into a swampy region, where he knew that they, helpless in mud and water and in want of their own kind of food, would soon give up. But the Ol'Goomun-Ol'Goomun, watching from the sky, felt sorry for them, gathered some little stars, which are celestial flowers, and scattered them along bits of ridges in the swamp, to show them the way out and also to feed them in the process, since she attached a sweet little yam to every flower as a root. The stars shone only during those couple of hours before daybreak when Wanji has to sleep, and vanished completely with the dawn, so that he could not track them, baffled as he was by the onset of rain again.

In fact, the diaphanous stuff of the swamp morning glories surrounds a silver star. As the rain eases with approach of dawn, the tightly furled buds, pointing like long slim fingers since midnight, open while you watch, unfurling into perfect pentagons in which shape they glow and shimmer as with inner light and seem thus to float along the ground—"Like leedle ballerina," as Rifkah said. With daylight they fall into rags, to dissolve like wafers in the ooze created by rain now falling like warm tears shed for the reality that beauty is for ever transient. Prindy made up a song about it, which they sang together while gathering mushrooms. [P. 870] There is no symbolism here (although there may be some tonal intimations of approaching tragedy) beyond the legendary meaning. The description contributes to the sustaining of the magical dimension and adds yet another detail to the vast landscape picture.

More often, though, the legendary enters into the action which it helps to shape. The following incident occurs in the journey of runaways from Port Palmerston (Darwin), Prindy, a quarter-caste boy, his half-caste mother Nellyeri, her tribal sister Queeny Pegleg, and his tribal uncle, King George (named after the King who remits his prison sentence):

> The women had really little to complain of, but so little to do as to need to complain. It was useless telling them they were loafers like the birds cawing and clucking and whistling around them and had never had it better, as George frequently did through his medium for talking to them, because their answer was that they were not bloody blackfellers and wanted to be on their way to the Beatrice and the civilized things belonging to it that became more and more alluring as talked about.
>
> How long it might have gone on was anybody's guess, considering the pigheadedness on both sides. Anyway, it ended quite suddenly, even shockingly, by reason of what seemed to be involved, the cause of it an old-man goanna, of the large spotted rock kind, a *prindi*, called Warradabil by George.
>
> The creature had been seen about for a couple of days, having come to join the feasting with the other bush scavengers. No one had molested it, because it was Prindy's Dreaming Mate and could not be killed without his permission, which he wouldn't be able to give unless the others were in real need of food. Mungus had had a go at it, but only to get a good fright when the three feet or so of its scaly white belly and throat reared over him, with claws extended and what looked like a hundred sharp teeth bared, and then to get a cuff from Prindy and lecture on the ethics of the thing. He repeated what George had said, that Warradabil might well be Prindy's dead Daddy's Shade, called *Lamala* in western lingo.
>
> The birds were interested in the goanna only as a rival,

he being much too big and ferocious a thing for any of them to tackle even in a gang . . . that is to say the feathered scavengers. For there was that other, the eagle, Watagarra. The great bird would know everything that was going on below and be biding his time. Then there he was, that morning, hurtling down over the rocks in a dive. The scavenger birds saw him and gave the alarm. The goanna, well out in the open, started a bee-line for the rocks. But it happened that Queeny was sitting on a rock just there, and not knowing what was going on, thought the huge lizard was attacking her, and leapt up with a yell and struck out with her crutch. But only lightning or an eagle could hit a goanna really on the run. With all that wood about her, he must have thought Queeny was a tree, and needing the first cover he came to, shot up her, hung for a moment staring into her face with talons hooked in her breasts, while the eagle went over. Then with her shrieking and spitting right onto the long forked tongue he was listening with, and her pounding his armoured back with the head of the crutch, he was moved to shin up further, grabbed an ear and a loop of her knotted hair, and there he was sitting on top of her head, forepaws extended and head turning from side to side, as if delivering a lecture, horny tail round her neck for better support. The three people watching whooped with sudden laughter. The birds took it up. Mungus barked. Queeny shrieked, "Tek him 'way, tek him way . . . kill him!" But the others were helpless.

Now the goanna was watching his baffled foe spiralling aloft. Then Queeny raised the head of her crutch and started beating with it wildly. The goanna grabbed it, probably thinking it a limb of the odd tree, shifted onto it, and as it fell with his weight, came down in swift arc, to land on his back on a slab of rock with the crutch on his belly. He lay jerking, with the wind knocked out of him.

Queeny raised the crutch, screeching, "You bloody bastard!"

George yelled, "No-more!"

Prindy gasped, "Don' you, Aunty!"

But with all her considerable strength she brought the crutch down and caught him in the side just as he was rolling over. Again he fell back winded.

"Eh! Eh!" yelled George and Prindy.

But she pounded the stricken creature with a succession of swift sharp strokes, so that his belly opened up and guts and blood came bursting out. With a mighty contortion he gained his feet, shot for the rocks again, reached them, went clawing up, got his trailing entrails caught on a projection, heaved himself round to get clear. Again the birds gave the warning. The great head came up. He tried to run for it. But there was Watagarra with great wings out to brake his dive and the wind whistling through them and talons outflung to grab. *Swish!*—and there was poor old Warradabil, with guts trailing behind him, having his first flight.

No laughter now. Even the birds were silent. Prindy, looking up, muttered, "Poor-feller, my mate!"

Then George turned on Queeny, as a brother is entitled to in extremes of bad behaviour, and roared, "Wha' for you do like o' dat, you bloody cranky rubbitch."

"Shut yo' bloody puggin' mout', you black bastard!"

"I shut yo' mout' for yo' by'n'by, yo' bloody stink-shit woman." When she raised the crutch to him he yelled, "Yo' look-out . . . I give you spear."

"Yo' try it, blackfeller!"

"I don' try it time I do . . . I *do* it . . . properly, yo' bloody halfcaste rubbitch!"

He turned to Prindy: "We got 'o go. Spone dat-one daid daddy belong 'o you, he mek him trouble long o' we. Come on. Gitchim swag, lil bits tucker. I wipe him out track." Even spirits need tracks to find those they would haunt. There was no doubt about the fear of those two unbelievers in Blackfeller Bijnitch, the care they stepped with in clearing out. George told them to stay behind and take the consequences. They ignored him. He was compelled to erase their tracks along with his own by means of his magic brush. Anyway, Prindy, working with his own brush would have done it for them, would have had no choice in the matter, indeed, so close did they stick to him during the exodus; and surely he would have wanted to do it. [Pp. 425–26]

Here, it might seem, we have the Herbert of *Capricornia* over again: the vitality of violent incident leaning towards burlesque and the gory, yet controlled by the sharply observed (if bizarre), balancing details. We have this, with greater control, but with much more as well. In *Capricornia* this kind of event would have been one link in a loose chain of incident, but here, as with all that happens to the wandering party, the incident has a surer place in the total scheme, it

contributes directly to the legendary or "marvellous" am-
bience and to the sustained narrative of the journey. The
world of spirits informs the incident through the natural
creatures involved and the attitudes of the characters. Because
the goanna is Prindy's dreaming mate its death serves to move
the party on, and Queeny's attack on it develops a crucial
underlying tension of the novel: as a partly "civilized" (and
partly Christianized) Aborigine—she has been commercial
"queen of the compound"—she and Nellyeri are resistant to
the "blackfellow ways" that George and Prindy are only too
pleased to escape back to. This tension between cultures is
to be linked with divisiveness between the sexes found in both
races and running throughout the novel. To make a final
comment on this passage, it shows how Herbert builds in
substantial blocks of incident and scene; the incident needs
to be quoted in full to do justice to it, though it is a tiny
part of the total design.

Something of this design can be suggested by a glance at
the three main characters, their deployment throughout
various locales, and aspects of theme which bind all together.
Prindy, the first character we meet, is of exceptional sensitivity (especially to music) and intelligence. As a quarter-
caste he stands between the two cultures, both of which try
to claim and initiate him into their ways. The opening pages
show his initiation into some of the Aboriginal magic by a
full-blood who seems to materialize out of the roots of a
banyan tree:

> He [Prindy] turned, to reach for a grubby cotton flour-
> sack hanging in the roots—to stiffen in that attitude. Only
> an eye of extraordinary sharpness could so quickly have
> discerned anything untoward, so much a part of the back-
> ground was that which had intruded into it—or materialized
> out of it, as seemed as likely.
>
> It was of human shape, greyish, or blackish made grey
> with dust and ashes and ancient body hair, so as to appear
> kindred to the crawling roots. It had stick legs, with shapeless
> lumpy feet and knobby knees, arms like a mantis, a tuft of
> grey hair sticking up like the crest of an angry bird out of
> a grubby ochred head-band, and whiskers plaited into a long
> goatee about slivers of cane or grass, an almost flat nose with
> slit septum dangling loosely from enormous nostrils. It

seemed to be sightless as a death's head—till suddenly there
burnt within the black caverns what looked like live coals. . . .
Not a move from either. Both might have been spellbound.
[P. 10]

This is the dramatic entrance of the Pookarakka, the witch-
doctor of the male Rainbow-snake cult with its god
Tchamala, something of a Lucifer figure in the Aboriginal
creation myth, except that he played a part in the creation
of the world and that his intervention in human affairs can
be protective to the "good" as well as destructive. This
Pookarakka is known by whites as Cock-Eye Bob or more
commonly as Bobwirridirridi. The novel shows retro-
spectively that he has been alternatively a prisoner and
fugitive from white "justice" before the novel begins, a
pattern to be repeated throughout, with Prindy also being
caught up in it through the competition of various groups
and individuals for possession of him: welfare authorities,
police, Aborigine-sympathizers, Communists, nationalists,
Catholics, all summed up in a jingle to the rhythm of a train:

Catholicism, Communism,
Anachronism, Despotism,
Christians, Pagans, Fascists, Jews,
Dominus vobiscum, and same to yous!
Hey, out the way there, Kangaroos,
Here come de Revolutionism!　　　[P. 1000]

Bobwirridirridi is an amazing creation, a character who
exists vividly for the reader but more as a *presence* than
someone we get to know, as befitting a Pookarakka. In the
scene in which his function is explained in the first chapter,
he is a hovering presence, glimpsed rather than seen, if
sighted at all, and he is to retain throughout a mysteriousness
that has nothing of the bogus about it. Though we see a
great deal of what he does, he maintains a secretiveness that
is part of Aboriginal life; we don't know what goes on in
his mind, as for instance we don't know exactly what goes
on between him and Prindy—when they talk significantly
in their meeting in prison we don't know what is said. Prindy
is similarly presented from outside (though in much more
detail), without being simply an external creation, He is a

character of great delicacy and appeal, expressing unspoilt, childlike imaginativeness, the capacity for wonder so vital and vulnerable—though he is no angel.

As well as contending with the competing "isms", Prindy is to be wooed by Judaism to which he is initiated by Rifkah, a Jewish refugee and mother-figure to him, offsetting the kindly paternalism of Jeremy Delacy, his white grandfather. Jeremy is to make genuine attempts to guide and succour Prindy without interfering in his destiny. His role as "sorcerer's apprentice" and his moving between the two main cultures (there are Indian and Jewish as well) greatly assist the initiation of the reader into Aborginal belief and his involvement with the clash of cultures.

In Prindy we see the tensions between Western individuality and Aboriginal tradition which "naturally cancels out originality", as suggested by his recurring chant:

> . . . *My Road, My Rown Road*
> *I go look dat Road, my Rown, my Dream Road*
> *Road belong 'o I, must-be find him by-'n'-by*
> *My Road, my Rown Road. . . .*   [P. 26]

Jeremy comments: " 'your Road is the way you must go through life as the reincarnation of a Dream Time ancestor. . . . But calling it My Rown Road . . . Own Road . . . suggests that he's seeking a Road of his own.' " (p. 26). Aboriginal magic wins Prindy's allegiance as against the passing attractions of the magic of Catholic ritual and belief, or of white technological culture—such as the wireless, electricity, and aeroplanes, which figure importantly in the novel as well as trains. This allegiance is shown through his dedication to Bobwirridirridi, though the individuality reinforced in him by white culture is tragically to prevent his full assimilation of Aboriginal ways.

Prindy's individuality is to be linked both to the social theme and to a preoccupation in all Herbert's work—cultural and personal identity. Prindy is the individual set apart by his racial inheritance and by his special gifts, including artistic ones. These are expressed especially through his musical ability. His imaginative attraction to the magical or wondrous aspects of various culture beliefs—not mentioned yet is the eastern, as represented by the Indian hawker and birdcatcher Barbu, who catches him in a bird-net—is accompanied by his chameleon ability for imitation and imaginative participation, as shown by his skill in picking up by ear the music associated with each.

Although Bobwirridirridi has his place in the traditional Aboriginal society, it is the unusual place of the especially gifted or chosen, a reconciliation of convention and individuality:

"The blackfellow's conception is similarly diverse and vague. The Cult of Koonapippi constitutes the Credo. All social behaviour is based on it. All males are initiated into it, and females, although rigidly denied communion, bound to observe its injunctions. The cult of Tchamala is something quite different. It mightn't even be a cult in the proper sense of the term, which I take to mean a sort of congregation . . . and so the Anthropologists and police might be to a large degree right in saying it's only a sort of lurk worked by heads, as smart ones are called. That's why I want to find out more about it from the old man. How one becomes a snake man I've no idea. There's always one about somewhere. You don't have to be a *koornung* to be one. In fact Bobwirridirridi's the first I've known who was. A Snake Man, although leading an ordinary tribal life, more or less, is supposed to be in league with spirits that do Tchamala's bidding. In being so he can be dangerous. He can arrange for one's being bitten by a poisonous snake, taken by a crocodile, drowned in a flood, struck by lightning, or merely inconvenienced by being harassed by mosquitoes, sandflies, marsh-flies, leeches, ticks, all creatures of Tchamala's . . . or washed out of his humpy in the middle of a black night and have his fire put out and nothing to start another with. In a society where it is implicit that everything is controlled by magic, it's handy to have it known that you are in league with occult powers. At the same time, there is the disadvantage of being too greatly feared to lead a normal tribal life. . . ." [P. 36]

The ambivalence of the witch-doctor's power is brought out here: it can be traded on, it can be destructive, and it sets him apart as feared and as cut off from "normal" community life. Here again we have the problem of individuality and of artistic powers. And there is, it is suggested, a dash of madness in Bobwirridirridi, who, having been almost poisoned by arsenic-spiced flour—a common trick that this time recoils on the white man by killing his own kind —is believed to be not quite right in the head as a result. He considers that he himself as retaliatory agent of Tchamala has been responsible for the deaths and thereby visited with special powers. There is a gap, once or twice a ludicrous one, between magical pretensions and his cunning practicality, but the novel convinces us that this practical ability to deal with the natural world is enhanced by magical belief. It is a source of vitality and spiritual fulfilment—a real "power of mind".

Early in the novel Jeremy explains the role of the mangan, a native plum, in Aboriginal folklore: it has the power to attract and spellbind lovers, "you fall in love only through magic . . . *Charada*, as love-magic is called" (p. 24). When asked by his sceptical listener Bishoff whether he believes in this, Jeremy replies: "I certainly do. It's a power of the mind . . . the greatest force in the Universe, surely" (p. 25). Something of this "power of the mind", again allied to the artistic, is achieved by Jeremy, who is also used to pose among other problems that of individuality. His role as "scrub-bull" has less to do with never-failing attractiveness to women as with his fate as a solitary who must live away from the herd because his oddity or freakishness demands it. He himself is not at home with the herd, and it can resent his difference to the point of destructiveness (though inevitably there is some of this in him as well). Disillusioned by his failure of involvement through political activity, he returns to the bush to achieve another kind of identification: he sees his Yalmaru or Shade in the form of a blackfellow, as Aboriginals can do on special occasions. While the novel allows that this experience has the reality only of hallucination, it nevertheless stresses its reality and significance as "a manifestation of a state of mind" (p. 1092). It is suggested that Jeremy's yearning for identification with the land and its indigenes, hitherto like an unfulfilled love affair, has not been all in vain—though it is to be shown as tragically incomplete.

In the novel the expression of individuality and imaginative fulfilment are shown to be endangered by sexual love. The story appears to support the Aboriginal belief in sexual taboos, especially during the initiation stage of puberty for males; sexual love only causes trouble, because it is too "personal", with resulting self-indulgence and battles for dominance. It is considered to be law-breaking, stepping outside the laws of relationship governing sexual union. (It is interesting that this Aboriginal view of love as a passing and tragic thing is borne out by all the love affairs in the novel, as though Aboriginal love is here used as a criterion, not as the imaginative model it is elsewhere.) It is the indulgence of Prindy's love for Savitra when both reach puberty that helps to prevent his full initiation into the Rainbow-snake cult, and to lead in fact to the violent deaths of both of them as well as of Jeremy, who allows the indulgence in spite of his knowledge of Aboriginal custom and against his own better judgement. The possessive Savitra intrudes on male ritual, as had Queeny Pegleg and Prindy's mother. But it is not only the women who are at fault. There is the male failure in Prindy to be temporarily continent, and the failure of proper guidance of elders in this respect. Temporary abstinence, it is suggested, is a necessary part of masculine maturity and in Aborigines contributes to a richer cult life (pp. 1304–5). Thus the connection is made between sexuality and artistic power (a preoccupation of Herbert's, especially in his autobiography, *Disturbing Element*). The interference of Jeremy in the initiation ceremony in a magnificent but horrifying scene of ritual violence, the novel's climax, shows a failure in his own character as well as in his attempt to identify fully with the Aborigines. Prindy also is prevented from doing so completely because of his entanglement with white culture. In this scene, which also involves the ritual rape of Savitra, the Aboriginal ways are preserved with a shocking ruthlessness that is paralleled in white society, where, however, it takes exploitive (as against defensive) forms such as greed and egoism.

To summarize the roles of the three main characters—Prindy, Bobwirridirridi, and Jeremy—they express a theme of identity: there is the important socio-cultural level (on which more must be said later) of the destructiveness of white society, and linked with this to the individual level involving the attempted preservation of powers of mind akin to the artistic—the magical, irrational powers that can keep man in touch with the marvellous in his own existence and in all existence. Only in Aboriginal life as a society does the irrational work fruitfully with the rational instead of against it, the worst sort of violation or destructiveness. In *Capricornia* a half-caste son seeks identity by moving between a foster father and a prodigal father, as well as between the two cultures. In *Soldiers' Women* this problem is presented through a female character, Pudsey, who has real artistic powers albeit limited ones (she is truly "enchanted" in potential, as is Alfie in *Poor Fellow My Country*). She flees a possessive mother (one of the novel's "witches") and an impotent father only to be crushed by the society in which she seeks to play out successive fantasy roles (including sexual ones) of her power. In *Seven Emus* whites try to steal an Aboriginal totem, symbol of dreaming power. In *Poor Fellow My Country* the identity theme has become more overt and complex, just as the criticism of society to which it is allied has increased in vehemence and scope.

The social concerns, so far only glimpsed, can only be indicated by providing further glimpses, an outline of main characters and parts of the story. One role of Jeremy's is as expositor of all that is wrong with Australia: throughout the novel he delivers a jeremiad using as touchstone a "True Commonwealth" in which a genuine ethos promotes the common and the individual good by relating him to his fellows and the natural world. Around him are grouped a number of others with social views and roles.

Alfie (short for Aelfrida) Candlemass combines the artist (the writer) and the patriotic reformer. After spending some time in the north as teacher in an Aboriginal compound she returns to Sydney as an activist, hoping to help to remedy Australia's colonial dependence on England. She feels she has "a continent to win . . . a nation to build" (p. 556)—as Herbert has said of himself when he returned from London in the early 1930s after writing *Capricornia*.[4] She becomes caught up with the "Free Australia" movement, obviously meant to parallel the Australia First movement of the thirties for which P.R. Stephensen became main spokesman. He in turn is paralleled by the would-be leader of "Free Australia", "the Bloke".

This strand of the story helps to draw Jeremy to Sydney and Melbourne, cities being from "a practical point of view . . . the Real Australia" (p. 1074), and at the same time to show how a genuinely idealistic, and potentially good, national movement (not nationalistic) can be captured and distorted by warring factions of the Left and the Right. These play into the hands of die-hard traditionalists, who in this case have a second world war to strengthen support for them by stirring up false but strident nationalism. This interplay can be illustrated by an excerpt from a Sydney meeting aimed at "founding" the "Free Australia" movement. This Jeremy attends as main speaker, not to found a political party as expected by both sides but to say why he thinks it is too late to try and realize the concept of a True Commonwealth:

> "While I was in jail I had plenty of time and need to think . . . and gave my thoughts largely to this matter of love of country . . . Patriotism, Nationalism. . . . "
>
> "National Socialism!" was shouted from the left.
>
> "Shit Commos!" came from the right.
>
> "Shut up . . . or out!" bawled the sergeant.
>
> Jeremy kept on at the main body: "Patriotism, of course, comes from *Pater*, Father, one's Fatherland. Although I've called myself a patriot in the past, I'm inclined to reject it now as jingoistic . . . despite the fact that its dictionary meaning is 'One zealous for the freedom of one's country.' Nationality comes from *Natus*, Birth . . . so, the land that has borne me. But that's come to stink somewhat, too . . . . "
>
> "And it's yoour jab to stop stink, ee?" a loud voice demanded from the left.
>
> Jeremy swung to it. "What d'you mean by that?"
>
> "Sticks oot a mile, choom!"
>
> "I'm not your chum . . . but explain yourself. I'm sure there's a meaning behind your words. Enlighten me . . . and stand up and do it . . . like a man!"
>
> A big hard-faced man rose slowly. He looked official somehow, at any rate better dressed than most of the others. He said in a grating voice, "You can't poot it o'er uz, snoozer."

"I'm not trying to put it over anyone. Come on . . . out with it!"

"Yoou're heere to wheetwash the Free Awstreelia Fascist Movement."

"Aw, rubbish!" Jeremy turned back to the mass. "I was talking about those words, lovely words, really, but distorted by rogues and fools . . . and therefore I'll avoid them, and use instead the simple expression Love of Country, clumsy though it is. I don't think anyone can object to that . . . even our immigrant friend over here who can't shut up and can't sit down . . . what a pity I called on him . . . I should've known better than to call on a Liverpool-Irish Commo!"

The man was still jabbering and gesticulating. The sergeant had to go halfway in to where he sat to shut him up. . . .

The man shouted, "You coom 'ere to launch yoour party. All reet . . . gi' uz yoour party policy."

"I belong to no party. I'm here to talk of Love of Country. . . . "

"This 'ere meetin's advertoised to launch yoor Free Australia Party."

"Don't you believe in a free Australia?"

"I doon't believe in no dirty National Socialist Fascists workin' their way in to teek o'er country loike bluidy Hitler."

Cheers from the left. Hoots of anger from the right.

"You sayed yo'self this Love o' Country stoof's only anoother neem for Nationalism. . . . " It ended in a compact *Plop* and a gasp, as an egg, thrown from the right, hit the speaker fairly in the broad face. Amidst the howls of wrath the action roused in the man's supporters were whoops of disgust at the smell. The egg was very rotten.

But it was not only the right who were armed for conflict. An egg went flying back from the left. More eggs from the right. Both factions to a man were on their feet. Tomatoes and other vegetables were flying—and abuse—*Fascist Bastards—Commo Shit!* The police were hurled aside or trampled down. The factions were at grips. People at the back were shouting, screaming. Those on the rostrum were on their feet, staring, gaping like actors on a stage who suddenly see the drama stolen from them by the audience. Press cameras were flashing and popping at the back.

Then there was the drama back on the stage, its actors not the staring ones to begin with, but the Bloke, with that big Liverpool-Irishman after him, the Bloke all eyes and

GOSHEN COLLEGE LIBRARY
GOSHEN, INDIANA

mouth, squealing, "Help, help!" the other all eyes and teeth and reeking egg-yolk, grabbing at his flying coat tails. The coat came off in the pursuer's huge hands, with the sleeves ripped out and dangling foolishly down the *Führer's* arms to make them look like a chimpanzee's. [Pp. 1076–78]

In the above scene, Jeremy (as does the novel as a whole) does try to distinguish "love of country" from jingoistic nationalism. Nevertheless, the passage illustrates certain qualities of content and methods that are likely to meet with resistance from Australian readers, for more than once Australians have been called a nation of mockers, and they are well known for the cynicism about idealism (and ideas) and politics. If a narrowing nationalism seems to emerge in the making of a Liverpool Irishman a typical kind of disrupter, and a Communist, this, and the violence, can be more accurately seen partly as a challenge to another potential sentimentality, a kind of "internationalism", or the view that emigrants or Communists (as with any other political group) are all "good blokes". There are plenty of "native" Australians in the novel who show political and other forms of opportunism and violence. Since the climactic meeting is a crowd scene, and since views of the Right and the Left have been brought out elsewhere through individuals, here we are entitled to see them played out in group action. But the nature of the riot as a performance does, for Herbert, invite not only the dramatic but the theatrical. I think the last paragraph is too close to stage caricature. A later, similar scene, of a war rally in Hyde Park on Jeremy's second visit to Sydney, is better managed, though the above example is effective if uneven.

Offsetting Alfie is Rifkah, an ex-Communist Jewish refugee who suffers from anti-semitism (even in the Australian bush). This allows the novel to explore the similarity between anti-semitism and the discrimination against Aborigines and the sustaining magical or spiritual belief inherent in both races. Rifkah moves among the Aborigines as a sympathetic friend but fails in the end to be accepted by them (as happens to Jeremy) because, as the novel unsentimentally shows, they don't want outsiders except to make use of them. They don't want pity ("they only exploit it when it's given") or sympathy, for they are a deeply proud people, proud in being themselves (p. 736). Although Rifkah's efforts to understand and commune with them, reaching beyond Jeremy's in some ways, assist the reader's understanding, she is seen finally as a failed Daisy Bates and yet another unfulfilled person, both in her loves and her social role:

> Her intention to become a sort of Queen of the Blacks had not been the success her prototype, the late Daisy Bates, had made of it. The blacks had not wanted her, except in extremes of illness or trouble with the missionaries of the several mission stations now dotting the coast. Perhaps Mrs Bates's blacks would have been the same, only that being desert people they depended more on her stores, which she was able to replenish, that she had the backing of police, and that, being English, she might be less sensitive about not being wanted. [P. 1457]

Around the central trio of Prindy, Bobwirridirridi, and Jeremy, and of prominent characters such as Alfie and Rifkah, there are a number of other characters of almost equal importance and many minor figures. The novel covers the period 1936–42 (with a final chapter, or epilogue, bringing us up to the 1970s). As the drift into war is a major drift of the novel, skilfully recalling World War I as a crisis in national identity, there is scope for involving the military and the police, including the new Commonwealth force who operate in the bush as well as in the city, as do communist and fascist organizers. Included in the picture is the exploitive commercialism from abroad of the beef industry (seen in Vaisey's monopoly), and the pallid attempt of religion to play a social role. Catholicism is looked at sympathetically on the whole, including the quality of its "magical" belief, but found inadequate.

The keeping of this mixed pot of concerns simmering and blending, the deployment of characters and invention of incident to develop theme, is one of the masterly achievements of the novel, its architecture, and shows how Herbert had learned from his earlier works: in *Capricornia* there is a wealth of materials amounting to prodigality; in *Soldiers' Women* more emphasis (perhaps too much), on a patterned control of such material; in *Seven Emus*, in the despoliation of the Aborigines' sacred places, the germ of the great theme and exciting narrative of *Poor Fellow My Country*.

The structure of the latter relies on recurrent motifs, images, places, incidents of a similar pattern which stimulate that harking backwards and forwards so essential if a novel is to maintain a shape that guides its progression. The locales are important as structural centres. There is Jeremy's home, Lily Lagoons, more of a conservation reserve than a station, and the adjacent bush township of Beatrice River, which is connected by rail to Port Palmerston to the north-west. Another centre is the Leopold Islands mission station, north of Lily Lagoons. Between these and their environs, especially the painted caves and the plateau near Jeremy's, there is a continual and carefully plotted traffic. And Jeremy is inevitably drawn to the vortex of the city, as we have glimpsed.

Of the unifying devices, the most basic is probably the legendary meanings with which both the natural world and events are invested. This dimension is constantly expanding as new details, such as the morning glories, are added, but after the adumbration of the basic legend of creation in the early pages (pp. 34–5), key elements recur both as a reminder of the enveloping world of spirit and as atmosphere, including the portending of events. For instance Tchamala is a frequent presence in storms and in water, with both of which he is mythologically associated as the creator of "all that is bad and wrong and uncomfortable and dangerous" (p. 36). As a sign of the reader's entering into this imaginative world, the moon soon becomes for him Igulgul, the moon Spirit, associated with love and the Wrong-side business, and a warning of possible mischief. Rainbow Head, a dominating feature of Port Palmerston, is not just part of the scenery: it accumulates an atmosphere foreshadowing strange and terrible events before Rifkah's crucifixion on the beacon is acted out there, leaving the serpent Head's symbolic presence intensified in preparation for the later scene of the bombing.

Probably the most important unifying element, in terms of recurrent events, is the Beatrice River Races, a natural community centre for gathering large groups together for the purposes of putting characters into new relations with one another and of initiating action. And the sense of bush community reaching beyond the towns that is built up is one of the novel's many virtues and a great improvement on this aspect of *Capricornia*. There are three of these annual race meetings: 1937, 1938 and 1939; in 1940 a communal listening by radio to the Battle for Britain is substituted, and in 1941 a memorial service for those killed in Greece.

More numerous and full of narrative interest are the escapes and captures that pulsate throughout, leading us into familiar or into new country. Prindy and Bobwirridirridi are the main fugitives, but Rifkah is involved in a chilling flight in Port Palmerston harbour, and Jeremy in an escape from political violence in Sydney harbour. Several of the other escapes are by train, the railway bringing out Herbert's ingenuity for narrative contrivance (every time the train leaves or reaches Beatrice River it is an event); an escape from bombed Darwin is in an old engine, the Sand Fly, which Pat Hannaford speedily gets back into working order. (Pat is a staunch and genial Communist and one of the most vivid *characters* of the novel.)

A frequent but imperfect sanctuary for these Aboriginal fugitives is the "painted caves" near Lily Lagoons. These caves are used skilfully in suggesting the mystical element of the novel, the sense of being in touch with great mysteries, as awe-inspiring as infinity, which can be conveyed by Aboriginal art. This is achieved progressively, and yet not mechanically, through four visits by different parties.

Love is another main part of structure—it certainly helps to make the world of *Poor Fellow My Country* go round. Jeremy and Rifkah are both centres for this, falling in love with each other as well as attracting others, but the love entanglements are too complex to be more than touched on here.

The novel is a historical one, not simply in the sense that it is set in the recent past, but also because it aims to represent the main forces in Australian society, the implication being that these are responsible for Australia's spiritually and socially bankrupt present. Herbert is able to weave in most of the important social and political issues still confronting Australia, including, for example, those aired at the time of

Whitlam's victory in 1972: treatment of the Aborigines, foreign ownership, dependence on outside powers, conservation, monopolies, and social justice. The historical dimension is achieved largely by the freedom of the fictional story, which follows social history and at the same time uses sparingly actual historical events and personalities, sometimes directly (e.g., Menzies and Mannix), sometimes through fictional parallels. We see in the novel the building up of mining interests in the north, and the British beef empire of Vaiseys has already been mentioned, as have the "Free Australia" movement and the clash of Right and Left. There is also the clash between British and local militaries, and we see something of the infiltration of German and Japanese interests. Among historical parallels which may appear to be sheer fiction are the plans for a settlement of Jewish refugees in the north, the abduction of a missionary by the Japanese (as Glascock is), and the presence and influence of high-ranking British personnel (there is a General Esk in the novel, there was General Squires in real life). The military machinations in the novel, supported by the police, are no doubt manipulated and heightened for dramatic purposes, but just as they reflect on social realities, they would appear to be based to some extent on realities.

The basic stuff of the novel helping to make it more effective, for organization cannot be divorced from the material it organizes, includes an immense factuality, a grounding in reality on which there is almost a tedious, obsessive insistence (as some have found in *Moby Dick*).[5] This naturalism, in which fact is sometimes just fact, at other times transfigured with the meaning of the significant image (Herbert does not seem to deal much in symbolism in the usual sense), is felt to arise from the extensiveness of the author's first-hand knowledge and his implicit appeal to its authority. It is as though his extraordinary range of bush experience had been unconsciously equipping him for this huge work. But Herbert's experience is not limited to the bush. He was, for instance, a first-hand observer of, if not participant in, the Australia First movement, and he did participate in the nationalism of the thirties through his work.

The novel's naturalism comes out mainly, however, in the

detailed features of the bush and its variety. Herbert can register its "signs" as an accurate, scientific observer as well as being able to invest them with legend, as we see in the extraordinarily close detail of hunting customs. An early passage in which Jeremy introduces the land to a sceptical outsider, Lady Lydia (though most readers are in the same boat), suggests the realistic closeness that is maintained:

"What colour is it to you"

"Grey . . . no, green-grey . . . a drab green-grey. Does that offend you?"

"Not a bit. It's the way most people see it . . . people born for generations in it . . . not truly native, of course. To me it's filled with colour." For once he indicated with his hand, sweeping it over the whole scene. "To start with, it has a blue iridescence over it. It's always like that in bright sunshine from about eleven to two. Then there are the bits of deeper blue and the quality of their depth. See!" He pointed with his finger "There . . . there . . . there! and the browns . . . see . . . and shades of green . . . and all meaning something. You can mark the watercourses if you concentrate, see where the sandstone ends and the limestone begins, by the change in colour. There it's schist. That litmus blue streak is the ridge where we saw the old blacks. The green that seems to be in the sky marks the lagoons . . . the billabongs. That yellowish patch . . . that's the Rainbow Pool."

But she was paying more attention to his animation. She said, "You truly love it, don't you?" [P. 141]

This naturalism is also apparent in the building up of the main locales and social centres of action, as with Beatrice River with its pub, stores, "big house", police station, hall, railway and railway workers, ostracized "mixed" families, Indian hawker and Chinese gardeners, and its Aboriginal camp.

In presenting its own kind of picture, the novel largely forgoes the techniques, condensing as well as serving other ends, that most twentieth-century novels rely on: the non-linear use of time; a dense, allusive, poetic language; varying degrees of the stream of consciousness; and the continually changing point of view and centre of consciousness.[6] Rather than changing points of view in this sense, Herbert relies on the varying content of the narrative "in itself", presented by an omniscient author; the tensions that in many modern novels are presented as coexisting within a dominating, complex personality are embodied in conflicting characters. As has been remarked of *Capricornia*, which set some basic aspects of Herbert's methods, there is little attempt to explore though processes or inner complexities of character. That "actions speak louder than words" (and, one might add, than psychological analysis) is rather the directing spirit of his novel. As a result, his talent—and the broad and complex concerns (an epic breadth) of *Poor Fellow My Country* require that amplitude, that development by careful accumulation of instances rather than stringent selectiveness, of those monsters, large nineteenth-century novels, though (*pace* James) Herbert aims to make his full-bodied in the sense of big-boned and meaty rather than fat.

The success of Herbert's methods, as outlined above, is shown in one of the peaks of the novel, a *tour de force* of dramatic narrative, though the great skill lies not simply in the peaks but in the gradual ascent and descent, the preparation and resolution they involve. The episode, necessarily sizeable, concerns yet another capture of Prindy by police-Sergeant Cahoon (Coon-Coon), another would-be father to him, and black-tracker Jinbal. Here we see the rich combination of vivid "fact" with a hovering magic and significance:

> They went splashing in to make the crossing. It was never deeper than to the horses' knees and mostly not much more than hock-deep, even though the strangely iridescent limey water swept over the ledge with the same smooth strength everywhere. Here was practically no rough, the rock mass having been worn smooth as a weir by the wash of ages. No trees at all on the crossing. There were biggish trees upstream a bit, but down only the permanently dwarfed and hump-backed things, just now but shivery islands of foliage. Immediately over the ledge the water was not so deep, as could be seen by the swirling weeds there and whiskery masses of moss. The deep was over another ledge.
>
> It was out about the middle that the Pookarakka, that time while crossing slung broken-legged on a pole, had tried to do his famous disappearing trick again. Here the water was knee-deep. They reached it. Was it the fact that the horse

Prindy was riding had taken part in that event which caused it to play-up now? Whatever it was, the beast's rearing jerked Coon–Coon's manacled hand and startled *his* horse, causing him to yell above the watery din, "Hey . . . what's goin' on?" He swung round, to see Prindy sliding out of his saddle on the off-side, that is the down-stream side, the right. He wheeled his horse round, to the left, the only way he could. That slacked the chain. Prindy took a flying leap over the ledge. He probably wouldn't have heard Coon–Coon yell, "You treacherous little bastard!" With both chains tautening, what began as a dive ended with a gutser. He went down. But almost on the instant, Coon–Coon, taking a grip on his end of the chain, jerked him up again, this time so that he floated on his back.

"Haul him in!" Cahoon bawled at Jinbul.

Jinbul had to lean well over to reach his chain. As he did so, Prindy grabbed his end of the chain, jerked. Jinbul, already almost overbalanced, came flying out of the saddle. His startled horse reared, slipped, could not recover its footing, since shackled to its rider, fell on its side, with helpless Jinbul half under it.

Cahoon, fairly screaming now, moved back to lend a hand. "You bloody little bastard . . . I'll belt Christ out of you for this!"

The Little Bastard was only a small yellow face with wide grey staring eyes.

What with the pouring water and the dragging weight downstream, the fallen horse hadn't a hope of rising especially with the led-horse performing behind.

Cahoon went first to the led-horse, slipped the clip of the lead-rope, then swung back, yelling at Jinbul, who was lying on his back, flapping the water to keep his head up, "Pull your foot out, *mungus*, and slip the stirrup-leather off the catch-bar."

The stirrup-leather was only semi-attached, for the very purpose of easy release of a rider pinned by his fallen horse. However, it meant being able to bend sufficiently to slip a hand under the saddle. Jinbul, looking strangely grey of dusky face, only kept beating the water with his hands, calling back to his master, "Break him my artch-bone, I stink, Boss. . . . "

He had to say it a couple of times before Coon–Coon heard, when he howled, "Jesus bloody Christ!" and this without any of that breast-striking.

Coon–Coon dismounted, leapt off the ledge, braving the fallen beast's thrashing hoofs, flung himself on its belly, tore up the saddle-flap, snatched at the girth-buckles. The horse went mad again with release of the pressure of the girth, tried to rise. Coon–Coon stilled it with a boot in the guts. He had yet to free the surcingle. He was a bit slower with this, bawling curses over the strap. Then the surcingle gave. Pressure of water against the upraised flap and the pull of Jinbul beyond, tore the saddle away. Jinbul went with it, and Prindy ahead of it, all with a jerk that pulled Coon–Coon over the horse's slippery wet body and after them all.

It was all so swift. There in a moment were they all, out in smooth shining water, riding the long swell of it, past the hunchback trees that bobbed to them as if in deference, while they looked back in astonishment at the distance-dwarfing horses that stared as astonished at them.

Strangely quiet out there, the only sound a sort of continuous hissing, but beyond it somewhere a growing roar. Perhaps it was this that roused Coon–Coon from what appeared to be a stupor of unbelief. He yelled at his Man Friday, "Get the chain round a tree!" Several biggish ones were coming up. He himself struck out across the current, to make sure of their being caught. But Jinbul, the grey-faced, accepting the inevitable, had sunken eyes only for what lay further ahead, a dark line, like a thin lip, and instead of striking oppositely, went drifting after. So they missed the tree, all of the trees. Cursing, Coon–Coon saw the staring, not only of the black eyes but the grey, and turned to look. Plainly it was a lip, quivering as if with suppressed laughter over the presumption of little men who thought they themselves so powerful, over the retribution always the due of traitors. But blind as he must ever be to the realities of the Unknowable, he saw it as a rock, and screamed "A rock, a rock . . . let's get to each side of it . . . swim, man, swim!"

No need to swim. As the lip opened to reveal the maw, those on the extremities of the chain were swept around as it sucked from both slides, leaving the chosen one, the mid-link of this magic chain, to fetch up against what for a fact was a shelf of rock even if serving as a laughing lip.

Prindy, slammed up against the lip, looking over it, saw it all. So near were they, the wanted ones, measured by man's reckoning, a couple of fathoms, plus a half for that outstretched three-striped arm and a bit more for the leg with its whipping saddle attached—and yet as far as Eternity, as could be seen by the agony of death in those eyes, blue and black, gazing up at him in the long, long little moment it took for their engulfment.

No, they were not gone clean away. There were their shades hovering.

The maw was like the throat of a flower, shining with light, to trap unwary creatures—like *Gwangu*, the Fly-catcher. The Shades hovered down inside like insects digesting in the false nectar that had trapped them.

The Sun rose up and up.

The water was falling.

Bits of the sugary marble peeped.

The sky was vivid blue, with white clouds sailing.

A straw-necked ibis came sailing along from where the flooded billabongs would be, saw, croaked with alarm, turned and went flapping back. A flight of white cockies, heading down from the Sandstone glimpsed, shrieked, wheeled and went screaming away eastward towards Catfish.

The Sun climbed up. The water fell.

Suddenly the chain on the right hand slackened. That meant being jerked sideways, dragged along the slippery rock a little way to the left, till the taut chain jammed in a crevice. It could be seen, silvery in the green whiskers. Now there was only one ghost below.

It was a long while before Prindy dared to haul in to see which it was had left him. It would have been that of the late Tracker Jinbul, because the handcuff was fairly wide open and a rag of moleskin hung on the saw-tooth projection like bait on a hook from which a fish has broken free.

How long would Daddy-o Cahoon's Shade be in taking itself off? Where would it go to? He might be right with his Old Jesus, but what about Old Tchamala, and Old God, who it seemed was a Jew—and Coon-Coon called Jews Sheeny Bastards?

At this point the narrative briefly catches its breath before it sweeps on again, the flying glance at Prindy's thoughts, though—or perhaps because—unrevealing, making it more effective.

What were the thoughts of the small executioner, as he lay against the marble lip, with hair now flying golden in the breeze, while he was chained by the neck to a dead man who probably had loved him?

Then Daddy-o went with suddenness that caused the chain to jerk out of the cleft. Prindy wasted no time in pulling in this time, because it was getting hot there with the Sun directly overhead and the water steaming and beginning to stink. But he stopped dead when a waxen hand appeared, outstretched as if in waving farewell, giving a blessing, or Heiling Hitler. He stared at it for a long while before he dared again. First the handcuff, well back on the black-haired wrist. Then the buttoned cuff of a khaki sleeve. Then the sleeve with the three chevrons of the sergeant who might have become an inspector. Then rags of cloth and flesh.

Who could trust the hand of Coon–Coon close enough to grab, even if it had no more than a torn-off arm behind it? Prindy could only keep it at a distance, and stare.

The problem was suddenly solved by a rush of wings. Prindy looked up, to see a brown white-breasted osprey diving to grab what he mistook for a fish. The buggers would often snatch one off your line. The long black talons seized it, raised it to the limit of the chain, which snatched it back, so that it came hurtling down and struck the hard rock— *Crack!* It was the cuff that struck. The lock was sprung. The manacle opened. The arm pulled by the waiting Shade drew the hand out of it, down into the maw. It was gone so quickly, that the osprey, hovering for another strike, whistled in protest. Prindy looked up to meet its angry yellow eye.

Now the ledge that was the crossing could be plainly seen as a dark ridge. The crippled trees were straightening up as best they could. The horses could be seen in the higher country to eastward, moving about amongst the timber there, with the angry restlessness of their kind when hungry but unable to crop properly with bitted mouths. From staring around, Prindy looked back at the maw. It was gone. All that lay before him was flat water, bound on the other side by a slab not dissimilar to that he was on, water that in its running round the rocks seemed to be laughing, perhaps over his having been tricked out of seeing how the magic had been wrought.

Bottom could be seen now. He gathered his chains together, slid down from the rock, began to work his way from shallow to shallow towards the horses, but looking back often whence he had come, as if expecting to see something odd. There was nothing. The falling water reflected the blue and white and silver of the sky. [Pp. 978–81]

The limitations and dangers of Herbert's methods are brought out clearly in the character of Jeremy. In a novel that has a strong polemical aspect (unusual in the modern novel, not only in Australia) Jeremy is the main spokesman as critic and apologist. The danger is obvious: he may talk too much and become Herbert's "mouthpiece". While this represents a problem not altogether overcome, it is I think an awkwardness, not a major flaw—more an occasional irritation. It can be too readily assumed (as did some reviewers) that Jeremy is simply a stand-in for the author. Certainly one needs only a passing acquaintance with Herbert's opinions aired in public at the time of the novel's publication to easily spot a number of similarities, but to press such an identification, and the criticism of Jeremy–Herbert as prophet–preacher that has accompanied it, is to ignore two basic points: that first, Jeremy is a failure, and his opinions are by no means totally endorsed by the novel; secondly, other recognizable aspects of the author are embodied in the views of other characters, such as Alfie, Rifkah, General Esk, Fergus Ferris. Besides Alfie's fervid patriotism, there are parallels, such as the irony of her winning the sesquicentenary novel prize with her *Australia Felix* (and Herbert's first name is Alfred). As with Jeremy's own idealistic opinions, Alfie's end in bitter disillusionment, the result of flaws of character as well as the negative forces of society. She is basically a sympathetic character, but demanding egoism can warp her views, as in her anti-semitism and her willingness to use the Aborigines. The failure of Rifkah's idealism has already been glimpsed. (What parts of the author may be represented in Prindy, Bobwirridirridi, Fergus, etc., I shall leave well alone.)

With Jeremy himself, his views and his character from which they spring are "criticised" by what happens to them and to him. His idealism cannot prevail—*Poor Fellow My Country* is a far cry from the facile Utopian novel—because of the nature of society and of Jeremy himself. Manning Clark has complained that Jeremy knows the answers.[7] He has plenty, but they remain largely theoretical and he himself cannot practise some fundamental ones. And Clark's comment failed to allow for an underlying uncertainty in Jeremy as well as for changes in him and his beliefs. His patriotism has to be rekindled by Alfie through her shared genuine sympathies with the "Free Australia" movement before it sours, and by Rifkah, who strengthens his flagging sympathy for the Aborigines. His hopes for Prindy are destroyed partly by his own possessiveness and interference. Although Esk has his own axe to grind in separating Jeremy from Rifkah, Esk puts to her a fundamental criticism of Jeremy:

> He's a man with a great capacity for love. Hence his deep disillusionment. This has bred in him a set of subtle hatreds. He's come to hate his country . . . through too demanding a love of it. He's long hated the countries of his origins, because he expected something of them they couldn't give. He would probably have come even to hating the Aborigines, to whom he's given so much for so little return, only everybody else hates them. He's perverse, you know. That mixture of Welsh and Irish. His last disillusionment, as I see it, was the boy Prindy. He speaks as if the boy is doing everything he expects and wants of him . . . which is probably intellectually true. But I'm sure he wanted the boy to accept him as his grandsire, to love him as belonging to him. The boy lives in a different world, of course. [P. 761]

This may go too far, but it is essentially borne out by the novel. It is part of the both sympathetic and critical presentation to show him as driven by disillusion, by an emptiness he tries frantically to fill. There is a desperation of unfulfilment behind his zeal that can make it obsessive. Jeremy's pain thus comes out mainly in indirect ways, but it is there; more internal dramatization would have demanded a different kind of novel. As Prindy is the unfulfilled artist, Jeremy is partly the unfulfilled leader, though leadership is a quality that in Australia evokes an unreasonable degree of scepticism; the novel distrusts it but mourns its difficulty and the lack of it.

If there is some occasional overflow of Jeremy's passionate polemics, this is a limitation that should be measured against the burden of argumentation he must reasonably bear in a polemical novel and bears well, for argument interacts effectively with dramatization. And excess is part of Jeremy's character, more as a strength than a weakness. Perhaps the main limitation is that sometimes when the authorial view-point and Jeremy's appear to be at one the reader will feel some separation is needed, that though he can see Jeremy's failings, the novel does not seem to be making sufficient allowance for them. Examples are Jeremy's contribution to Alfie's eventual enmity towards him and his occasional violence, mainly verbal. Yet though the latter does offend against the sentimentality that violence such as anger is never justified, and never found together with what is sympathetic, as in love, pain, or disillusion, it is in keeping with Jeremy's character and helps to keep him human. If he does not always come through as sympathetically as the author wishes, then the novel's achievement in coping with its greatest challenge in characterization outstrips the intention—some irritation with Jeremy confirms that he lives as a character. If the novel does not admit to his failings as much as it might, they are clearly shown.

Poor Fellow My Country as a whole is a novel of enormous ambitions, and though the work is not flawless, the ambitions are fulfilled to a remarkable degree. It is a moving threnody not only for a nation unfulfilled but also for man's incapacity to fulfil himself. Herbert's earlier works represented a kind of refusal to mourn, to see instead man's misused, or unused, power over his destiny as a ludicrous or grim joke. In his latest work "the spirit of the land", no mere label or landscape painting, takes on a vital life, expressing man's capacity for wonder, the magical power of the imaginative and the irrational within himself which he has denied. Similarly Australian society has failed to achieve a real ethos, its "distinctive" characteristics are only superficial and defensive. Instead of exorcising the demons of an alien country (to use Keneally's phrase),[8] demons reflecting those within men, the novel shows that the whites have "exorcised" a vital part of themselves; the Aborigines, through the land and their ethos, reconciled the good and evil spirits by accepting them in a balance of detachment (externalization) and involvement. Hence their belonging. Herbert's threnody rises above angry denunciation, the freakish and facile, through its grip on personal and social realities and through its passionate imaginativeness. *Poor Fellow My Country* dramatizes no less than an Australian tragedy.

NOTES

1. Thomas Keneally, "The Australian Novel", *Age*, 3 February 1968, p. 2. Subsequent references to Keneally's comments are to this article, an abridged version of which appeared in *Quadrant*, February 1977.
2. Judith Wright, "At Cooloola".
3. All references to *Poor Fellow My Country* are to the first edition (Sydney: Collins, 1975).
4. Xavier Herbert in conversation.
5. Here I have borrowed and adapted some phrasing from Laurie Clancy's article on Malcolm Lowry ("Malcolm Lowry's Voyages", *Meanjin Quarterly* 35, no. 3 (1976): 281). Apropos of a comment on *Moby Dick*, Clancy comments: "But one accepts the mythic and allegorical interpretations and dimensions of the novel partly because one is first convinced of its immense factuality, its grounding in reality, on which Melville insists with almost obsessive and tedious repetition."
6. Again I have borrowed and adapted phrases from Clancy's article above (p. 280), where his summary of techniques of the modern novel was convenient to my purpose of pointing out how Herbert instead makes his own use of "older" techniques, in no perjorative sense. The individual use of techniques and not the newness of techniques themselves can contribute to unique achievement.
7. See Manning Clark's review of *Poor Fellow My Country*, in The *Canberra Times*, 10 September 1975, p. 10. Though Clark's review is perceptive in some respects, it is too quick to conclude that the prophet takes over from the artist. This view is based largely on a misconception of Jeremy's role in the novel as a whole which I take up at the end of this essay. This misconception was shared by some other reviewers. All reviewers were at a disadvantage (though few acknowledged it) in having to cope with such a large novel which makes extraordinary demands on reading time as well as on a reflective reading. It is ironic that Herbert's aim as artist is similar to Clark's as historian in his 1976 Boyer Lectures where he attempts to explain the failure of Australians by returning to the past to look at the quality of intellectual and spiritual life. Though I have read all the reviews, I have chosen to ignore them in my own attempt to make a preliminary survey of the novel; an adequate appreciation will only emerge after some time and much discussion.
8. In comments on *Voss*, *To the Islands*, and *The Tilted Cross* in the article cited in footnote 1.

"The Splinters of a Mind Make a Whole Piece"

Patrick White's *The Eye of the Storm*

RICHARD WILSON

The notion that any given writer is really saying the same thing in each of his different works is familiar enough, and Patrick White has been charged with merely repeating in *The Eye of the Storm* what he has already said elsewhere.[1] Others may see a development in his treatment here of the formidable maternal figure that has been frequent in his fiction;[2] others again may deny that there is in fact this time also an improvement and that the spiritual states she is purported to embody are at all credible.[3] Such states, at any rate, would appear to be crucial. Their function in this novel may reveal itself if we look patiently at how indeed he has "got it all together" on this occasion and whether there is now a difference in degree of his artistic subtlety that produces a significant difference in his kind of fiction. Elizabeth Hunter's spiritual evolution may prove to be his central but by no means his exclusive interest; he is continually leading us outwards from her to the adventures in selfhood and identity experienced by her children, by all the others around her, and the agents by which he most persistently expresses his metaphysical interests may prove to be not people at all but the play of light on birds, jewels, and flowers.

We can at least begin with the old lady herself, keeping in mind that any commonplaces encountered are hers and not White's,[4] whether they be religious or artistic or, as in her thoughts of the storm itself, both: "You can never convey in words the utmost in experience. Whatever is given you to live, you alone can live, and re-live, and re-live, till it is gasped out of you."[5] Awakened by Sister de Santis from the half-asleep in which a fragment of the past has revisited her and become the greater reality, she denies that she has been dreaming: " 'Not dreaming—living' " (p. 211), and this is the mode White sustains for her throughout while we learn, very early, that "she would have liked to experience a state of mind she knew existed, but which was too subtle to enter except by special grace" (p. 16). This experience in her life has become the gauge for the rest of it and is what she looks forward to; "she had no desire to die however stagnant her life became: she only hoped she would be allowed to experience again that state of pure, living bliss she was now and then allowed to enter. How, she wasn't sure" (p. 24).

What she is sure about is that she yearned for it long before she first experienced it, and White takes pains to document the long history of this hunger. None of those near her understood it, least of all her devoted husband in those early years out at their property, "Kudjeri". She recalls how "she began going out of her way to avoid him, hoping to find in solitude insight into a mystery of which she was perhaps the least part" (p. 28). When he offers her freedom from the marriage, she writes that she didn't believe in "*a state of freedom greater than we know and 'enjoy'—at least, not in life*", then exclaims to herself, "but how you longed for it" (p. 103). Some suspected but none believed: "a few individuals, sensitive up to a point, had guessed at some mysterious, not religious or intellectual, some kind of spiritual aspiration, and labelled you a fraud when you couldn't confront them with, not spiritual, but material evidence" (p. 90). She remained at the mercy of their image of her. "If you could have said: I am neither compleat wife, sow, nor crystal, and must take many other shapes before I finally set, or before I am, more probably, shattered. But you couldn't; they would not have seen you as the eternal aspirant. Solitariness and despair did not go with what they understood as a beautiful face and a life of outward brilliance and material success" (p. 102). Not until a third of the novel has been devoted to her recall of her years of anticipation of it does White divulge that she "had experienced transcendence by virtue of that visit to the Warmings' island"

(p. 205); not until another third has been devoted to its implications for these last days of hers does White present it. Few scenes in fiction could less resemble a gratuitous "set piece"; no scene could be more organic in the whole of which it is one of the most significant parts.

What she transcends during the island experience is not so much selfhood as the imperfections of the one she had hitherto known. She fulfils her wish to "break out of the straitjacket and recover a sanity which must have been [hers] in the beginning, and might be [hers] again in the end . . . a calm in which the self had been stripped, if painfully, of its human imperfections" (p. 29). This is not the selflessness of the saints but a truer self, the kind she had glimpsed with as much fear as fascination in Odilon Redon's skiapod; "not her own actual face, but the spiritual semblance which will sometimes float out of the looking-glass of the unconscious" (p. 200).

When White does take up the great event itself, he does all he can to direct interest away from the overt drama and onto those implications that reach back through Elizabeth Hunter's long life of self-awareness and self-dissatisfaction. Getting up early on this day that begins so quietly, she finds herself alone, "not even herself for company" (p. 414). She indulges a pang of self-pity, recognizes "her own type of useless, beautiful woman" (p. 414), who had caused her husband fatal grief and who had "encouraged her lovers' lust" (p. 415). The scientist Pehl refusing to tell her where her daughter Dorothy is, she wanders into the bush, knowing that she can admit her faults only to herself, knowing her hypocrisy and keenly feeling the injustice of her innocent victims' not surviving while she continues to demand and receive. "For the first time she was disturbed by the mystery of her strength, of her elect life, not that frequently unconvincing part of it which she had already lived, but that which stretched ahead of her as far as the horizon and not even her own shadow in view" (p. 416). She walks into the rain forest, "walking more humbly, as much for her solitariness as for the powers and honours so unreasonably conferred on her" (p. 416). She responds to its flowers but finds she no longer wishes to possess them. "By allowing her inescapably frivolous and, alas, corrupt nature the freedom of its silence, the forest had begun to oppress her" (p. 417).

This whole prelude to the moment when the eye is to be focused on her continues to insist on the desperate egotism, aimlessness, and restless craving for attention and connection that have always characterized her. When she hears foresters, she must go to them and satisfy her "longing to talk to somebody, nobody, somebody quite simple, stupid even", needing to "reassure herself that she could still fit into the pattern of someone else's life" (p. 417); but she immediately realizes too that "it was going to be practically impossible to make herself credible" (p. 417). She succeeds in being again only "brittle and pretentious" (p. 418) and the foresters merely smile at the ground. When she returns to the house, she envies "the Warmings their complementary lives" as evidenced by the "smell of privacy" in their bedroom, and Dorothy's room is of course empty (p. 419). Despite her rearranging her hair and dressing for the evening, she feels "an irrelevant figure hanging around . . . for no purpose she could think of, and in what was after all a ridiculous get-up" (p. 420). Abandoned, insufficient to herself, she is presented at the nadir of her selfhood.

When the tumult of the first half of the cyclone begins, White further subordinates the sensational and even the seventy-year-old woman's physical responses, so that the violence, rendered for us indirectly and in low key, takes on a dream-like quality and the metaphysics dominate the foreground. Driven by buffeting wind and torrential rain to the shelter of the bunker, fully sensitive to "the highest pitch of awfulness the human spirit can endure" (p. 424), she has no fear of death. "She could not visualize it. She only positively believed in what she saw and was and what she was was too real too diverse composed of everyone she had known and loved and not always altogether loved it is better than nothing and given birth to and for God's sake" (p. 424). The prose falls even quieter as she is awakened by the sudden silence of the eye and goes out to wade through debris, while "round her a calm was glistening" (p. 424). She is "without much thought for her own wreckage"; she is totally concentrating on something else:

she was no longer a body, least of all a woman: the myth
of her womanhood had been exploded by the storm. She was
instead a being, or more likely a flaw at the centre of this
jewel of light: the jewel itself, blinding and tremulous at the
same time, existed, flaw and all, only by grace; for the storm
was still visibly spinning and boiling at a distance, in columns
of cloud, its walls hung with vaporous balconies, continually
shifted and distorted.

But she could not contemplate the storm for this dream
of glistening peace through which she was moved. [P. 424]

The eye withdraws its attention, the second half of the cyclone
returns, and when her rescuers explain it all to her the next
day, "she could hardly bother: nothing mattered beyond her
experiencing the eye" (p. 427). They are full of solicitude,
"as though guarding a treasure. . . . Whereas she was simply
herself again" (p. 427). Henceforth she sees all her other
identities in relation to this one moment of self-without-taint,
and White, who has provided for our seeing her as a girl,
wife, mother, adulteress, society hostess, and irascible invalid,
provides too for our seeing all these personae in her own
new perspective. We know her as White knows her; we
discover her as she discovers herself; and he thus authenticates
the paradox of such a destructive survivor finding grace. This
is the quintessential selfhood that she looked forward to all
her life and to which she now looks back, hoping to
experience it yet again before her life ends. As a characterization, it is the fullest and most credibly various that White
has ever achieved.

The presentation of each of his other characters, too, in
their respective encounters with selfhood is generally more
balanced and proportioned than in his earlier work, and there
are far fewer figures engaging merely one side of his talent;
most come in for all of it. The satire, the compassion, and
the metaphysical speculation are no longer so mutually
exclusive among the people whom he marshalls about his
protagonist: her daughter and her son, her nurses and her
cook, her lawyer and his wife—with the single exception of
the flat Badgery (fictive cousin of the Sugdens and the Duns)
—are presented in several dimensions.

Elizabeth Hunter's daughter, for instance, is established
not only as the Princess de Lascabanes and Dorothy Hunter

of "Kudjeri" via Gogong but also as hopelessly *deracinée* wherever she is and seeking in worldly comforts some recompense for her spiritual sterility. White gives us all sides of her; her snobbishness, meanness, priggishness, affectations, and ruthless selfishness to begin with, but also her pathetic self-insufficiency, her flashes of bitter jealousy of her flamboyant and superficially impressive brother Basil, her guilt over her non-relation with her father and her eternal competition with her mother. Basil sees her as "rigid" and "humourless" (p. 232) and "a thriving hive of self-pity" (p. 493); her mother sees her as "always knotted to the point of strangulation" (p. 66); Cherry Bullivant recognizes that this "friend" of schooldays would like to dispose of her mother at a nursing home as she herself had disposed of hers. Dorothy's perpetual efforts to escape self counterpoint her mother's perpetual quest to discover the significance of it. Overwhelmed by the impact of a foreign Australia, she laments "*I have never managed to escape this thing Myself*" (p. 49): Fleeing the ghastliness of Cherry's Australian welcome party, she decides in desperation that "if there was no running away from herself, she must at least escape from the Cheeseman house, with its implications, and downright accusations" (p. 297). On Brumby Island she had found momentary release from self while passing through the rain forest, a willing initiate; and when she reached the ocean there was a moment when she desired its oblivion in preference to "the paroxysms and alternating apathy of a lopsided existence" (p. 375). But she had fled this island, too; fled Pehl and the mother with whom she had found herself competing for his half-desired, half-abhorred attentions, and then had declared "blessed the anonymity which would clothe her at last in the great plane flying her back with speed and discretion to Europe" (p. 408). Belonging nowhere, "sometimes Dorothy Hunter suspected she existed only in the novels of Balzac and Stendhal and Flaubert, the plays of Racine" (p. 54). She retreats again and again into her favourite, *The Charterhouse of Parma*, to become Dorothy Sanseverina. Her mother tells her that the book was the father's favorite too, and that "he loved that woman".

"Who—Clélia?" she hoped.
"No. The other—the duchess. He admired her brilliance."
[P. 224]

Dorothy, who, unlike her mother, can be duchess only in
Stendhal's pages and so hopes that her father at least
preferred the other lover of Fabrizio, must reply, " 'I find
her dishonest in some respects.' " White relentlessly marks
the essential contrast between the mother and the daughter,
as she answers her:

> "This—Sanseverina was no more dishonest than any other
> beautiful woman, or—or jewel. An emerald isn't less beau-
> tiful, is it? for the flaw in it?
> It was Dorothy who was exhausted; she mumbled, "I can't
> think." In fact, her thoughts, her aspirations—which were
> also her dishonesties—were rattling round inside her like the
> loose seeds in a maraca. [P. 225]

The important discriminations are made as relentlessly as
the ironies are sustained, but there is also genuine compassion
in the total account of Dorothy. Her encounter with the
Warming family on their island, where she is alien, rejected,
and swamped by her mother, gives poignance to the time
she spends with the Macrory family during the nostalgic visit
she makes with Basil. There she freely plays out her mother's
role, even to the detail of wearing white (the colour that
everyone in the novel remembers the old lady by) and she
briefly enjoys Ann Macrory's yearning affection and the
adoration of the daughters whose dresses she makes (while
they stick pins—and even scissors—into the dressmaker's
form of her mother). "If she could have remained enclosed
by this circle of love and trust, she might have accepted herself
by living up to their opinion of her" (p. 511). But Dorothy
remains at the mercy of herself, and she is shown throughout
always to have been at the mercy of her mother. Shackled
by her cynicism, she is usually wrong: she totally disbelieves
her mother's account of the eye of the storm, regarding as
deceitful evasion the true account she is given of how her
mother learned the name of the noddy bird that saved her.
Though she says that the Dutchman she met on the flight
to Australia, the old seaman who had experienced the eye

of a cyclone at sea, calmed her fears during bumpy weather over the Bay of Bengal and struck her " 'as being . . . himself the soul of calm and wisdom' " (p. 72), she remains scornfully incredulous of her mother's experience.

Though, too, she tries to rid herself of her murderous hatreds and respond to natural beauty such as the bland golden light from the park opposite the house in Moreton Drive and the birds in its garden, she dooms herself by a philosophy that keeps her inaccessible to such forces: "as if you can possess the moment of perfection; as if conception and death don't take place simultaneously" (p. 221).

So with her mother at last dead, the money in the bank, and enjoying her notion of herself and of impersonality, she has no doubt how she will "occupy herself in her state of spiritual (and economic) emancipation" (p. 587): she will rid her shoe cupboards and bookshelves of the unfashionable, share gourmet meals with some "elderly, distinguished connoisseur", and exchange her present confessor for a brand new "spiritual preceptor" (p. 588). Our last glimpse is of her sick and frightened: "I am this flying shoebox the prayers rattling inside *grâce à Dieu on atterrira à Orly à 07h 05*" (p. 590). White's firm control ensures that she is not merely her lame metaphysics or her ludicrous values, because this minor figure's notion of a perfect state at last attained is seen in the context of the major figure's far different apotheosis, and so the sting of the satirical is ameliorated by a fine compassion that gives her a fully human stature. Her effectiveness as a study is surpassed only by her function as a vital complement.

The other complement similar in stature is, of course, Basil: the other negative to the mother's positive, who, confronted with a stop-over at Bangkok, wonders "how to keep himself company in the four-hour wilderness" (p. 130) and desperately plunges into the company of similarly stranded actors and actresses, only to discover again his own drunkenness and impotent lust. In his constant rearguard action from the challenge and the mystery of self, he is bitterly aware that "you only couldn't prevent mirrors mucking about with empty disintegrating faces", then argues that "emptiness is not emptiness when it serves a purpose" (p. 130) and he

rationalizes it as vital to his art as an actor, who could
otherwise not "fill", under inspiration, with emotion. He has
no sympathy with his first wife, the "cerebral actress to bury
other contenders" who agonizes *"I'm having such a terrible
time Basil with my self"* (p. 131). But he comes back
continually to his own nothingness; to his "hunger—for
what? For substance perhaps, for permanence?" (p. 251).
Failed by friendship, marriage, knighthood, and name, he
recognizes that the main motive for his return to Australia
is "to renew himself through bursts of light, whiffs of
burning, the sound of trees stampeded by a wind when they
weren't standing as still as silence" (p. 249), and "Kudjeri"
mud. When, unaware of each other's presence, he and his
sister come from their Goneril-Regan performance in the
family solicitor's office and sit in the Botanic Gardens on
either side of "a wall of evergreens", he "leant forward on
the park bench, trying to interpret the blades of grass. There
had been a time when he saw clearly, right down to the root
of the matter, before his perception had retired behind a
legerdemain of technique and the dishonesties of living"
(pp. 272–73).

He does "return to the source of things" (p. 417) and finds
that "to be passively accepted by your natural surroundings
is only temporarily gratifying", while "what he craved was
confirmation of his own intrinsic worth as opposed to possibly
spurious achievement". On the night of his arrival at
"Kudjeri", when he has "nipped out for a pee", he finds
that "the darkness continued to offer the kindly indifference
of nature at its domestic fringes, while the house behind
would probably never share its secrets with one who had
renounced life for theatre" (p. 477). Still he persists in
fossicking for the lost self, driven by something much more
desperate than nostalgia. Next day, alone by the dam, "the
empty sky . . . staring at him" (p. 491), he declaims a few
lines of Lear, listening to his own voice "and some of it
returned out of that extrovert blue" (p. 492). But chiefly he
misses on that spot his loving and unloved father who had
long ago cantered up to rescue him after he broke an arm
falling from a tree; now, after he has clumsily cut his foot,
he feels "abandoned by everybody. Stranded in his own

egotism and ineptitude. Though he listened for it, the reliable roan was not coming at a canter" (p. 494). In the former stables, now all dust, rust and neglect, he carries out again the "rituals of childhood" (p. 504) with splinters and cobwebs, sits again on the ancient harvester, even puts on an old boot and relives fragments of his relationship with each parent as he sits in his father's beloved 3-litre Bentley, until this fragile moment too disintegrates into farce when an abrasive Dorothy discovers him and they together struggle to get that boot off.

So his next boy-like escape is to "what used to be the orchard" (p. 516), taking with him, as used to be habitual, bread and cheese and Shakespeare. But it is the Lear of *"Is there any cause in nature that makes these hard hearts*? Some of the lines were flung back at him like stones": hence, this time the intruder is the mother who is not to be dismissed by any denial such as: "Stick to the text reality is a mad king not an aged queen whose crown won't come off for pulling whose not quite fresh eyes live by lucid flashes as hard as marble" (p. 516). There is thus no escape, certainly not in places; nor in time, for "reality is always present tense" (p. 517). Nor in people; not even with the sister who represents for him a final chance for reconnection. "This relationship had grown dovetailed, they were taking it so much for granted" (p. 518). " 'Oh, Basil! . . . What have we got unless each other? Aren't we, otherwise— bankrupt?' " On this their last night at "Kudjeri", they huddle pathetically in their parents' former bed, having come full circle, till Dorothy, horrified by her brother's casual awareness of this ironic fact, has to "tear open a darkness" (p. 526) by snatching the curtains from the window. As they are confronted with their native landscape that is " 'beautiful —but sterile' ", White confronts the reader with their abysmal isolation:

"That's what it isn't, in other circumstances."

"Other circumstances aren't ours." [P. 527]

One of White's greatest strokes in the whole novel is to have them awakened the next morning by the telephone that brings to that room the death of their mother—who has rewon those other circumstances. For Dorothy it is the end; she henceforth denies him, anxious only to expunge their moment of mutual surrender and dependence; and this for Basil is the final betrayal and abandonment in the entire "Kudjeri" gesture.

If he is to come to terms with himself at all it must be through his art as an actor—this is the notion he recognizes, confesses, examines throughout the novel—and so far he has never dared risk expressing the significant other fractions of that self. Lotte Lippmann, the German Jewess who cooks for his mother and grotesquely sings and dances for her some *Tingeltangel* routines, rightly assumes he agrees that the "drunkenness" of theatrical performance is as necessary to the performance as to the audience, and she pierces him with her desire for a second chance at life in which she "would ask to create one *whole* human being" (p. 148). He too "might have created a whole rather than a part. When all the parts were hanging from their pegs and out of sight, this whole might have reminded him that he was not wholly actor: he was also a whole human being" (p. 149). His sense of failure and incompleteness is acute. In a rare moment of honesty, mainly a response to the qualities of Sister de Santis, he confesses a wish to " 'reject the whole business of—of acting: all its illusions and your own presumption—not to say *spuriousness*' " (p. 345). To the totally self-conscious Sir Basil Hunter, whose every public move and gesture White has shown as calculated histrionics, there has come an itch for self-scrutiny that could even result in self-awareness, and there is high interest in which of the three possible options he will choose. There is first the challenge of Lear that he is fearful of accepting, for he has earlier confessed to having been already " 'one of the many premature Lears' " (p. 127) —even to having been " 'a bloody superficial' " one (p. 349) —and there is candour, self-knowledge, as well as a flicker of something approaching hope and grit in the way he offers de Santis the old Bradleyan cliché about the play:

> "Nobody has ever entirely succeeded as Lear, because I don't think he can be played by an actor—only by a gnarled, authentic man, as much a storm-tossed tree as flesh . . . So he can probably never be played . . . Blake could have,

> perhaps. Or Swift. That didn't mean you wouldn't have
> another go at it yourself. [P. 350]

But he shies away, saying the role calls for what he implies
he lacks, the tragic quality rousable only through "purity
of the inner man" (p. 235). He will play it only in drunken
dream-fantasy during his flight back to the only world real
to him.

There is, second, the far more terrifying challenge of Mitty
Jacka's notion of an improvised play: " . . . an actor tends
to ignore the part which fits him best *his life* Lear the old
unplayable is in the end a safer bet than the unplayed
I . . . " (p. 246). He is tempted: could this help him achieve
Lotte Lippmann's notion of creating one whole human being?
The idea strikes terror into the hearts of that gaggle of theatre
people in Bangkok. But it strikes deepest in Basil, who uses
his talents defensively, whose art is all protective, never an
expression of the fullest self but a screening of it. As he
explains to Mitty, it is like the screen his father erected for
him during a childhood illness, designed to ward off draughts
but in fact reflecting the night-light's shadows so fearfully
that he never dared satisfy his yearning to look behind it.
Beyond it could lie the awful flux and fluidity of living and
life, far beyond the controls of slick techniques; perhaps the
accident of self-revelation—perhaps Revelation itself, even
less to be dared.

The answer lies in the third option, as Patricia Clancy
makes so helpfully clear in her article, "The Actor's Dilemma: Patrick White and Henri de Montherlant".[6] There is
always *The Master of Santiago* and the role of the austere,
God-seeking Don Alvaro, in which he "made a fine figure",
therefore fitting him best as an actor though, ironically, fitting
him least as a man. "Impress anybody with some of those
lines—and your voice: *God neither wishes nor seeks anything.
He is eternal calm. It is in wishing nothing that you will
come to mirror God*" (p. 317). Elizabeth Hunter's son ("not
believing in 'God' " [p. 318] declaims them mentally as he
lies naked beside the sexually robust Flora Manhood. As Dr
Clancy so neatly sums up the options: "Mitty Jacka's living
theatre, *King Lear*, and *The Master of Santiago*. What he
could be if he dared, what he could never be, and what he

is."[7] What is so arresting in White's art is how, in each particular, these counterpoint the so much more positive daring of Basil's mother, who as well as being consummate in playing all the social roles that her life presented to her, created one whole human being by in spirit fully playing the "I". Reaching for God, as does Don Alvaro in his final scene, she could have composed, as well as spoken, those lines of his quoted above. And, most significantly, Elizabeth Hunter knows that screens exist only to be lifted and, having glimpsed the vision revealed in the eye of the storm, finds that it gives expectancy and purpose to the remainder of her life—finally, in fact, capping it.

Her son and daughter never come to terms with their own selfhood, never even know of her journey; others, not her flesh and blood but her "acolytes" during its final stages, are intimate witnesses who catch glimmers and flashes and whose reactions provide White with further variations on his theme as he shows—caustically, amusingly, compassionately, and definitively—how those around her misunderstand or half-understand what is happening to her. Flora Manhood, Lotte Lippmann, and Mary de Santis serve him well. Flora, whom Geoffrey Dutton justly describes as "a superbly realized character",[8] shares with Elizabeth Hunter the physical lust that drove her to seduce a younger Arnold Wyburd and to violate her sensibilities with Arnold Shreve. Flora's own vigorous carnality, partly sheer, vulgar health, partly restless experiment, drives her from the arms of Col Pardoe to the bed of Snow Tunks and her lesbian friend Alix, then to the farce of trying to conceive a child by Basil and at last back resignedly to Col—and his Mahler, his paperbacks, and his eternal chops. Selfhood is all too much for the robust Flora: "She wished she was a plant or something" (p. 86). Her lover and her patient cannot help her with it: *"Your trouble Flo you've got wrong ideas about yourself for that matter nobody knows what he really is.* Not according to Her: *only oneself can know that one is really like Sister.* So it was always this: hacking into you from either side" (p. 107). She humours the old tyrant, makes her up, complete with lilac wig, but something extra happens, and Flora is vulnerable to it.

> Momentarily at least this fright of an idol became the goddess
> hidden inside: of life, which you longed for, but hadn't yet
> dared embrace; of beauty such as you imagined, but had so
> far failed to grasp (with which Col grappled, you bitterly
> suspected somewhere in the interminably agitated depths of
> music); and finally, of death, which hadn't concerned you,
> except as something to be tidied away, till now you were
> faced with the vision of it. [P. 121]

There are other breaks in "the mists of senility", other
"inklings of transcendence" (p. 442) which almost whirl her
"to an understanding of mysteries such as love, beauty,
fulfilment, death" (pp. 442–43). She hungers for something
more than the deadly dull decent kindness of the Vidlers with
whom she boards behind that carefully scrubbed front step
in 21 Gladys Street. At the end, after the death, she gets
it straight: "Hadn't she loved, not Mrs Hunter herself, but
something she stood for? Life, perhaps. She whipped you
on" (p. 564). Finally, with Col, Flora unconsciously says
more about Elizabeth Hunter than about herself when she
tells him: "She understood me better than anybody ever"
(p. 573). And why would she not?

She understands her dancing cook, too, the unhappy little
Jewess Lotte, eternally unforgiving of herself for having
escaped the gas ovens, but has no wish to identify with her.
All they have in common is suffering. However, they use
it differently; Lotte, " 'the original masochist' " (p. 150)
according to her mistress, makes, in the Gandhian sense, little
progress with hers; there is little purity in it; it is as soft
as her perpetual *milchig-fleischig*, as oozily indulgent as her
Torte. The art of her German honky-tonk is indeed "a tiny,
satiric one—to find what in all things is ridiculous" (p. 82)
and it produces only the grotesque. She leans on her mistress
and learns little from her. " 'Yes,' " she tells Basil. " 'She
is all you say [evil, brutal, destructive]; but understands more
of the truth than most others. . . . And if I cannot worship,
I have to love somebody' " (p. 150). Yet it is as much a
soggy gratitude as love. Even worse, Lotte is *sorry* for her
and therefore never gets her straight at all. As she dances
for her, she sings sentimental rubbish about disillusionment
and celebrates maudlin self-pity.

Such defeatism repels and embarrasses the old lady, who eventually glares dismissal with, " 'There's too much of yourself tonight' " (p. 543), and as she herself grows more preoccupied with re-entering the eye, Lotte becomes for her "a steamy, devoted, often tiresome Jewess standing on one leg" (p. 544). Mrs Hunter dead, she is left with herself, whom she cannot face, so she goes to her room, hangs a towel over the mirror, rakes her cheeks with her nails and at last creates in the bathroom her own holocaust. "The heater, with its permanent smell of gas and flames roaring inside the copper cylinder, had terrified her in the beginning, but she had grown used to all such minor effects. Outside the window of the maids' bathroom the sky was more convincingly on fire, the blaze smudged by fingers of smoke from the chimneys of Alexandria and Waterloo" (pp. 606–7). When she has opened her veins in the bath she has, unlike her Mrs Hunter, entered a heaven totally infernal.

It is not Lotte or Flora who can in any sense accompany the old lady; that difficult privilege is earned by Mary de Santis, whose spirituality, in its rigour and austerity, utterly sunders her from these colleagues and receives respectful tribute from its chief inspirer. White has her open and close the novel and entrusts some of its most telling effects to her characterization. Just as he succeeds in authenticating those non-corporeal qualities that exist in the lusty body of Flora, so in this nun-like nurse he achieves a credible balance between her sensitive questing spirit and her human fragility, her spasmodic lust, her sense of guilt. Next to her patient, she is the figure who most develops a sense of being. She has from the first "an authority of the spirit" and a "deeper access to the heart of the creature round whom they revolved" (p. 19), a heritage from her keenly religious Italian and Greek parents. When her patient asks her what she understands by love, she offers a description of selfless giving that guiltily disturbs the woman who could never love her husband or her children. The old invalid adorns her with a turquoise sash, saying, " 'See? I haven't altered you. . . . Only heightened a mystery which was there already, and which is too valuable not to respect' " (p. 167). Awe gives way to bitterness when she envies the purer and younger woman's access to the dimension of love that she knows exists but had not till then found: " 'I wouldn't want to expose anyone of your worth and dedication—indefinitely—to a flawed character like mine' " (p. 168).

But Mary de Santis, for all her background and gifts, is well aware of being a seeker after grace rather than, like Elizabeth Hunter, a lucky recipient of it. She too is confronted with "her knotty solitary self" (p. 174). She had been united with her dying father "in a dangerously rarefied climate where love and suffering mingle" (p. 342) and, to her, Basil "was Papa: an elderly, distinguished, but weak man, asking for love and understanding as well as the drug he depended on;" (p. 338) and *"You mustn't touch the basil Máro Papa has planted"* (p. 174) are the words she keeps recalling from her childhood. Sinning in thought only, she must yet exorcise her lust by "a discipline of drudgery" (p. 207); knowing her motives so damningly mixed as she lunches in pathetic tipsiness with the ego-ridden actor, she fails to present her case against his mother's incarceration in a rest home; "she knew she would never find the strength or opportunity to bear witness to her true faith and plead for the one who was also, incidentally, Elizabeth Hunter" (p. 351). By the time that lady has died, Mary has found strength through assimilating the meaning of much that had hitherto checked her, and she expresses her love for the dead through service to the paralyzed young Irene, her next patient, who, savagely at the mercy of suffering, " 'only convinced by what is evil' " (p. 604), thinks all the sick are disgusting.

> "Mrs Hunter wasn't sick," Sister de Santis said. "She was old. She had been a great beauty in her day—a success. She was also cold and cruel when it suited her to be."
> "Was she happy?" Irene asked.
> "Not altogether. She was human. In the end I feel age forced her to realize she had experienced more than she thought she had at the time." [P. 603]

The nun's faith, "plain as a bedpan" (p. 643), is her work, and as well as serving White as an excellent foil to his flamboyant, restless, and indulgent central character, it is she who sees how, in the portrait in the possession-ridden house in Moreton Drive, "the face transcended a vulgarity of superficial, slippery paint, to reveal a correspondence, as will some of the semi-precious stones, or flowers, or phrases of music, or passages of light" (p. 20).

The play of light on birds, jewels, and flowers reveals in fact a special correspondence with Elizabeth Hunter's experience of the eye of the storm itself. Mentioned before and after that event, they are foreshadowings and reflections of it that become integral with the prose, deft reminders and easy underlinings of White's abiding preoccupations in the novel. The birds appear in the first mention of the eye. Dorothy's Dutchman, describing his experience, particularly mentions being " 'surrounded by hundreds of seabirds, also resting on the water' " (p. 71). Dorothy Sanseverina, to whom nature is raw and does not speak, finds the trees of her mother's garden "contentious", climbs "warily" the path through them and is "wary of the light too. Round the suspended terracotta dish, which the night nurse kept filled with seed, birds were hanging in fluttering clusters. Instead of the normal clash and shattering of light, here it glowed and throbbed like the drone of doves" (p. 365). She and her brother are later recognized by their victim-mother as cruel-beaked gulls, intent on their predatory plan to hasten her to a rest home, even if that hastens her death. The mother remembers that the thousands of birds resting between the waves scrabbled peacefully for food and that as she fed the seven swans floating fearlessly near, she sensed their recognition of her "lean and tempered spirit" (p. 425) during the ineffable moment. She remembers too that in all the intervening years, "the gulls had not deserted her" (p. 428) but chiefly she recalls it was the suffering of a bird that saved her. Telling her uncomprehending and disbelieving daughter of the noddy bird impaled on the broken branch of a tree, she says: " 'I think I was reminded that one can't escape suffering. Though it's only human to try to escape it' " (p. 409).

Pain is stressed in the recurrence, throughout the novel's accounts of this episode, of the words *impaled* (p. 409), *skewered* (pp. 425 and 427); *pierced* (p. 425); and "the death cry of the insignificant sooty gull gave her back her significance" (p. 425). Her understanding of the pain she had in her life caused and suffered provides the nexus, so that, in the final hours, the gulls are still part of her vision. " 'Oh, yes,' she smiled at her human satellites, 'I have only to learn to re-enter [the eye] and I shall be accepted. Their beaks were crimson, with staring nostrils, but innocent of cruelty' " (p. 446). After the death, the final act of de Santis, the companion of her night hours and sympathetic observer of her pilgrimage, is to go to the garden and fill the birds' dishes. "Light was strewing the park as she performed her rites. Birds followed her, battering the air, settling on the grass whenever her hand, trembling in the last instant, spilt an excess of seed. . . . The birds . . . scattered as she blundered amongst them, then wheeled back, clashing, curving, descending and ascending, shaking the tassels of light . . . ". The consummated spirit is manifest in "this tumult of wings" (p. 608).

The eye is also a jewel. During the supreme interval on Brumby Island, she had been refined to "a flaw at the centre of this jewel of light" that existed "flaw and all, only by grace" and she had known a "dream of glistening peace" (p. 424), a jewel so different from those she adorned herself with in her glamorous days as a society hostess and beauty. Those of course impress the crass Badgery, commanded to bring the box containing them, and Elizabeth Hunter admits to having been caught latterly "telling her once blazing, if now extinct, beads" (p. 43); (her favourite is the ruby-red pigeon's blood). Even for her final moment, seated on her commode-throne, draped with the robe of rose brocade and crowned with a green wig, she scrabbles as many rings as possible onto her old fingers. She ceases to be Elizabeth Hunter while arrayed as Elizabeth Hunter still. But, at a deeper level which increasingly prevails, she knows that though "she would have given anything to open a box containing the sum total of expectancy . . . she must expect her answers outside boxes, in the colder contingencies preparing for her" (p. 102). Display is for the Princess de Lascabanes, who attends Cherry Bullivant Cheesman's party adorned with the diamonds she blackmailed from her in-laws, and for the guests who had "emptied their jewel cases"

(p. 289) for that Warrawee orgy. Her mother has a more interesting way of using them, and so has White.

The Ethopian ring that Badgery remarks on her patient's thumb is the only thing Basil ever gave her. Its twin is discovered by him on the finger of Mitty Jacka, who urges his exploitation of his dying mother for the benefit of their new theatrical enterprise and who warns him that "aged saints are made through the waning of desire more than by the ripening of inherent sanctity" (p. 237). The agate seal featuring a phoenix is of course the appropriate gift for Mary de Santis, who characteristically declines it. She agrees to wear with the turquoise sash only the pearl and turquoise star. For Flora herself—"silly human Manhood" (p. 333) the old lady calls her—there is merely the pink sapphire ring "to belove her to her chemist" (p. 334) and there is here grand comedy involving a letter stating legal possession, and we have Flora's rejections—and misconceptions, in more than one sense.

The other sapphire, the blue one, the much rarer Star variety, is precious to the irascible old invalid; she especially wants to wear it on her "throne", has Flora scrabble under the bed for it. It is natural that she should identify herself with it; so does White. Her eyes, those "not quite fresh eyes" that "live by lucid flashes" (p. 516), the "terrifying mineral blue" (p. 10) in them intermittently giving moments "of splintered sapphires" (p. 11) are associated with her truest insights and with her keenest memories of the eye of the storm: "a bird's glistening call then the gulls scraping colour out of the sky" (p. 546).

No wonder then that Arnold Wyburd, the scrupulous family lawyer who had known passion once, illicitly with her, should steal it and find it a "torment", this "eye of the sapphire, with its bars, or cross, of recurring light" (p. 597). His good, dull, honest, unimaginative wife Lal, wearer of "donkey brown" (p. 529), receives the turquoise necklace which is extremely old, having belonged to Elizabeth's mother, and which was lent by her to young Sal Warming on the island and worn by her herself throughout the purifying ordeal of the cyclone. Arnold notices that it does not in the least suit or enhance his freckled wife. It suits in every sense his aged employer: the turquoise, one remembers, is sky blue and—of more interest—usually almost opaque and only sometimes translucent. Elizabeth Hunter's jewels reflect many lights.

And so do her flowers. Not of course the astilbe; that is the favourite of the not brilliant Lal Wyburd. " 'I was drawn' ", says Elizabeth Hunter, " 'to the more spectacular flowers' " (p. 191), and these do not include, she derisively recalls, the hardy mimulus Lal never succeeded in growing at Double Bay (p. 534). Mrs Hunter is interested in the Canterbury bell, the *Campanula* that resembles the small bells worn on their horses by the pilgrims, and is reminded of this flower as she wakes to find her veiled night-nurse kneeling in prayer. The saintly Mary is in fact the chief custodian of her flowers and brings her roses, the flower White mainly uses here. From her dreams early in the novel the old lady speaks aloud of their being " 'still only thorns. Locked buds. This long frost' " (p. 208). During the "Kudjeri" visit, the barren Dorothy finds in an "unkempt bed . . . one or two autumn buds, cold, tight, pointed, which would dry on their stems without opening" (p. 473). But Mary brings Mrs Hunter a "tribute of roses" (p. 209) from the morning light of the garden where she finds waiting her "a cloud of roses floating in its own right, none of the frost-locked buds of Elizabeth Hunter's dream, but great actual clusters at the climax of their beauty" (p. 208). She collects them in ectasy, suffering the gashes of thorns, resisting the sensual in the sensuous, aspiring to an absolute of adoration.

> Poured in steadily increasing draughts through the surrounding trees, the light translated the heap of passive roseflesh back into dew, light, pure colour. It might have saddened her to think her own dichotomy of earthbound flesh and aspiring spirit could never be resolved so logically if footsteps along the pavement had not begun breaking into her trance of roses. [P. 209]

The passing Greek stranger recognizes her spirit and appropriately concludes " 'Tí ximaíroma kánomay!' " (p. 210) (" 'What a sunrise we are making!' ") (p. 211) With which Mary, on rejoining her patient, is able to agree.

It was: the roses sparkled drowsed brooded leaped flaunting their earthbound flesh in an honourably failed attempt to convey the ultimate.

"Yes—our roses," Elizabeth Hunter repeated.

Which Mary de Santis interpreted as: we, the arrogant perfectionists, or pseudo-saints, shall be saved up out of our shortcomings for further trial. [P. 211]

As Lotte dances for her at a later point, Elizabeth Hunter slips into a fantasy where she is flinging rose petals. Hers are the roses of selfless celebration, unlike poor Lotte's. When she cuts her wrists in the bath, Lotte is "faced with a flush of roses, of increasing crimson" (p. 607), the roses of a self-indulgent death; and she sings, in cheap sentimental optimism, the German equivalent of: "The roses can never vanish away, Love makes them rise anew" (p. 446). But it is Mary and the paralyzed Irene who enact the final meaning of these flowers. In that ultimate garden scene already mentioned, Mary notices that "a solitary rose, tight crimson, emerged in a lower garden; it would probably open later in the day", and at the peak of her feeling for the soul of Elizabeth Hunter, she determines that "she must take this first and last rose to her patient Irene Fletcher. She would return and cut it before leaving: perfect as it should become by then" (p. 608). The transmission is effected. "Sister de Santis wondered how she would convey to this entombed girl, her future patient, the beauty she herself had witnessed, and love as she had come to understand it" (p. 607). The wings of birds and the petals of flowers now reflect and refract the pure morning light with the jewel-like intensity of the eye of the storm itself.

There is of course much more to say. In the total structure, all twelve chapters are disposed to lead up to and away from the heart of the subject, manifest in chapter 8, and each contains such effective contrastive detail. Chapter 1, for instance, gives such impulse to the theme with its introduction of de Santis pursuing and Dorothy fleeing Self; chapter 5 juxtaposes Elizabeth's memory of her husband's death with the imminence of her own. Chapters gain enormously by contrast, as when chapter 10, involved with Dorothy and Basil at the empty end of their spiritual road at "Kudjeri", is followed by their mother's reaching her deeply satisfying destination. For any writer to have sustained the line of interest and continuity amid such a diversity of effects is a remarkable accomplishment.

Dynamic is the word hovering over this exciting book. There is far greater suspense in it than in any of White's other novels, where we are never in any doubt about "the chosen", about who will ride in the chariot, or that Theodora will find grace in one form or another, that Stan will "arrive", that Voss will go straight to his goal, that Arthur and not Waldo will be "saved" and that Hurtle Duffield will "see" it all. But what the story of Elizabeth Hunter keeps persistently before us is the sense of chance and luck; even immediately before entering the eye, "she could not believe, finally, in grace, only luck" (p. 417). As she muses while Flora is settling her on the final ironic "throne", "Balance is always a matter of chance" (p. 549). What was given her once may *not* be given again. There is nothing ideal or heroic about her as there is in varying degrees about the other protagonists, and we are given her within a realism even more unrelenting than that of Voss's story. White chose his three epigraphs well. His Elizabeth Hunter was given her human body, so difficult to wear, by chance; she and those about her feel what could have been a tremor of heavenly love, and that is indeed perverse; and she, when there is so little time left for her, knows well that men and boughs break, that you must praise life while you walk and wake, for it is only lent. The shifting, changing, protean quality in the prose[9] keeps it all at high pitch. Surely Patrick White has satisfied in *The Eye of the Storm* "the desire of raising other men into a perception of the infinite."[10]

NOTES
1. Dorothy Green, "Queen Lear or Cleopatra Rediviva", *Meanjin Quarterly* 32, no. 4 (1973): 401.
2. P.R. Beatson, "The Skiapod and the Eye: Patrick White's *The Eye of the Storm*, *Southerly* 34 (1974): 222.
3. Leonie Kramer, "Patrick White: 'The Unplayed I' ", *Quadrant* 18, no. 1 (1974): 66.

4. Green, "Queen Lear", p. 403.
5. Patrick White, *The Eye of the Storm* (London: Jonathan Cape, 1973), p. 414. All page references are to this edition.
6. Patricia Clancy, "The Actor's Dilemma: Patrick White and Henri de Montherlant", *Meanjin* 33, no. 3 (1974): 298–302.
7. Clancy, "The Actor's Dilemma", p. 302.
8. *Australian Book Review* 11 (1973): 122.
9. I have tried to define this source of power in my article "The Rhetoric of Patrick White's 'Down at the Dump' ", in *Bards, Bohemians and Bookmen*, ed. Leon Cantrell (St. Lucia: University of Queensland Press, 1976), pp. 281–88.
10. William Blake, quoted in the epigraph to *Riders in the Chariot*

Tourmaline and the Tao Te Ching

Randolph Stow's *Tourmaline*

HELEN TIFFIN

In what seems to have been a fit of authorial desperation, Stow published in 1966, three years after the publication of *Tourmaline*, twelve poems entitled "*From* The Testament of Tourmaline: Variations on Themes of the *Tao Teh Ching*". The twelve poems of this "Testament" correspond to particular verses in the *Tao*[1] designated by the corresponding number in Stow's versions. Stow had thus provided critics with a clue, or as he later termed it, a "key"[2] to the meaning of the novel.

This key was used by A.D. Hope in two very illuminating articles[3] in which, by introducing readers unfamiliar with the *Tao te ching* to that text and some of its tenets, he showed that Stow had written a philosophical novel based on the opposing ideas of the *Tao te ching* and Christianity. In pointing to this basis for the work, Hope answered some of Leonie Kramer's earlier objections to it[4] and moved closer than any critics had previously done to that "deeper meaning" whose presence Geoffrey Dutton[5] and others had sensed. Hope linked *Tourmaline* with some of Stow's earlier works, in which he discovered embryonic oppositions between peace and aggression, noise and silence, action and inaction, and went on in his exploration of these themes in *Tourmaline* to identify Tom Spring as the chief "spokesman" for the Taoist point of view, and the diviner as the representative of an opposing messianic way.

While this opposition is central to the work, its existence alone does not explain how Stow arrived at the two specific philosophies he chose to place in opposition, or to what particular end he opposed them. When Raja Rao in *The Serpent and the Rope* (1960) placed Hinduism in confrontation with Buddhism, he did not choose two differing metaphysics arbitrarily. The drifting apart of the protagonists, symbolizing the rift between the two systems, had a historical basis in the Hindu origins of the Buddhist School.[6] While there are obvious metaphysical and ethical oppositions between philosophical Taoism[7] and Christianity, there would seem to be no comparable historical basis for their opposition. Stow does not, however, choose two differing systems arbitrarily and set them down face to face in an improbable Western Australian desert. He has his historical precedent too in the nature of colonial sensibility and activity. Law, government, and religion are in the colonial experience transplanted from their place of origin and grafted onto the new environment. This introduced system, evolved out of the history and geography of another place and another time, may be wholly inappropriate to the rhythms of the new land, and to the ethics and metaphysics eventually evolved out of it by a people who establish some new and harmonious spiritual relationship with it.

In some of his earlier works, Stow seems to be feeling his way towards an expression of the incongruity inherent in the clash of old world values and an altogether new world. In *A Haunted Land* Beth Maguire and her daughter Anne are no respecters of the land. Beth loves to shoot kangaroos, and she and her daughter Anne are associated with introduced animal species like the fox. Anne more or less rapes an Aboriginal station hand, and out of her own shame has her brother kill him. That the property on which the family live is called "Malin" is not surprising, for their influence on the land and its original inhabitants is indeed malign. Both Andrew and Beth Maguire enslave others to their purposes and become prisoners of their own aggressive desires. The association between dependence, enslavement, aggression, and rape of the land is important. It is as if Stow is suggesting, as he does more directly in *To the Islands*, that, historically, British–Australian settlers raped the land and its people, setting in motion a malign cycle of aggression which historically and emotionally alienates the usurper from the ways of the land, and from the right perception of "the land and its meaning".[8] Conversely, certain of the less aggressive characters, such as Adelaide in *A Haunted Land* and Keithy in *The Bystander*, have a dim half-conscious perception of its rhythms. But in the action of the novels, the malign cycle of aggression overwhelms these tendencies.

In *To the Islands* Heriot journeys from his mission station in order to expiate his obsessive racial, historical, and personal guilt, which on all three levels relates directly to the Aboriginal people. However, Heriot's journey ends not with expiation but with the glimmerings of a new insight into the true ways of the world. Re-educated out of his old Western tradition by his Aboriginal guide, Justin, and by the desert over which he stumbles, he learns that guilt for aggressions committed in the past will not stop the cycle. Such guilt can only lead, as it has done for Heriot, from a general crime to a personal re-commission of it. The massacre at Onmalmeri, for which Heriot's mission service is a kind of personal atonement, is almost re-enacted at the more horrifying personal level with Rex. What Justin and the land teach Heriot is that one kills only to live, and with necessary but passing regret. Heriot in his Western way longs for what is beyond the immediate, plays with dependence on and independence from others in an attempt to find peace. In the end, he has moved towards though not reached "the islands". He has moved from raving towards silence, from action towards inaction, from rejection of the land towards acceptance of it. At the last there is still something of the aggressive desire to dominate, but it is passing slowly as he moves towards the death that will finally release him.

Heriot learns the hard way what Stow's earlier "bystander" characters like Adelaide and Keithy intuited. The land has its own meaning, and man to find peace must put himself in tune with that rhythm. Thus Heriot discards not just the symbols of the aggressive aspect of the "civilization" he is slowly rejecting (the Western, Australian, one) such as the gun; he also discards the cultural trappings of the civilization (the Lyke Wake Dirge, the hymns) evolved by different generations, out of a different relationship between man and a very different land. Heriot begins to achieve through Justin an intimate acquaintance with the rigours of his environment, a new and "original relation"[9] to the universe. Significantly, characters like Adelaide and Keithy in the earlier works, the quiet ones, the non-aggressors, those not concerned to uphold law and conscience or a particular religious system and specific social code, are the ones who can unconsciously begin to perceive the new land's meaning, without the need for Heriot's lengthy and arduous journey of initiation. It is as if in his earlier works Stow is moving from an intuitive perception of the colonial dilemma to an interest in exploring its process. The movement is from what is alien and imposed to what is naturally evolved out of the new.

Stow's earlier novels, then, suggested a connection on the one hand between non-aggression, silence and quietness, and anonymity and understanding of land, and, on the other, between adherence to codes, laws, or religions evolved elsewhere (dependence on the old, not independence in the new), and a lack of understanding of the land. The aggression usually, though not always, is intimately associated with the maintenance of these social mores, religion, law, or custom. People who reject the realities of the land and adhere to the latter are frequently depicted as prisoners of one sort or another—of their own aggressive tendencies, of their obsessive exercise of power over others—and the consequence is that they blame the land itself for this, seeing themselves as prisoners of the real object of their aggression, its heat, its dust, or its space.

Already the lines of opposition have been drawn between certain types of characters in Stow's earlier novels. In much of Stow's poetry too, where narrative is naturally minimized, the dominance of the land is accentuated. It may seem anthropomorphically dangerous or aggressive, depending on human attitudes to it; but it is also surprisingly companionable or beautiful. And usually, even in its tiniest and most insidious form, dust, it asserts its quiet dominance over talkative and powerful man. The land seems to Western Christian man, with his Biblical brief for it, something to be overcome, used, and dominated. But, Stow seems to assert, to Australian man it should be more obvious than to most that the land's meaning is that it will endure. Silent, non-aggressive, it will reign in the end, and man and his cities will disappear in dust. "Body", as Stow says in Variation VII[10] "is land in permutation", an emphasis prefigured in the earlier works and upheld in *Tourmaline*. The connection is patent, between those individuals who are non-aggressors, the quiet bystanders, and the land itself, as is the historical connection between the assertion of dominance and the spread of aggression, with despoliation of the land and alienation from it. By the time Stow wrote *Tourmaline*, he had thus historically and geographically arrived at the basis of the Taoist–Christian philosophical opposition.

While the direction of the lives of Madeleine and Rama of *The Serpent and the Rope* comes to stand for the two opposing sides of the metaphysical clash between Buddhism and Hinduism and for the historical parting of the ways of Buddhism and Hinduism in India, so the Christian/Taoist opposition provides Stow with the philosophical ground-plan for the Australian colonial experience. As in the case of Rao's work, the philosophical oppositions in Stow's are anything but arbitrary, and their lines of opposition are effectively drawn even without the terms *Taoist* and *Christian* ever being applied, though a knowledge of the basic philosophical oppositions enriches the reader's understanding of Stow's purpose.

The *Tao te ching* was composed in China in about 479 B.C. by an anonymous sage generally referred to as Lao-tzu. On one level the *Tao* is an attack on Confucian practices, but like the *Analects* of Confucius it was designed as a handbook of survival during the destructive wars that had rent China before and during Lao-tzu's lifetime. Its eighty-one verses have posed endless problems of precise interpretation, but translators and commentators do agree on a number of basic ideas which it upholds.[11]

In this period of social upheaval, tyranny, and slaughter, agression between the warring states had evolved into a self-perpetuating cycle. The author of the *Tao te ching* is concerned to find a way out of this apparently endless cycle. The analogy of the wheel for such a cyclical pattern is inappropriate, as the cycle with which Lao-tzu was concerned, while seemingly universal, was not inevitable, but was governed by cause and effect, stimulus, and response:

> Humans and human societies are thus highly responsive to challenge. So when anyone, ruler or subject, tries to *act* upon humans individually or collectively, the ultimate result is the opposite of what he is aiming at. He has invoked what we might call the Law of Aggression.
> . . . The operation of cause and effect in human affairs is . . . complex. In its vast complexity we discern certain causal chains of challenge and response which represent the functioning of the Law of Aggression. It is this law, not the mere passage of time, which is the reason for the cyclical pattern of life.[12]

The Taoist's response to this pattern, his way of coping with the cycle, is to do nothing about it. The answer to survival and to escape from this "law" lies in humility, compassion, and indifference to such Western Christian concepts as good and evil, truth and falsehood. The Taoist believes that good not only implies or presupposes evil, but that it actually creates it—all extremes or opposites invite their converse. In every so-called lie, the Taoist believes, there is necessarily contained a truth, in the reason for that lie. Polarization is always to be avoided. The Taoist does not commit aggression because of a difference of opinion, nor does he assert his own rightness over that of another, for to make another feel inferior is the essence of aggression. The sage knows what his own way is, but makes no attempt to integrate all his reactions, trying to understand, if he cannot acquiesce in, ways that are different from his own. He can, for instance, pity others in their fear and suffering, or death, but can regard his own death impersonally. Consequently he cannot endorse the operation of laws and governments that assume collective agreement on a set of rules based on concepts of right and wrong, truth and falsehood. Lao-tzu believed that man's original nature was kind and mild, but that it had become aggressive as a reaction to the force of legal and moral codes. In his system, the single soul was to be honoured. Ambition was to be annihilated, and similarly desire for anything beyond the here and now. If we did not prize rare and valuable goods, or better still if we did not know of their existence, greed and ambition, inferiority and superiority, the exercise of power by one individual over another would disappear. A ruler or leader should thus keep his people innocent of desire and ignorant of power and riches. He himself should be like the sage Lao-tzu, virtually anonymous, exercising his guidance not by law and command, but by questions and silence as a wordless teaching.

XVII
The best of all rulers is but a shadowy presence to his subjects.

> Hesitant, he does not utter words lightly.
> When his task is accomplished and his work done
> The people all say, "It happened to us naturally".

II
The whole world recognizes the beautiful as the beautiful, yet this is only the ugly; the whole world recognizes the good as the good, yet this is only the bad.

> Thus Something and Nothing produce each other;
> The difficult and the easy complement each other;
> The long and the short off-set each other;
> The high and the low incline towards each other;
> Note and sound harmonize with each other;
> Before and after follow each other.

Therefore the sage keeps to the deed that consists in taking no action and practises the teaching that uses no words.

> The myriad creatures rise from it yet it claims no
>   authority;
> It gives them life yet claims no possession;
> It benefits them yet exacts no gratitude;
> It accomplishes its task yet lays claim to no merit.

> It is because it lays claim to no merit
> That its merit never deserts it.

Lao-tzu in his own work never urges his views as "right" or "good" but only on the basis that if we do not follow them we invite disaster.

In this summary of the *Tao*, I have been emphasizing the ethical at the expense of the metaphysical implications of the text. While these are indeed present, they are less obtrusive than the ethical in a philosophy dealing in survival in the here and now.

It might be said that to the extent Tao [The Way] is considered divine, the metaphysics becomes a theology and Taoism a religion. . . . It is not based on faith, but on direct experience of God [The Way]. It has no place for ritual or priests or church. It promises no response to prayer while we are in this world, and as to the next world, that does not exist—unless it be the state of non-being. . . . It vigorously attacks morality and government—two institutions that religion generally supports. And most curious of all, the mystical experience it offers is not ecstatic, but dark, neutral, and uncertain.[13]

Even in so brief an account, the differences between a Western Christian way of thinking and that of the Taoist are obvious. Although, as commentators have noted, the Christian and the Taoist might act alike in a given situation, they would do so for entirely different reasons. If the sage is to teach "naturally", to lead wordlessly, and if, as the *Tao* notes, "good words are not persuasive; persuasive words are not good",[14] how then is Lao-tzu able to teach a "way" by his text? One obvious method employed throughout is the use of image and metaphor, and secondly, by simply presenting "that which is naturally so". Lao-tzu provides, in the interests of human harmony, the obvious examples of the harmonies and rhythms of the universe:

XXV

Man models himself on earth,
Earth on heaven,
Heaven on the way,
And the way on that which is naturally so.

XL
Turning back is how the way moves;
Weakness is the means the way employs.
The myriad creatures in the world are born from
Something, and Something from Nothing.

X
When carrying on your head your perplexed bodily
     soul can you embrace in your arms the One
And not let go?
In concentrating your breath can you become as
     supple
As a babe?
Can you polish your mysterious mirror
And leave no blemish?
Can you love the people and govern the state
Without resorting to action?
When the gates of heaven open and shut
Are you capable of keeping to the role of the female?
When your discernment penetrates the four quarters
Are you capable of not knowing anything?
It gives them life and rears them.
It gives them life yet claims no possession;
It benefits them yet exacts no gratitude;
It is the steward yet exercises no authority.
Such is called the mysterious virtue.

VIII
Highest good is like water. Because water excels in benefiting
the myriad creatures without contending with them and
settles where none would like to be, it comes close to the
way.

.   .   .   .   .

It is because it does not contend that it is never at fault.

I have deliberately chosen these examples from the particular verses of the *Tao te ching* on which Stow bases his own
"Variations", but were any number of images and metaphors
to be chosen from the eighty-one verses, one general idea
might be seen to be behind them all. They express the process
whereby the apparently yielding, the non-aggressive, the non-
combative, the silent, the soft makes its way through, endures
after, or invites disaster less than the aggressive, the hard,
the determined, the forward thrusting. Favourite Taoist
images are thus those of the newborn babe (weakness,
ignorance), the uncarved block (returning to one's original
roots, or the state of the newborn babe) the female, the valley,
and water, the most yielding of substances which yet carves
canyons. In *Tourmaline* Stow takes over some of these

images: the newborn babe, the silent stone, and giving a
Taoist image a local habitation and a name, has his narrator
remember the pink frail lilies which break the hard caked
earth before the earliest rains.

The *Tao te ching* is not, however, a novel, and like the
Bible and similar texts, its power depends in part on its
gnomic quality. It must have the versatility of interpretation
the oracular needs for wide appeal and credibility. It does
not need to deal in plot and character: indeed, true to its
anonymity, it mentions no places, no names, no dates.
Moreover, it expresses a philosophy of non-action, of silence,
of quietitude, of non-combat. Its exponents, unlike other
sages, must be silent and uncontending; they must teach by
seeming to "happen" naturally. All this presents enormous
difficulties for the novelist who wishes to endorse the Taoist
point of view and demonstrate its success in a medium more
usually dealing in action, in character, and in words. It must
end by asserting (silently) the virtues of acceptance of
imperfect conditions, of inaction, dryness, and death, over an
active life of progression and aggression, and the promise of
Eden, of paradise regained. And this must be done without
preaching, without naming, by the sage who necessarily is
stumbling and inarticulate, and in this case, in a recognizably
Australian idiom. There is a further problem, too, which
Stow has set himself, in that he wishes to show that place
is more important and enduring than the people who inhabit
it. The bodies must be the land in permutation. The epigraph
to *Tourmaline* translated, reads, "O people of little weight
in the memory of these places".[15]

Now, while the *Tao* stresses the necessity for harmony
between man and the universe, and the fact that man is only
a very small part of "the myriad creatures" or "the 10,000
things" (as opposed to the Judaeo-Christian idea of man's
dominion over the beasts of the field), and while it stresses
the need for man to observe nature closely to find the Way,
nevertheless, there is considerably less stress on land, and on
specific qualities of the land in the *Tao* than there is in Stow's
"Variations". In Stow's verses—

I

The loved land breaks into beauties, and men must love
them with tongues, with words. Their names are sweet
in the mouth.

But the lover of Tao is wordless, for Tao is nameless:
Tao is a sound in time for a timeless silence.

Loving the land, I deliver my mind to joy;
but the love of Tao is passionless, unspoken.

Nevertheless, the land and Tao are one.
In the love of the land, I worship the manifest Tao.

To move from love into lovelessness is wisdom.
The land's roots lie in emptiness. There is Tao.

IV

The spaces between the stars
   are filled with Tao
   Tao wells up
like warm artesian waters.

Multiple, unchanging,
   like forms of water,
   it is cloud and pool,
ocean and lake and river.

Where is the source of it?
Before God is, was Tao.

VII

The loved land will not pass away.
   World has no life but transformation.
   Nothing made selfless can decay.
The loved land will not pass away.

The grown man will not pass away.
   Body is land in permutation.
   Tireless within the fountains play.
The grown man will not pass away.

XVI

Deep. Go deep,
   as the long roots of myall
   mine the red country
for water, for silence.

> Silence is water.
> All things are stirring,
> all things are flowering,
> rooted in silence.

XL
> There is no going but returning.
> Do not resist; for Tao is a flooded river
> and your arms are frail.
>
> The red land risen from the ocean
> erodes, returns; the river runs earth-red,
> staining the open sea.
>
> Before earth was was molten rock, was silence.
> Before existence, absence. Absence is Tao.

As well as the shifted emphasis regarding the land, there is a corresponding change in the view of man's relation to it. While in both the *Tao* and Stow's variations on it man may read in the physical processes of the universe a metaphysical message, Stow emphasizes in his poems a sort of feeding cycle between man who understands the rhythms of the universe and the land itself. This relationship is less socially oriented and more land oriented than that in the *Tao*. Moreover, the images of that land are specific: "Tao wells up like warm artesian waters" (IV) "Go deep, as the long roots of myall mine the red country for water" (XVI). Within the more specific cycle, though, is contained the complex interaction of land, man, silence, water, earth building up, erosion, and returning to the source. Out of the darkness, "rooted in silence", "fountains of being" start. The fountains feed back into the land, eroding it, changing it, returning it and the water into the soil again, to the silence and darkness out of which it grew. The general physical process is as in the Tao, a metaphor for the physical and psychic life of man.

I began by asserting that *Tourmaline* is a novel of philosophical debate between Christianity and the *Tao te ching*.[16] The Christian side of the debate does not pose for Stow any of those problems associated with the *Tao*. "Poor little talkative Christianity"[17] has never relied on "the silence between words" for its praise. It is an aggressive evangelical religion whose ideals and ideas have largely formed our ideas of ambition and worth, good and evil, government and the moral law. Living in a Christian capitalist society, and writing for such an audience, Stow can take the ideas, and their symbols for granted and express this side of the debate in familiar and conventional terms. But the Tao side demands a different kind of literary shorthand. The philosophy of the Tao itself must be expressed through hints and questions; through signs and symbols and not by direct statement. Why then does Stow, through his "Testament", refer the reader so directly to it? It is not too fanciful, I think, to suggest that Stow's personal metaphysic which grew out of his observations of man and the land found reliable philosophical systematization and a ready-made symbolic framework in the *Tao te ching*. Through Tom Spring's statement of the core of Taoist thinking, the reader is given a key to the image shorthand of *Tourmaline*, and an alternative philosophical background against which to set human motive and action in the novel. The cycle of aggression which the Tao sets out to diffuse and which is the pattern behind much of the action and discussion in *Tourmaline* can best be understood through a knowledge of the *Tao te ching*; while the diviner's career and its outcome is best appreciated through Christian analogy or an affinity with messianic religions generally.

Tourmaline lies in a "coma" from which it is awakened by the entry into the town of the diviner, Michael Random. He is close to death as a result of, so one is given to understand later, his own predilection for self-destruction. Like Tourmaline he lies in a coma until revived by the townspeople, and reverenced as their potential saviour. It is important to remember that Stow suggests several times in the work that what happens to Tourmaline is part of a cycle; it has all happened before. Almost all the inhabitants are to some extent trapped, not just in the general coma, but in some cycle or state of mind and being from which they are unable to release themselves. "I thought I'd never come to Tourmaline" (p. 167)[18] Byrne sings, but most of the characters in the novel have not only "come to Tourmaline", as a state of being, but, Stow suggests, have been there before. Tourmaline's geography, as well as its history, is fuzzy at the edges—Like Lacey's Find, with which its connections are ambiguous, it passes (like body) from dust to dust. The narrator speaks of his age as "aeons" (p. 131) and is told by Tom Spring, whose point of view is the one Stow seems to be endorsing in the novel, "Poor old man. . . . Your memory's going. You've been cured once already" (p. 148). The narrator hasn't been cured in the course of *this* story, so Spring must be referring to some process in the past. But most of all it is the action initiated by the diviner which seems to have happened before. Spring tells the diviner, "You're dangerous. You're wrong. And it'll all begin again, all those terrible things" (p. 133). Later he pleads with the narrator, "Haven't we had enough of these . . . black and white men?" (p. 147). Even Kestrel knows the routine of repetition: " 'She'll go to the witch-doctor,' he said; not with resentment or as an accusation, but almost idly, as if recalling dull history" (p. 101).

What happens in *Tourmaline*, then, may have happened to the town of Tourmaline and its inhabitants before.[19] What happens this time is told to the reader by a character simply called the Law, who sets out as historian and conscience of the town to write its "testament", or rather, his own testament. It is of course both, and the Law tells of the arrival in Tourmaline of the diviner, his resurrection from a state of near death, and his elevation by the town to the position of leader and saviour. The town recreates their "diviner returned from the dead" in this role, and Michael Random (his name suggesting that almost anyone would serve their needs) is all too willing to take on their purification and castigation as a step towards a recreation of a paradise. Random, the diviner, replaces the town bully, Kestrel, as leader; and Kestrel, after the desertion of his two disciples, Deborah and Byrne, leaves the town. Random, promising water, finds only gold. The messianic cult he has begun in the town dies, its promise unfulfilled. Robbed now of his "virtue", his "prepossessing" qualities, the diviner leaves Tourmaline presumably to die in the surrounding desert. Kestrel, as if by a magical intuition, returns, bringing with him water-divining equipment and diggers. He will again be chief, and a more frightening one than the diviner. The diviner with his "rod" and his enslaving of the souls of the town has shown Kestrel, the "new" bird of prey, how to enslave on a bigger and better scale. The cycle begun out of the town's desire for water has led it to the creation of a diviner, and the imposition of his rule of law, conscience and humiliation. Even though this promised paradise is not achieved, the aggression and enslavement born out of the need of that hope of paradise remains in potentially more frightening form with the return of Kestrel. Both whites and blacks in Tourmaline and on its outskirts succumb to this dream of paradise, and allow the diviner as the new saviour (Christ for the whites, Monnga for the blacks) to "take charge" of their lives. In so doing they commit, for Stow and for the *Tao*, the gravest error: "There is no sin but cruelty: Only one. And that original sin, that began when a man first cried to another, in his matted hair: Take charge of my life, I am close to breaking" (p. 174).

The narrator, the Law, is the speaker here, but the reader may assume, I think, that here he speaks for Stow, for this is the cardinal sin in many of Stow's works. Both the diviner and Kestrel are guilty of cruelty, and most of the townspeople are all too ready to commit their lives to another; to conjure up their own "saviour". Only Tom Spring and Jack Speed, the two characters associated with the Way of the *Tao* in the novel, do not succumb to the need for a paradise beyond; hence, neither participates in the "creation" of the diviner or defers to his laws and charisma. "Good luck to you, Mr Frankenstein—it's a fine healthy boy", Spring tells the narrator (p. 146). The Law and the other inhabitants have recreated a monster out of hope, from fragments of their own "bitter heritage" (p. 7).

Although Random is any messianic saviour, Stow uses Christian motifs to identify him. When Random is rescued from the tussle with his God in the wilderness, he lies for three days as if dead, but on the third day rises into Tourmaline still coated with the unguents with which the women have anointed him (p. 31). He is told that Tourmaline looks to him for salvation, and he speaks often (and familiarly) of hell. Other characters, too, associate him with Christ, even those like Kestrel, who did not participate willingly in his recreation. Kestrel "welcomes" the diviner

to his bar with "Get me to the River Jordan. . . . You've
made a lot of converts here" (pp. 46–47). They are, of course,
not so much converts as willing accomplices in his rise and
maintenance as familiar saviour. It is not noted that Byrne
has a "Christian name" until the advent of the diviner, nor
is his discipleship to the diviner confirmed until Random
washes his wounds and takes off his shoes. The
Law–narrator takes the diviner to the hill and offers him
Tourmaline in prospect—the gaol, the church, and the
garden in just that significant order. Finally, in the climactic
scenes in the church, the diviner is actually named as
"Christ" and "Monnga". But by using the double designa-
tion, one for the white and one for the black population of
Tourmaline, Stow reiterates the point of naming his diviner
"Random". Christianity merely provides one example and
a convenient symbology for the type of aggression he wishes
to explore and reject.

Almost every feature of Random's nature and career that
makes him a Messiah leads him directly away from the Way,
the true path of the Tao. In Tao terms he cannot be wrong,
but everything he does leads him and his community away
from harmony with the rest of the universe, and thus invites
disaster. Of leaders and rulers the *Tao* says: "The best of
all rulers is but a shadowy presence to his subjects",[20] but
Random is constantly described as "shining" and "prepossessing". He encourages total dependence on himself and initiates
a kind of cargo cult[21] of which he pointedly takes charge.
He knows he has seen God and has direct access to him
because God has made him "suffer" (a Western Christian
idea), and having suffered himself, will make Tourmaline
burn too on its path to the false paradise. Thus he commits
more and more Taoist "sins", using humiliation and dependence as means to conversion. It is important that the
humiliation of Deborah is achieved through invoking a very
traditional and unimaginative kind of moral law which
results in maiming—Spring describes Deb in her new
"happy" converted condition as a "hunchback" (p. 147). The
diviner's self-inflicted wounds, are, significantly, not on his
hands and feet but near his heart, suggesting that he has
attempted to stifle the true promptings of real love of

humanity and succeeded only in scarring his own capacity to feel. The people of Tourmaline, then, have conjured up the diviner in the image of their own need, but once he is formed and elevated, he manifests a lust for power that far exceeds Kestrel's former dominance of the town. The diviner should be a saviour—instead he is a destroyer, and Stow has to show this failure through a narrator who began as one of the creators and chief supporters of Random. It is this narrator, the Law, who designates the diviner "Christ" in the church scene. But the same narrator is Stow's chief instrument for equivocating Random the Saviour. There is of course the obvious disapproval of Spring and Speed; and there is, towards the end, the narrator's increasing awareness that things are not going as he'd hoped with the diviner. But it is through the unconscious perceptions of the narrator and some of the other characters that the most significant comment is made on Random and on aspects of his Christ-like career. I shall take up this point presently.

The first "law" that the presence of the diviner initiates in Kestrel's bar is the law of aggression. Byrne, arch convert and disciple, wants to "wrestle" the diviner. The mock-heroic way in which the struggle is treated acts as a reminder of the importance placed on aggression-fighting in the Western world, or rather the elevation of it to something heroic and magnificient. The mock-heroic treatment adds to the humour of the situation, with its punctuation of spectator comments and oaths; "For the love of Jesus, someone put him to bed" (p. 51). Stow is noted for his excellent and always appropriately "realistic" use of dialogue, but it is not too fanciful to suggest, I think, that the mention of Jesus in connection with this mock-epic struggle acts subliminally to connect the two. Such a connection is made more explicit later when on the night of Kestrel's "orgy", Charlie remarks with enthusiasm, "There gunna be some fighting tonight, by Jesus" (p. 110). In a novel of philosophical debate between two opposing systems, such ironic use of blaspheming in Australian idiom is a particularly suggestive way of stressing one of the central divisions between the two systems: the dependence central to Christianity and the aggression thus involved in its practice, and the independence–non-aggression nexus of Taoism. And, by Jesus, and for Jesus, fighting and dissension do occur in Tourmaline.

The diviner with his gold hair and his blue eyes is associated with these two colours throughout the work.[22] Sometimes the yellow "burns" or shines to red or gold, fire or metal. The blue of his eyes can be similarly metallic, and burn, or it can have the opaque quality of windows opening within and without on vacancy. The blue can also be "ice" blue, corresponding to the termperature range in Random's vicinity as in the confrontation between himself and Deborah, where the extremes of heat and cold are expressions of emotional states. Two things in particular are suggested by these colours and their associated qualities. The burning gold and the ice blue with which the diviner is associated link him with two extremes, both of which, the *Tao* would say, are bad because they *are* extremes and because, like good and evil, one necessarily produces the other. Fire will be fought by fire in an aggressive world of extremes, and metaphorical fire is fought with actual fire by Random during Kestrel's "orgy". Secondly, the blue and the gold are associated with the water the diviner seems to promise and the gold he actually finds, and just as blue and gold are combined in the diviner's physical and spiritual being, so the gold and water are linked in the novel in a particularly significant way. We are tempted to think of water as good, and gold as bad, with the concomitant idea that the diviner's finding gold instead of water indicates his own spiritual poverty, for all his talk of bringing a new "spring" to the town. While this is of course one meaning of the association between the two symbols within the one character, there remains the problem of whether Stow means us then to see Random as part angel, part devil, and the apparent water-gold connection remains puzzling until considered in Taoist terms.

As far as the Taoist is concerned, both the water *and* the gold are the delusions and desires which lead Tourmaline astray, and the desire for water is the more dangerous one. Tourmaline's desire for water is closely associated with its desire for "paradise"; for the lost Edens imaged in the general garden references and the references to the green glory of the narrator's youth. Existence is not a problem; there is water enough even in the surrounding desert, as Dave Speed and Bogada show. The water, then, is not the necessity, but the dream of Tourmaline, the key to the lost paradise. From the Taoist point of view, paradise, which was always here in this world for us to find through harmony with the Way, has been lost between desire for too much (promised usually in the next world by messianic religions) and the moral laws which make a pilgrim progress towards paradise through actions based on discriminations between good and evil. Any carrot held before a donkey is basically antipathetical to a Taoist view, and in reaching for the carrot, for the pie in the sky, or water even, man is led into dissatisfaction, ambition, dependence, and aggression, all that ensues from Tourmaline's desire for water and its creation of a diviner to provide that water.

It is not necessary for the reader to know the Taoist point of view to make this connection. By combining the gold and the blue in the person of the diviner, and in the outcome of events in the novel, it is possible for the reader to see the destructive force of greed whether it be for gold or water. Need and greed are closely related here. Tourmaline's need for water is not a need directly related to survival; it is a desire for *more* water. Against this town point of view on the need for more water, there is Spring's equivocation, and Dave Speed's assertion: "If the water comes, it'll be when we've stopped needing it", (p. 70)—a Tao view that it is dangerous to desire, and only when active desire is eschewed will what is desired happen naturally in its course.

This extensive use of colour exemplifies an important technique Stow uses in the novel. Much of the meaning of *Tourmaline* must impinge on the reader not through logic, direct statement, or connected incident, but through images and their associations and their placement in the work. One such set of images is those of imprisonment, associated, as we would expect, with the aggressive and dependent characters. I suggested earlier that Stow wants his readers to understand that Tourmaline has happened before. Through the law of aggression, the *Tao* teaches, man traps himself in an endless cycle of cause and effect into which he is led as a prisoner of his own desires. He thus becomes a prisoner within and without. Tourmaline is a collective image for the state of being of man caught in such a double cycle, yoking him to the perpetual need for "black and white" men such as Random. Tourmaline is conjured out of the dust by the narrator and passes back into it at the end, this particular phase of a recurring cycle completed. It is as if the air clears for the space of the novel through the agency of the Tao to let us perceive the mistakes always made by people imprisoned in such a cycle. Man will destroy himself, the *Tao* warns, if he remains imprisoned in his history.

The narrator, a prisoner of his own limited conscious understanding, his own past, and his dream of a lost paradise, for "esprit de corps" (dependence on others), is thus appropriately the Law, the conscience and historian–narrator of the Tourmaline condition. But others are trapped too. In Kestrel's bar the flies are imprisoned, and the windows of the pub and of many of the buildings in Tourmaline seem "stone blind". Kestrel is trapped in his own power struggle and cycle of aggression intimately related to the diviner's. Deborah is caught first by her love for Kestrel and then by her obsession with the diviner, and Stow uses the image of the trapped flies superimposed, as it were, on the image of Deborah to suggest the nature of that busy, futile, repetitive obsession. After talking with Deborah, the narrator returns to his kitchen where "the kettle boiled on the rusty stove, and a solitary fly crossed and recrossed her distant figure climbing the hillside" (p. 87). Byrne is described as "tied", while other Tourmaline tenants seem trapped by the heat, the day, the timelessness, and the general torpor of the Tourmaline condition.

The diviner too, though he enslaves others to his cause, is himself trapped. He sleeps on an iron bed with a "grey broad-striped blanket" (p. 88), an image suggestive of prison bars, and is described by the narrator in that flash of intuitive perception as "a criminal of quite extraordinary distinction" (p. 163). Random is obviously trapped by Tourmaline and its needs, at once gaoler and prisoner of the Tourmaline experience.

There is an interesting relationship in the novel between

two different levels of consciousness in the narrator's mind. On the one hand, his connections between image and event may be basically logical. He consciously sees Deborah as imprisoned in her love for Kestrel, and it is logical that he would associate her with the trapped flies; but it is her "progress" up the hill towards the diviner's hut on which he superimposes the image of the futile movements of the fly. He is thus half-consciously perceiving the nature of the thrall in which the diviner is holding the town. He is more startled, however, to find himself suddenly thinking of the diviner, the saviour, as a criminal of quite extraordinary distinction. The connecting process in his mind here does not have even a quasi-logical basis. Such perceptions suddenly well to the top of the narrator's consciousness almost in spite of himself. These intuitive perceptions—and they are almost always expressive not of the conscious view of the narrator but of the point of view of Tom Spring—would provide, if he would let them, the key to his release from imprisonment in the state of Tourmaline.

Kestrel is the diviner's "dark underside". He and Random are, as Tom Spring says, "two sides of a coin" (p. 147), the self-haters, the humiliators and enslavers of others. Acceptance of self and of the inviolable individuality of self in others are central tenets of Taoism. Though Kestrel leaves the town at the rise of the diviner's power, he returns as it collapses to take up the potential and develop it further. With his new water-divining equipment to replace the diviner's home-made rod—mechanization and mass production are to replace cottage industry—he will enslave others on an even vaster scale. " 'Honour the single soul' ", Spring pleads. " 'I think in thousands . . . and tens of thousands,' ", says the new Kestrel (p. 172). The Tao teaches that once power struggles begin, they can only grow worse. Random may be "diviner" than Kestrel, but the darkness of Kestrel is the inevitable other side of any divine light. Kestrel is never, of course, a disciple of the diviner: though the two are naturally linked in the dependence–cruelty aggression cycle, they inhabit a world where there is room for only one "divine" at a time. Kestrel, as the blindness of his own pub windows suggests, is imprisoned too in the Tourmaline condition.

Against all this activity, power, ambition, morality, dependence, and aggression, Stow has to show the doctrine and
operation of the philosophical alternative: the Taoist view
based on harmony with the universe and with the land, not
a rape of it, or too great an expectation of it. Taoism, as
I have already noted, is a non-aggressive, non-assertive ideal
grounded in non-action and in silence. It is a philosophy that
proposes that "good words are not persuasive; persuasive
words are not good". These values must be depicted and
endorsed within a work dealing of necessity in words, and
by convention, in some action. Stow presents the Taoist aspect
of the novel in three major ways: through direct statement
of the Taoist ideal; through Tom Spring and Dave Speed,
who represent the point of view of the *Tao* and Stow's own
variations on it, and, most important of all perhaps, through
the use of a particular type of narrator.

The Tao never teaches by direct statement, but there is
one instance in *Tourmaline* where Tom Spring goes about
as far as the sage of the Tao may go towards explanation
and teaching. The narrator says that Spring "unveiled his
God to me", and typically he does not preach or proselytize.
It is noteworthy that it is the narrator who *reports* this
passage. Stow does not present the *Tao* doctrine to the reader
in direct speech. As the true sage, Tom Spring would have
every difficulty in stating his belief, and had he presented
it in the novel as a stated creed, Stow would have been doing
violence to the matter by his method.

> "Can I cure you?" he wondered, hopefully.
> "You can try," I said, to placate him.
> And he did try. But so stumblingly, so clumsily, that it
> was difficult to attend. He unveiled his God to me, and his
> God had names like the nameless, the sum of all, the ground
> of being. He spoke of the unity of opposites, and of the
> overwhelming power of inaction. He talked of becoming a
> stream, to carve out canyons without ceasing always to yield;
> of being a tree to grow without thinking; of being a rock
> to be shaped by winds and tides. He said I must become
> empty in order to be filled, must unlearn everything, must
> accept the role of fool. And with curious, fumbling passion
> he told me of a gate leading into darkness, which was both
> a valley and a woman, the source and sap of life, the temple

of revelation. At moments I thought I glimpsed, through the inept words, something of his vision of fullness and peace; the power and the darkness. Then it was hidden again, obscured behind his battles with the language, and I understood nothing, nothing at all; and I let my mind wander away from him to the diviner, at the altar, brilliant by flamelight, praising a familiar God, through the voice of a ritual bell.

When Tom stopped speaking, I made no remark.

And he said, wearily: "That was meaningless to you."

I was candid, and said: "Almost."

"Words can't cope," he said. And he added, rather bitterly: "Your prophet knows how to cut the truth to fit the language. You don't get much truth, of course, but it's well-tailored." [P. 148]

Verse LXXXI of the *Tao te ching* is one used by Stow for his "Variations". It is the final verse of both the *Tao* and of Stow's verses and therefore focal.

LXXXI
Truthful words are not beautiful; beautiful words are not truthful. Good words are not persuasive; persuasive words are not good. He who knows has no wide learning; he who has wide learning does not know.
The sage does not hoard.
Having bestowed all he has on others, he has yet
    more;
Having given all he has to others, he is richer still.
The way of heaven benefits and does not harm; the way of the sage is bountiful and does not contend.

Like the wise leader, the sage is unobtrusive, and his teaching is unobtrusive. It is never new and startling because it points to the rhythms of the universe which have been and will always be there. All that is necessary is right observation. Consequently the narrator has been, to use his own and Tom's phrase, "cured before" (p. 148), presumably by observation of the harmonious principle of the universe, but has now again fallen by the messianic wayside in pursuit of past dream and present hope.

Tom Spring's "cure" is the only direct statement of the Tao philosophy in *Tourmaline*, but it is clear that this philosophy underlies the novel totally. Much of the operation of Tao principles occurs in *Tourmaline* through the attitudes,

and more rarely actions, of two characters, Tom Spring and
Dave Speed. Both Spring and Speed are apparently isolated
from most of the action of *Tourmaline*, unobtrusive in every
sense. Yet their attitudes and opinions remain curiously
pervasive. Neither alters the course of events in the novel
to any significant extent, yet because they remain such a force
in the consciousness of the narrator, even at times when he
would prefer to reject their attitudes utterly, their force on
the reader counteracts the more flamboyant diviner-Kestrel
side of the debate.

The likening of Tom Spring to the "ivory statue of a sage"
(p. 75) has already been noted by A.D. Hope, as has Spring's
serenity and peace. He is never "prepossessing" in the sense
in which the diviner is; obtrusively bright with overtones of
"possessive" and "possessed". Whereas the diviner is constantly associated with blues and golds, the colours of the
double dream of Tourmaline, Spring is most commonly
associated with the red softness of the dust, and with the
grey-green leaves of the actual environment. While the
diviner allows himself to become a leader and potential
saviour, Tom refuses to lead, in particular to lead towards
false hope to the familiar chant of moral rightness and
humiliation. He lets Deborah go her way, always offering
but never insisting on sanctuary for her in his home. He
questions the diviner's purpose and method rather than
preaching against it, and, though he has seen the problem
of Tourmaline occur before, and knows it will occur again,
he pleads only with the narrator not to be the instrument
of the reinstitution of that aggression cycle. Tom maintains
his own independence and his tolerance for other views,
disliking these "black and white men" who are " 'like the
Chinaman who invented gunpowder. "Just a few rockets for
granny's birthday," he told them. Boom!' " (p. 148), but by
the terms of his own philosophy he cannot take up a gun
against them. He understands the town's craving for more
and better water but will not accept the price to be paid
for that water. His beliefs are not based on vapid faith but
on direct experience—what he has seen before. He has no
time for ritual or priests or church. He does not, as he says,
"understand divining". He does not support morality and

government, and his mysticism in so far as it may be categorized, is of a "dark, neutral, and uncertain nature". Tom Spring, in spite of his refusal to participate in the action of the novel, does act as a one-man chorus on the action, and his attitudes provide a foil for the conscious enthusiasms of the narrator and the rest of Tourmaline. He does not like "esprit de corps", and, unlike Kestrel and Random, he would "honour the single soul" and so refuses to participate in the diviner's mass revival rituals.

Not only do Spring and the diviner differ in name and in way of life—Tom Spring is the true spring, not the false fountain the diviner promises, and Tom is naturally a "spring", while a "diviner" must search for water—they differ also in death. Death is a central concern of *Tourmaline,* the tale of a town caught in a cycle of living death. The town celebrates the day of the dead, and the narrator is himself frightened by the processes of time and by the prospect of decaying into death. Death is a major fear for the narrator because he places his emphasis, like most of us, on self. He worries that when he is gone there will be no one to take his place. He mistakenly thinks that this prospect worries others also. Random the diviner seems to have been in the habit of flirting with death and suicide, again placing an important premium on the difference between the two states, with death as a form of punishment for failure and moral dereliction in life. For the philosophical Taoist, though, "body is land in permutation", "nothing made selfless can decay". Spring is "perishable", but this is part of the accepted process of life. Consequently Tom dies quietly, emanating a calm even in death, and is already being absorbed by the covering red dust of the land when the narrator finds him. The diviner on the other hand, who has already extended his quarrel with God into the realms of potential sefl-destruction, is last seen heading towards death defiantly, flying in the face of the natural processes of the earth, still an aggressive rebel against its harmonies. "The diviner broke into a sprint, and leaped the trailing barbed wire of the fence, and ran away laughing, into the gathering wind" (p. 170). It is a humourless laugh, for the diviner has "no sense of humour at all" (p. 168). On the other hand, Tom, after refusing to succumb to the blandishments of the returned Kestrel, dies quietly and peacefully in and not against, the gathering wind. "Tom was asleep at the counter, his head resting on his forearms. There was dust in his thinning hair. So peaceful he looked. I felt calmed" (p. 173).

Thus the sage passes as quietly and naturally out of life as he had existed in it. Only Tom Spring at the end of the novel, and Billy Bogada (coffined in the box marked "SPRING—PERISHABLE") at the beginning are able to escape from the cyclical hope–dependence–aggression state of Tourmaline into the peace of death. We might presume that the diviner dies, but he has already shown a talent for resurrection as well as self-destruction, and we know also that he and his kind will rise again to play their habitual role in the cycle. Tom earns his release, for philosophically he has only been at most a fringe dweller of the state of Tourmaline.

There is another important "outsider" on the Taoist side of the philosophical debate. It is, in much of Stow's work, the outsiders and the "bystanders" who see and understand most of the game, and in *Tourmaline* they are Dave Speed and his Aboriginal companion Jimmy Bogada. It is Billy Bogada who dies in the beginning of the novel, and Jimmy Bogada who lives the life of the land with Speed. Thus Spring and Speed are closely associated with the Aboriginal people in life and in death, while the narrator "never visits the camp", and to the diviner the Aboriginal people are only potential converts on the path to his God. At this stage in Tourmaline, they have become partially divorced from their traditional way of life, a way, like that of *Tao*, once intimately associated with the land and its meaning. They are now a foster people, dependent and dying. Deborah is a fitting representative of this half-way house state. She has been nurtured by the Springs, who are her foster parents, but she is seduced from their true kindness and harmony into a state of domestic war with Kestrel, and then into an obsessive and humiliating hero worship of the diviner. Just as Gloria Day keeps the oleander "improbably" flowering outside the church by a natural use of available water, while caught up in the teachings inside the white man's church, so Deborah is caught between the steadiness of Spring and the excitement and volatility of dependence and destruction. Because of the closer connections between the philosophy of Speed and Spring and the land itself, it is not surprising that they are the only whites in the novel who have any enduring connection with the Aboriginal people.

Dave Speed is left heir to the Tao estate of Tourmaline on the death of Tom Spring. Throughout the novel Speed and Spring are seen conversing when Speed does come to town, and it is obvious that they are both on the same philosophical side in their rejection of the diviner and his cult. But there are important differences between these two characters. While Dave may be Tom's heir, he is never his disciple in the dependent, possessed and possessing, dog-like sense. Neither is he his dark shadow in the sense of the relationship between the diviner and Kestrel. Kestrel is the diviner's heir as Speed is Spring's, but in a very different sense. The differences between Spring and Speed seem to stand for something of the difference between the verses of the *Tao te ching* and those of Stow's "Variations". While Tom Spring introduces the reader to the Tao in its pure philosophical form, Dave Speed is Tao in localized action, in full and perfect harmony with the particular environment. He never "unveils" his God to anyone, but he has the natural acceptance of conditions in the here and now, and he lives out of them and enjoys these harsh conditions. He "seems" to "preach passivity" (p. 71) to desert conditions, but it is not submission; it is an equal partnership. He rejects the cube of gold (p. 55), but accepts the traditional Taoist image of the uncarved block.[23] He wishes to approximate the way of the earth—to be a tree, or a stone. Dave's reaction to news of the diviner, and the subsequent conversation, is worth quoting in full:

> Dave listened poker-faced. When Tom had done, he breathed out a sort of sigh.
> "It's the end," he said.
> "You're a queer coot. Everyone else says it's the beginning."
> "You too?"
> "I don't know. Yes, I do too. We like water, don't we?"

"Sure we like it," Dave said. "But do we like strangers blowing in and sending the word round they got special powers to change the place?"

"He never said that. We wouldn't know he was a diviner if the Law hadn't dragged it out of him while he was sick."

"He's a fake," Dave said.

"I don't think he is," said Tom. "Or if he is, he doesn't know it."

"What's he like? Big talker?"

"Not a bit of it. Quiet. But not," Tom added after a moment, "not still. Know what I mean?"

"Sounds like Kes."

"You're right," Tom said. "Funny. Hadn't thought of it."

"Kes in favour of him?"

"No. He's the only one."

"It's the end," Dave said again.

"You want us all to go native," Tom said. "That's what you've got against him. Just enough food and water to keep us alive and no distractions. Dave Speed's Utopia."

"And what's wrong with it?" Dave demanded. "I know what I'm talking about. All the years I spent when I was the town drunk, wanting to be a tree."

"Seems to me you've got there."

"So now I want to be a stone. And I'll get there too."

"Won't we all?" Tom said. "It's death you mean."

"Maybe," said Dave. "Well, you can't get much quieter than that."

He swung his legs to the floor and stood up. "Better go and see young Jack. Be back in the morning." [P. 69]

Speed looks towards his own quiet end with hope, but not to the "end" of Tourmaline at the hands of the diviner. Unlike the Law–narrator, Speed does not fear age. " 'Time flies,' he said. 'And who'd want to stop it if they could?' " (p. 66). The narrator senses in Speed something of the same quality he found in Tom Spring. Speed, living outside the town, is even less obtrusive than is Spring; he is "outstanding" in his own natural element, not prepossessing in the deliberate way of the diviner. "Something about him, in spite of everything, drew one's attention, like a bird in the Tourmaline sky" (p. 66). The Law knows also that Dave "was as much a native as Jimmy Bogada, and had learned the same tolerance of deprivation" (p. 67). Speed's "Utopia" is the "Utopia" of the *Tao*, individual, not collective, and based on full acceptance of the here and now, the land as it is, not on the prospect of an after life, or a regained paradise in this one.

In Speed's acceptance of natural conditions, his attitude to the land, particularly to the water, his isolation, his knowledge of deeper truths (the "outcomes" of *Tao*), and in his general inarticulateness, he is Tao in action in a particular environment. Just as Stow's "Variations" give the *Tao* a local habitation and name, so in the novel Speed is Stow's variation on Spring, the specifically local adaptation of the creed of Spring. Hence the philosophical Spring dies, leaving the ground to Speed, and this heritage, though barren, is anything but bitter. The bitter heritage belongs, in the narrator's opening words, to the other sons of Tourmaline caught up in the messianic religious cycle of aggression.

The nature and purpose of the narrator Stow uses in *Tourmaline* has been something of a puzzle to critics. The Law-narrator is the self-styled "memory and conscience" (p. 42) of Tourmaline. Tourmaline was, I suggested, symbolic of that state of mind and place in time to which man comes through the law of aggression. The inhabitants of Tourmaline represent the remnants of the last active cycle of destruction which must soon come again. The Law, then, as memory and conscience of that state, represents two attitudes quite antithetical to the Tao point of view.

In the first place, the Law likes law, government, the moral code, and his hobby consists in reading the crimes and punishments of the past. It is only towards the end, and fleetingly, that he sees himself and his career through different eyes: "I see myself again as a boy; a long solemn face, obsessed with responsibilities never more than an illusion, wearing unreasoned habit like a straitjacket. I was a good lad, alas. A tool, a dupe. What price have others paid for my arrogant simplicity?" (p. 113). This Law-narrator who invokes right and wrong is like the diviner (into whose service the Law is naturally pressed), one of these "black and white men", so potentially destructive in the way in which the *Tao* sees all obtrusive government and hard and fast moral law as being. The Law feels himself and his laws

to be outworn relics until the diviner convinces him of their
viability. Random will reactivate this false "spring" in the
Law, and by making Tourmaline "burn", ironically hopes
to find water.

In the second place, as historian and recorder—the memory
of Tourmaline—the Law-narrator is potentially a destructive
influence. *Paradise Lost* is placed between the Bible and
Pilgrim's Progress on his grandfather's shelves, and it is this
ancient dream of a long-lost garden which becomes the hope
of Tourmaline, causing its citizens to conjure up the diviner,
become dependent on him, and foster the concepts of good
and evil in a collective pilgrims' progress to a paradise lost.
Through this dream, true need and greed have become
confused. The Law-narrator's yearning for a lost green is
of course an expression of his age yearning for youth; of
man's perpetual yearning for what lies beyond his present
condition and understanding; and on a more local level, it
is the colonial's dream of the motherland, where the grass
is naturally greener. Many of the inhabitants of Tourmaline
listen long-sufferingly to the Law's reminiscences and
dreams, and in his so-called memory of the former greenness
of Tourmaline an interesting distinction is apparent. The
Law has specific memories of his youth and of Tourmaline
—the pepper trees, the black dog crossing the street, the frail
pink lilies. But he is also inclined to generalize to a dream
paradise, and it is this particular section of his "memory"
that Dave Speed calls into question. These memories are
always less specific, of "birds" or "trees" or "greenness"
suggesting the ultimate confusion in the Law-narrator's mind
between an ideal dream and a specific past—between what
might have been and what he hopes will be. He associates
his love of the past with his being "half in love with ruin".
By adherence to the past, and to the laws and dreams of
that past, he is indeed unconsciously allying himself with ruin
in terms of the Tao.

It would seem on the surface that by training and
inclination the narrator is squarely on the "diviner" side of
the debate, but while on the one hand he "creates" the
diviner, tempts him by showing him Tourmaline from the
hill, becomes subject to his power, participates in his ritual,

and agrees, as moral law and government have traditionally done, to act for good or ill in the name of a higher purpose, he is nonetheless the chief agent through which the Tao point of view is expressed by Stow, and even Spring's apologia is recounted by him.

Knowing "more than he knows",[24] the narrator finds that Tao values will out. If Tao is the true way of the universe, then, the narrator will unconsciously express this way, even as he consciously follows a very different path.

The Law begins his Testament on the day Kestrel leaves Tourmaline, the beginning of the day of the diviner, which is also, apparently coincidentally, the day of the dead, over which the Law traditionally presides, as he has done over the "creation" of the diviner. This juxtaposition associates the diviner with the guilt–victim nexus of the day itself. Characteristically, Spring and Speed have as little time for the woolly, guilt-ridden celebration as they do for the diviner. The Law is hurt by Spring's rejection of his sentiments, but he retains throughout a respect for Spring's views even while he cannot fully understand them or accept what he can understand. This respect for Spring, this sense of his importance in the action in spite of his apparent withdrawal from it, is unconsciously expressed by the narrator in a number of ways.

Though he begins to write his Testament on the day of the diviner, he sets his tale back in time and begins his character sketches with the love–hate power struggle of Deb and Kes, and follows this with a description of Spring's real strength and peace:

> Tom Spring, on a rickety chair, behind the counter of his store, sleeves rolled up on his thin strong arms. A small strong thin man, Tom; quiet, so quiet one might stop and listen, in surprise. A deep Quaker quiet, an act of religion, that might help his soul to become like a great cave and trap and amplify the faint whisperings of God—that was the silence he was building, behind his quiet eyes, under his thinning hair. Imagine him there. [P. 12]

Spring's is the first human habitation to be described, and it is situated opposite, or opposed to, the war memorial. The

Springs have a cat, which, unlike Kestrel's dog, is independent, acknowledging no owner, though associated with Spring. Kestrel's dog, the narrator observes, changes his allegiance from Kestrel, to Byrne, and back to Kestrel again. Although the narrator does not appear to see that the dog stands not just for Byrne and his devotion (first to Kestrel, who treats him badly, then to Random, who treats him with contempt, and back to Kestrel again), but for the whole town, he nonetheless makes the initial connection, directing the reader's attention to the comparison. He completely fails however, to see the significance of the black dog who appears to be the sole occupant of the Tourmaline street in the photo he shows the diviner. The dog is, of course, a fitting image of the utter dependence and devotion that has led to the destruction of Tourmaline and will do so again. In associating the cat with Tom Spring, and the black dog with Tourmaline's past and fate, the narrator is showing the reader more than he himself consciously perceives.

An image that recurs to the narrator is that of "smooth pink lilies, so tough, so delicate, that sprang up leafless from the baked ground, before the earliest rains" (pp. 75–76). The image and sentiment are traditionally Taoist; the soft or quiet which penetrates the hard and the unyielding is the classic example of the Way. But more interesting than the image itself are the occasions when it occurs to the narrator. Twice it is connected with the diviner, but in both instances it arises in direct contradiction to what the diviner seems to represent. The illogic occurs to the narrator in the first instance, and prompts him to ask: "Why, in my great hope, did I remember the easter lilies in our old garden; the smooth pink lilies, so tough, so delicate . . . ". In the second instance, he does not draw attention explicitly to the anomaly, but the reader might by now be expected to note it for himself. Of the diviner, the narrator says,

> Because, even when my disbelief was strongest, he could disarm me. Suddenly, turning to speak to someone else, I would catch sight of him. And the brightness then, the force, seemed beyond resisting; and my mind would go back, through years like buried roads, to the kingfisher-flash by the creek, and the frail pink lilies, breaking the baked gound in my father's garden. [P. 162]

"Turning back is how the way moves";[25] and in turning back, the narrator has arrived instinctively at the right image of the Way. The diviner with his brightness and force may be the kingfisher flash, but he is not the fail pink lilies, and his way is not theirs. It is thus at points of his highest hope in the diviner that the narrator instinctively returns to the image of the successful way of the universe: the one that offers true hope for life in this world. Man must look to the land and its meaning, as the *Tao* does, and not to the diviner and his inappropriate one, if he is to survive.

In Stow's "*From* The Testament of Tourmaline: Variations on Themes of the *Tao Teh Ching*" it is the land itself that is emphasized; images of dryness and water in particular are used to express the traditional *Tao* ideas. But the "Variations" by necessity deal in the relation between water and baked earth, and the philosophical Tao implications are thus expressed in *Tourmaline* terms. Like Dave Speed, the "Variations" show that man in the state of Tourmaline can find his answer through the Tao. There is not, has not been, and will not be, any necessity for a diviner. The *Tao te ching* is an appropriate text for Tourmaline conditions. Stow's "Variations" are a "Testament" to the appropriateness of the philosophy to the Western, Australian, situation. If they are the "testament" of Tourmaline's people, they represent their unconscious contemplative chorus of right perception, even while in action they follow the way of the diviner.

To begin, the narrator says, "I must imagine and invent" (p. 12), and *Tourmaline* might be seen then as a kind of debate in the mind of a narrator who, while consciously clinging to codes, laws, and a religion inappropriate to his experience, unconsciously perceives the harmony of the universe. He cannot help doing this, as the way of the Tao does "happen naturally". The message is one of colonial dilemma and adaptive growth. Though I have referred to Tourmaline as a novel of philosophical "debate", and to "sides" for the sake of convenience, it is not essentially a debate. While Stow endorses one way of life at the expense of the other, there is never a real confrontation between the two. The main action exists not in the streets of Tourmaline, but in the narrator's mind—and the action is a slow process towards a more conscious perception of harmony between man and land. Like Rao's *The Serpent and the Rope*, then, *Tourmaline* does not yoke by violence two arbitrarily chosen philosophical systems. The clash the narrator "imagines" and externalizes as action in a small dry town in Western Australia is representative of a historical clash—that of the dilemma of transplanation and adaptation inherent in the colonial experience.

Tourmaline is remarkable in conception and achievement. For all this philosophical seriousness, the dialogue remains witty, plausible, and down to earth; the medium is not philosophical, but colloquial. Like the Tao it endorses, it is firmly rooted in the realities of daily living. Remarkably, Stow has managed to assert successfully the values of silence, inaction, death, deprivation, and acceptance of the here and now, in the face of charisma, speech-making, action, and promised paradise here and in the hereafter. He has achieved this through the use of conscious and unconscious perceptions on the part of the narrator, and more rarely through statement and significant action. He has shown through action the triumph of inaction, and through dialogue the values of silence.

In a recent interview, Stow was asked whether he felt that the "bystander" character had a positive value. He replied: "Well, I did think so at the time, now I have my doubts rather. I did at that age believe that innocence was a virtue and that non-involvement was also a virtue. I also believed in an uncomplicated way, in the doctrines of Taoism (that the fool is the wise man, the weak is the strong). I doubt that I would write in the same way now, at least not with the same security."[26] While I think there is no doubt that Stow considers in *Tourmaline* that the way of the Tao is the way of life, and that what goes counter to it is, to put it in Taoist terms, not wrong but an invitation to disaster, he has not found it necessary or practicable to explore its possibilities further in the novel. But just as the road to *Tourmaline* is paved with *A Haunted Land* and *To the Islands*, so his later works such as *The Merry-Go-Round in the Sea* and a number of his poems contain echoes of Taoist thought. Stow himself has presumably continued to feel some affinity with its ways: "I really have nothing to say about poetry in general (except that mine tries to counterfeit the communication of those who communicate by silence)."[27]

NOTES

1. Stow gives the full title the spelling *Tao Teh Ching*, though the more usual form is *Tao te ching*. I have chosen to use the latter, and its shortened form *Tao* in this account. While *"Tao"* signifies the original text of Lao-tzu itself, "Tao" refers to the general philosophy embodied therein.

2. John Beston, "An Interview with Randolph Stow", *WLWE* 14, no. 1 (April 1975): 228:

> Concerning "The Testament of Tourmaline": do you mean it to be closely tied in with the novel?
> Yes, it is, in fact it's something of a key to the novel. . . .
> Since it deals with Taoism, what reading would you recommend as a background to it?
> Just simply the *Tao Teh Ching*, the Taoist "Bible". There are lots of different translations of it. I've read it often over many years. The poems in the "Testament of Tourmaline" are numbered according to the sections of the Tao Teh Ching.

3. A.D. Hope, "Randolph Stow and the *Tourmaline* Affair", in *The Australian Experience*, ed. W.S. Ramson (Canberra: Australian National University Press, 1974), pp. 249–68; and "Randolph Stow and the Way of Heaven", *Hemisphere* 18, no. 6 (1975): 33–35.

4. Leonie Kramer, review, *Bulletin*, 6 July 1963, and *Southerly* 24, no. 2 (1964). *Tourmaline* was published in 1963 and was received by critics with puzzled enthusiasm on the one hand and qualified dislike on the other. Geoffrey Dutton's reaction is typical of the first response, while Leonie Kramer's approach exemplifies the second. This second view generally accuses Stow of failing to integrate the realistic and symbolic levels of his writing, so that in all his novels, but particularly in *Tourmaline*, the meaning of the whole remains obscure and wanting in "human interest". Professor Kramer does attempt to penetrate this obscure meaning but feels that, given Stow's basic confusion of conception and method, any such attempt is necessarily doomed to failure.

5. Geoffrey Dutton, "The Search for Permanence: The Novels of Randolph Stow", *Journal of Commonwealth Literature*, no. 1, (September 1965): 146: "It is difficult as yet to judge this book critically, there is so much in it, such poetry of the imagination, such depth of meaning. Admittedly the narrative method is at

times a trial, yet the novel's immense suggestability remains
unimpaired. It is an extraordinarily original work."

6. Hence Madeleine's conversion to Buddhism grows out of her
interest in Hinduism, as the Buddha himself evolved his new path
out of his Hindu background.

7. In using the terms *Taoist* and *Taoism* I am using a convenient
adjectival and noun form of Tao, the Way, as originally set down
by Lao tzu in the *Tao te ching*. I don't intend the terms to include
the later developments of Tao into a religion usually referred to
as Taoism. Stow is obviously interested in the original text of
the *Tao*, and not the technicalities of its later religious practice
in China. The terms *philosophical Tao* or *philosophical Taoism*
are sometimes used to distinguish this from later "religious"
Taoism.

8. Randolph Stow, "The Land's Meaning", in *Outrider* (London:
Macdonald, 1962), p. 20.

9. The term is originally Emerson's but has been given general
currency as an expression of a particular colonial process by R.E.
Watters in "Original Relations", *Canadian Literature* 8 (1961):
6–17.

10. Randolph Stow, "*From* The Testament of Tourmaline: Variations
on Themes of the *Tao Teh Ching*", Variation VII, in *A
Counterfeit Silence* (Sydney: Angus & Robertson, 1969), p. 72.

11. For specific quotations and general commentary on the *Tao* I am
largely indebted to Holmes Welch, *The Parting of the Way*
(London: Methuen, 1958). I have also drawn on Arthur Waley,
*The Way and Its Power: A Study of the Tao Te Ching and Its
Place in Chinese Thought* (New York: Macmillan, 1934); and
on D.C. Lau, trans, *Lao Tzu: Tao Te Ching* (Harmondsworth
Mddx.: Penguin, 1963).

12. Welch, *Parting of the Way*, pp. 20, 21.

13. Welch, *Parting of the Way*, p. 87.

14. Lau, *Tao Te Ching*, verse LXXXI, p. 143.

15. *"O gens de peu de poids dans
la mémoire de ces lieux ..."*
St-John Perse: *Anabase*

16. In providing critics with a "key" to *Tourmaline* three years after
the publication of the novel, Stow might be seen to be laying
himself open to the charge of having written an unintelligible and
esoteric dialogue with himself. The question is naturally raised
as to whether the novel can stand alone without Stow's "Variations" and without a knowledge of philosophical Taoism. While
we have been as critics prepared to accept the symbolic shorthand
of the Christian tradition, we have been impatient with personal

symbols. In asking us to have some knowledge of the Tao, I would suggest, Stow is doing no more than asking us to know something of a philosophy which has been as important in the East as Christianity has been in the West. There have been almost as many English translations of the *Tao te ching* as there have been of the Bible, hence there is no problem of availability of the text. We gain added meaning from the work by noticing the implications of the Christian symbolic references, and Stow might well expect his readers to gain the same from knowledge of Taoism.

17. E.M. Forster, *A Passage to India* (Harmondsworth, Mddx: Penguin, 1936), p. 148.
18. Page references are to the Penguin edition (Ringwood, Vic., 1965).
19. And will happen again. Hence, the novel is set, as Stow tells us at the beginning, in "the future".
20. Lau, *Tao Te Ching*, p. 73.
21. A.D. Hope also applied the particularly appropriate term *cargo cult* to the diviner's religion.
22. There are other characters associated with blue and gold in the novel, particularly with blue. Blue is almost a Tourmaline uniform, particularly for the diviner's "converts". Deborah is always dressed in blue, and so is Byrne. Byrne's devoted discipleship is indicated by the Law's statement that he could hardly tell the two apart as they make between them that significant symbol of divinity, the divining rod. The diviner has, however already been described by him as fair with blue eyes, and Byrne as "dark".
23. Another classic *Tao* image is associated with Speed—the newborn babe. " 'I'm a drongo' said Dave. 'I'm a kid. I don't know anything' " (p. 70).
24. Stow, "Country Children", in *A Counterfeit Silence* p. 6.
25. Lau, *Tao Te Ching*, p. 101.
26. A. Rutherford and Andreas Boelsmand, "Interview with Randolph Stow", *Commonwealth Newsletter* (Aarhus), 1973.
27. Alexander Craig, ed., *Twelve Poets 1950–1970* (Brisbane: Jacaranda, 1971), p. 175.

Victims Black and White

Thomas Keneally's *The Chant of Jimmie Blacksmith*

CHRIS TIFFIN

Race relations in Australia's past, and, by implication, present are the accepted theme of *The Chant of Jimmie Blacksmith*, and discussion of the novel, whatever success it is seen to have, has started from this assumption.[1] There are, however, two further ways in which the book needs to be seen to appreciate how it explores beyond the social-racial level, and to pinpoint more accurately the role of Keneally as narrator. The first of these approaches is to set the Blacksmith story against that of its historical prototypes, the Governor brothers; the second is to see Jimmie not as fictional black or half-caste, but as the most successfully drawn of Keneally's recurrent sensitive, oppressed, ultimately self-destructive victims.

Keneally has stated he drew upon contemporary newspapers, citing the *Sydney Mail*.[2] In the text he pretends to quote also from the *Bulletin* and the *Sydney Morning Herald*. A more proximate source, however, which seems to have had considerable impact on the novel, is the retelling of the Governor story by Frank Clune.[3] Clune synthesizes from the newspapers of 1900 the events of the killings and the pursuit, the interest in approaching Federation, and the interest in the Boer War, and combines these with an attitude of unsympathizing horror at the killings. Keneally adopts this nexus, makes some changes in narrative, many in sympathetic stance, and produces a novel which is still his most accomplished and arguably his greatest.

Keneally's changes to his sources would be of less interest and importance if he had not retained so many details of the original events. The household the Governors attacked, for example, consisted of almost the same occupants as the Newbys', including a schoolteacher with a German name. The menfolk were staying the night at the old homestead a mile from the new one, and the murders took place on a Friday night in July. The deaths and injuries correspond with those in the novel, although one of the daughters and Miss Ketz the schoolmistress were killed outside the house. Jimmy Governor had only his uncle, Jacky Underwood, with him at the initial killings, while his brother Joe was responsible for a killing later. Jimmy Governor had previously been a police tracker and was fencing for the Mawbys at the time of the attack. Jacky Underwood and Ethel were quickly apprehended while Joe and Jimmy Governor evaded the police till October. A week after being outlawed, Joe was shot dead and Jimmy captured after having been shot through the mouth.

Keneally, then, adopted more than just the bones of the story without alteration. The changes he made are of three types—racial, narrative, and psychological or thematic. In the first place Joe, a half-caste and Jimmy's full brother, becomes Morton, a full-blood and Jimmie's half-brother. The result of this is an increase in Jimmie's isolation from both the black and the white world; it shows him to be as excluded from the tribal beliefs as he is from the community espousing the white values. The black religion he uneasily dismisses as "horseshit" (p. 75),[4] and seeks purposeful life in the alternative values of possession. In this quest he is encouraged by the well-meaning Mr Neville, who counsels a racial form of social climbing: " 'If you could ever find a nice girl off a farm to marry, your children would only be quarter-caste then, and your grandchildren one-eighth caste, scarcely black at all' " (p. 7). Jimmie is convinced, but when he tries to convey the idea to Newby he is firmly repulsed:

> "How yer goin' to raise yer piccaninny, Jimmie?"
> "He be no piccaninny, boss. He three parts white."
> "Yair. And his kid'll be an eighth black and his a sixteenth. But it doesn't matter how many times yer descendants bed down, they'll never get anything that don't have the tarbrush in it. And it'll always spoil 'em, that little bit of somethink else." [P. 61]

These parallel speeches indicate the tension between two sides of a contrast which, as W.S. Ramson has shown, is explored from the first paragraph of the novel.[5] Jimmie's plight as half-caste is, in fact, worse than it would be as a full-blood, for his white side gives him the awareness that Keneally associates with the desire for possessions—the desire to "improve" himself. While there are obvious advantages for the fiction itself in using Mort as a way to highlight Jimmie's tribal side, there is a further point in its use. Clune's account of the Governor killings is far from a simply factual one, and he enthusiastically condemns them as "murderous curs—slayers only of women, children and old men".[6] Moreover, he specifically rejects any extenuation for the Governors on the grounds that they were blacks retaliating racial wrongs. They were not really blacks at all, says Clune, but half-castes. Clune's complete withdrawal of sympathy on this point prompts Keneally's dwelling upon it and his elaborate use of Mort and Tabidgi to enshrine the tribal beliefs and customs from which Jimmie is partly distanced yet by which he is partly still entrapped. Mort and Tabidgi kill instinctively and impulsively when they are placed by Jimmie in killing situations, and their response to killing is instinctive horror. Jimmie is more conscious; he has insights into what he is doing even as he wields axe or gun, with the result that his horror at his own actions is far more complex. It is as though Keneally associates Jimmie's racial dislocation with a moral awareness. The whites are never called upon to answer for their crimes or examine their motives. Mort and Jackie are incapable of the self-exploration necessary for Keneally's particular idea of hell. Only Jimmie is sufficiently self-conscious, disadvantaged, dislocated, and imposed upon to be made coherently desperate. It is this desperation which Keneally explores to show just how irrelevant is a rhetorical question like Clune's, "If murderers could foresee the sorrow that their crimes cause, would they pause in their impulses of hate?"[7]

Inevitably, there are numerous small narrative changes from the Governors' story to the Blacksmiths', but two are important enough to warrant mention. The first is the capture of Jimmy Governor, who was taken sleeping by a

fire, not in a convent; the second is the protracted incident
of the hostage McCreadie. Keneally's version of the capture
allows him to encapsulate the earlier religious parallels in
the book and to insinuate into the paralleled rebirth ceremo-
nies of Easter and tribal initiation, the further idea of
initiation into guilt.[8] Keneally opens the novel with a
reference to Jimmie's initiation tooth, and later makes explicit
the parallel between that initiation wound and the wound
he receives from the marksman. Here in the delirium it
becomes associated with the actual moment Jimmie fell from
grace, or perhaps that at which he reached his greatest moral
degradation.

> He slept and his wound pained on. As any rebirth wound
> could be expected to.
> When he was conscious and remembered how he had got
> the wound, he fell into a worse delirium.
> Often it was the lurid corner where Mrs Healy had died
> between the dresser and linen cupboard. Those he loved were
> there considering with shoppers' interest the bloody remnants.
> And Mort—trust Mort!—was the first of them who got
> the idea of painting himself with tints from the rotten traces
> of Jimmie's old hatreds. [P. 173]

Jimmie clearly sees the wound as retributive for his
"earlier indecencies" (p. 78) the worst of which are brought
together in this penitential delirium: the destruction of Mrs
Healy and her child, the corruption of Mort, the abandonment of Harry Edwards to Farrell, the attack on Verona.
Thus the finale in the convent is a "hell" in a theological
sense, for Jimmie is tortured not only by the pain in his
mouth but also by the knowledge and memory of his guilt.
He is his own accuser, turning the nuns' chant into:

> God have mercy on poor Mort Blacksmith,
> Taught to kill women by his bastard brother Jimmie.
>   [P. 170]

When he is discovered at last by the nuns, their judgement
of Jimmie's whole career is much more tempered than any
he has met in his life: "My poor man, you've done so many
evils and suffered so much."
The introduction of McCreadie into the Blacksmith story

is Keneally's most daring gambit, because it exposes the Blacksmiths' psychology over a considerable time and in close detail. Until McCreadie enters, the story has been basically episodic with no sustained and close study of a changing relationship. Keneally has been able to sketch brief incidents, bear in upon them for the insight or irony he wants to portray, then move on to the next. "The McCreadie-Blacksmith connection", Keneally's own phrase, is more than just such an incident. Psychologically it allows for a richer presentation of the tensions between Mort and Jimmie as they flee, and provides a ready method of exposing Jimmie's need for some self-image to conform to. But McCreadie also acts as spokesman for the wider historical view of the Aboriginal in Australia, a role Clune could take but which is impossible for Keneally's narrative viewpoint without excessively excusing Jimmie. Clune had pointed out that the Constitution, which was so much celebrated in the Federation preparations, "made no provision or even reference to the aborigines".[9] While McCreadie does not volunteer that particular instance of neglect and incomprehension, he evinces both a sympathetic interest in Aboriginal beliefs and an awareness of the statistical results of the first hundred years of racial conflict in the country. He provides the overt reminder of facts that undercut the cornucopian headiness of the new Federation depicted in the final pages. Keneally intends his historical fiction to "find evidence in earlier events for the kind of society we have now, wishing to tell a parable about the present by using the past".[10] The events (as depicted) of Jimmie Blacksmith's career, the historical facts supplied by McCreadie, the abuses of Senior Constable Farrell, the cautions and doubts in Mr Neville's rejected letter to a church paper, and the exuberant optimism of officially egalitarian Australia are the chief elements Keneally presents as modern Australia's birthright.

The third set of changes Keneally makes on the original are concerned with the motives of the participants. Predictably, perhaps, these are designed to make Jimmie more attractive and to undercut or at least neutralize his opponents. Jimmy Governor's motives for the killings are obscure, although the trial records seem to indicate that the most substantial reason was retaliation for ridicule both of himself and of Ethel about their marriage. This line, at any rate, was used by defending counsel to try to establish provocation and thus gain a plea of manslaughter. Relations between the Governors and the Mawby men were apparently cordial: the Governor brothers used to play cricket with the Mawby boys. There was no dispute about payment for the work done, nor evidence that Mawby refused supplies; in fact, Jimmy did not take any food from the Mawby house after the killings. Other possible contributing motives include a domestic argument in which Jimmy accused Ethel of involvement with his brother, and some idle talk about "going bushranging". At any rate, whatever prompted the original killings, Keneally's Jimmie Blacksmith is much more severely provoked and is made much more dignified in his response to that provocation than is his prototype in the newspaper accounts Keneally drew on, while Clune allows scant dignity to "the yellow cur".[11] After the event, similarly, Clune shows Jimmy Governor calculatingly and without compunction implicating Joe,[12] whereas Keneally's Jimmie struggles, falls, then achieves salvation on this very issue, as I shall argue shortly.

If not as moving, at least more entertaining are the changes made to the other characters, their motives and psychologies. These are to some extent implied in what has been said above. Mawby's attempts to insult Jimmie into leaving without payment interspersed with gruff almost-kindnesses, the universal meanness and toughness of the selectors, Petra Graf's high tone and invidious kindly offer to Gilda are all Keneally inventions or modifications of historical characters. There is none so sustained in the book, however, nor so splendidly executed as the schoolmistress's fiancé, Herbert Byers or as Keneally portrays him, Dowie Stead. Byers was a kangaroo shooter from Ulan who pursued the Governors until Joe's death (which occurred after, not before, Jimmy's capture). It was he who wounded Jimmy in the mouth (and also, in fact, in the buttocks). The newspaper accounts give little information on Byers, but Clune features him as a combination of outraged and bereaved lover and relentless, implacable vengeance. Whereas Clune portrays his continual criss-crossings as dogged but often unlucky, Keneally's Stead

is a hollow character acting roles, galloping aimlessly
backwards and forwards, and always arriving a little too late,
like a comedian who has the door constantly shut in his face.
If Byers is Clune's Spirit of Young Australia, determinedly
avenging cowardly and vicious murders, then Dowie Stead
is a Young Australia that takes shelter in the practical and
material, for it is uneasy with the received ideals, sensing
their hollowness:

> There was a functionality about his body; and people knew,
> having beaten drought and fluke, grasshoppers and banks to
> own what they owned, that functionality mattered. . . .
> Dowie Stead should have felt vastly angered. Instead he
> felt elected to give chase. This sense of election outweighed
> his guilt at feeling no grief of his own; which lack of response
> —he believed—was a judgment on him for rolling lubras in
> Gulargambone.
> It did not fully occur to him yet that he might not have
> loved Miss Graf, for everybody said she was good and wise
> and handsome. Like Gilda, Dowie had always been awed
> by her. It worried him that he was lightened every time he
> remembered that now he did not have to marry her.
> [P. 90-91]

There is no element of the original story which Keneally
undercuts more than the retributive zeal of Herbert Byers.
Sometimes his alterations become almost a satire on Clune's
own moral comment, as though the proximity of Clune's
account to the present makes its attitudes more real targets
than the now forgotten horror of the *Sydney Mail* or the
Mudgee Guardian. On this point the following comparison
is instructive. The first passage is Clune's, the second
Keneally's.

> On the way to Breelong, Bert Byers had cashed a cheque
> for sixty pounds, in five-pound notes, to keep him and his
> mates in provisions.
> He was allowed to look for the last time on Helena's face,
> as she lay in her coffin—her battered face and head.
> Emerging from the house, Byers was almost demented with
> grief. His friends stood by him to comfort him, but he mastered
> his emotion, and said with chilling calm, "I'll follow him . . .
> and I'll get him . . . and I'll shoot him like a dog . . ."

Then, giving strange emphasis to his words, he put his
hand in his pocket and brought out a piece of paper. It was
a five-pound note. I'll soak this in his blood," vowed Byers,
"and I'll keep it in memory of the girl he killed!"[13]

> In Gulargambone he had cashed a cheque for sixty pounds
> at the Squatters' Club. Today he wondered whether he
> should not take out a new, blue-hatched five-pound note and
> say that he would not cease the hunt until he had rinsed
> it in Jimmie Blacksmith's blood. It was a little wild and
> imaginative, and Dowie was not at all sure that it should
> be done. But it might soothe the Newbys who were bona
> fide mourners.
> Mrs Newby however died during the inquest, making the
> gesture inappropriate. [P. 91]

Clune's account (and I suspect it is his interpolation, as I
have failed to find any contemporary reference to the
incident) is external, reporting what was said and done, the
only internalizing being the motive of supporting himself and
his posse in the pursuit. By contrast, Keneally reduces much
of the incident to tentative thought. The result is an attack
not only on the rhetoric of romantic love, but on the parade
of emotion which is assumed or claimed but not felt. The
force of Clune's account is dismantled principally by sub-
stituting the thought for the rhetorical word, but Keneally
goes further than that. Even Dowie's contemplated gesture
is paler—*vowed* becomes *say*, *soak* becomes *rinse*. Detail
enters to distract. Byers's prop for the gesture is simply "a
five-pound note". Dowie is made to linger over the thought
of "a new, blue-hatched note" as though its pristine state
might make it more appropriately unreal for such a gesture.
Clune simply states the cheque was cashed. Dowie cashes
it "at the Squatters' Club", a detail which not only detracts
from the expected emotion, but introduces a note of com-
fortable élitism to counter that of supportive mateship in
Clune.[14] Gulargambone, moreover, is the scene of Dowie's
adventures with lubras, which have, he thinks, made it
impossible for him to feel grief at his fiancée's death. But
Keneally's final sentence is disturbing. One can admire the
deftness with which the melodramatic gesture of a conventional lover is undercut, and respond to Keneally's superb

satire of the self-aggrandizement that all except Mr Newby draw from the catastrophe. But the problem remains that this satire is supported and maintained at the expense of any compunction for the deaths themselves, which become events or details almost as minor and simply functional as the introduction of the Squatters' Club a few lines earlier. To kill off half the Newby family in order to show that the other half become swept up in the rhetoric of the event—"They were insatiable for words like *monstrous, unspeakable, black butchers*" (p. 89)—is, even for a fiction-writer, a curious manner of proceeding.

To some extent the explanation, but not the solution, of this problem lies in the context in which Keneally is writing, as I have set it out above. Keneally inherited not only a skeletal story with considerable narrative detail but also an interpretation of the events and characters. At the time of the murders, the *Mudgee Guardian* commented under its running title "The Black Horror":

> In Mudgee Joe Governor would not have been regarded as a blood-thirsty character by any means, and one not likely to be guilty of the terrible crime credited to him at Breelong. But this can be said of most aboriginals, who seem harmless and innocent beings under ordinary circumstances, but when the inbred passions of the savage nature assert themselves and greed and lust is uppermost in their minds, few, if any Australian aboriginals will shrink from committing murder.[15]

This is typical of the attitudes of the time, although most accounts did not misjudge the incident so obviously as this. Clune's retelling of the story rebuts the idea of lurking racial violence as an explanation for the crimes partly on historical grounds and partly on the grounds that Jimmy was a half-caste anyway and should therefore be judged as a white, which he curtly proceeds to do, without any concession that, even on the evidence of the 1950's, Jimmy's treatment may have been less than that accorded to a white worker. However the story is told, an attitude to Jimmy's crimes is implied. Keneally's retelling is in part a polemic against the Clune version, which had left Jimmy in fact worse off than the "savages" attitude at the time of the events; and with such a strong focus on the rehabilitation of Jimmie, the fact of the murders is minimized as much as possible.

But the recurrence of casually treated violent death in Keneally's novels is too pervasive for any single instance to be satisfactorily accounted for by contextual explanations. It has been noted frequently, and even where it is not noted it is sometimes responsible for a discomfort and even a querulousness which readers feel with Keneally. On the face of it, Keneally simply delights in violent death, and it has been suggested that Keneally himself is Ted Knoller in *The Chant of Jimmie Blacksmith*.[16] There are, however, more cogent reasons for Keneally's constant return to this motif. The first death in his first novel is depicted thus:

> In the shocking dirt of the cement floor, Wally lay now, indiscriminately felled amongst the piglets, prostrate on his stomach with his head on his side. Someone had battered him about the head and then strangled him with a noose of thin rope. His tongue was a large red indecency. The sow had chewed at his right cheek, adding her own touch to the extraordinary state of the corpse. Wadell had never seen anything that suffered so heavily from its own stinking mortality.[17]

Although this has been a violent murder, Keneally is clearly more concerned with the indignity of death. The pig-pen surroundings, the lolling "indecent" tongue, the savaged cheek are all summed up in what is a focal phrase for Keneally's work, "stinking mortality". Keneally is fascinated by the tenuousness by which physical man maintains his hold on life, and by extension, the ease by which one man can destroy another's life. This is what Jimmie discovers as he hacks Miss Graf (p. 79), what Tabidgi tries to tell the people of Dubbo (p. 129), what Byrne learns from the "barbarous fluidity" of the bayonet in *Bring Larks and Heroes*.[18] The ease of death and of causing death must be reinstated as a factor in our concept of life, although we have become progressively insulated from a sense of the imminence of death. But this is only the ultimate manifestation of a condition that Keneally sees operating in all human consciousness, and it is in this that his interest in death finds meaning.

Keneally continually sees human relationships in terms of dominance and vulnerability. When people interact they play out a more or less tangible power struggle, and the situations in Keneally in which people exercise control or power over others are far more important than those which depict lateral or co-operative relationships. A significant incident recounted in an early novel shows a St Trinian's–like boarding schoolgirl decoying the class goody-goody out of bounds so that she is raped. The temptress herself escapes, exulting in her victory: " 'I can remember . . . feeling deliriously on-top-of-the-world. I had been chosen to show the stupid where they stood, to upset the balance of things, since it was a makeshift hypocritical balance anyhow. I *felt* myself chosen.' "[19]

Power to manipulate others is, and Keneally would agree with Orwell on this, exhilarating and self-justifying. Often it is enshrined in institutions, which adds a level of complexity to the simple agressor-victim pattern into which Keneally sees most relationships falling. The difference between the career priest Costello and the non-career Maitland in *Three Cheers for the Paraclete* is the temperamental ability or lack of it to exploit the forces or powers available within the institution. The relation of individuals to and within institutions seemed initially to be Keneally's chief concern, but later perspective has modified this view somewhat. In fact, as early as 1965 he claimed as his theme the flavour of life of the underprivileged and radical.[20] One can be underprivileged and radical in a number of contexts. Some of Keneally's protagonists are indeed, in Maitland's words, "institutional beings";[21] others are victimized as members of a social group set apart by poverty, race, or religion. But whatever the means of victim-determination, all are subject to parallel pressures and manifest similar psychologies. As the narrative viewpoint is aligned to the victim, we see Keneally's vertical relationship from the bottom and are encouraged to sympathize there. From that viewpoint the other party appears enigmatic even if predictable, insulting, self-contained and remote, sometimes ludicrous, and sometimes malicious. In fact, the central ambivalence in Keneally is his inability to decide whether human certitude is more comic or more diabolically sinister. The victim is aware of the power to which he is subject, tries for a time to resist or circumvent it, hankers after the certitude that seems to underlie it, and eventually precipitates self-destruction with some degree of self-awareness. One course this takes is for the victim to seek power himself, for the Keneally victim is aware that power not only corrupts, but *is* corruption. The meek may inherit the earth, but the moment they try to do so their meekness is forfeited and thus their claim. The rewards handed out in Keneally novels are meagre indeed.

This pattern of human relations needs to be borne in mind when approaching *The Chant of Jimmie Blacksmith*, for it modifies some of the conclusions reached by reading the novel, as it usually is read, as one concerned overwhelmingly with race problems. Jimmie is as much a radical, underprivileged victim as he is a racial victim, and the novel has as much to say about power, vulnerability, and guilt as it has to say about Australian racism.

Jimmie's goals in life as he articulates them to himself at the outset of his career are possessions: "The Nevilles had succeeded so well as to make Jimmie a snob. In the mind of the true snob there are certain limited criteria to denote the value of a human existence. Jimmie's criteria were: home, hearth, wife, land. Those who possessed these had beatitude unchallengeable. Other men had accidental, random life. Nothing better" (p. 15). His commitment to these criteria is hardened by the dispossessed lot of tribal people and the indignity of their existence which he equates with dispossession. Through marrying a white, "a nice girl off a station", he hopes to achieve the vague status of "Mr Blacksmith". These are his thoughts as he makes his second foray out from Brentwood station. But his attempts at economic self-establishment are frustrated in part by economic factors and in part by psychological ones. Economically the plan is hopeless because he receives so little—either the salary is constant but meagre, as when he is a tracker on 7s 6d per week; or he is short-changed, as he is with Healy and Lewis; or when he is with less indigent employers, as in the shearing-shed, his wage seems completely arbitrary. More important, though, he is repulsed by the continual psychological attacks. The whites have certain expectations of him, and part of the reason for their grudging wages is

that they expect equally unsatisfactory work. When Jimmie
works well he contradicts expectations in a way that is
construed as a return of the insult embraced by the original
expectation. It is a sophisticated form of "give a dog a bad
name".

> After a week he had post-and-railed a hundred yards. Such
> fast work didn't quite accord with Healy's mental budgeting.
> Boundary-riding on a big splay-footed grey, Healy stopped
> to measure at random the distance between two of Jimmie's
> fence posts.
> "That isn't so bad at all," he murmured, but as if Jimmie
> were undermining him. [P. 19]

This suspicion of undermining constantly provokes re-
prisal. Jimmie is sometimes sensitive to the danger, as when
he warns Mort that even his laughter might antagonize the
whites and get them the sack simply because the whites could
not understand it. At other times, though, he is unable to
calculate the sort of threat he might be posing. When he goes
to arrange the wedding, a brief power display is forced on
him. Mrs Treloar, the minister's wife, sees him first, assumes
he is looking for work, and tells him there is none. He
explains he wants to get married. Assuming he means
immediately she stands ready to rebuff him on that score.
When he passes that test, too, she applies an economic one
which he also passes. The penalty for his not being indigent
and shiftless, that is, for not fulfilling Mrs Treloar's expectations, is that he is set to cutting firewood for four hours and
threatened with the police should he desist. Only by such
a demand can Mrs Treloar reassert her dominance. Gilda,
too, although less intelligent than Jimmie, becomes aware
that she is subject to the expectations of others more powerful,
and that any divergence from those expectations will make
her liable to punishment. And like Jimmie she cannot
understand how her attitudes and conduct could matter to
people whose health, wealth, comfort, and certitude dwarf
her own. "Why did large, tough women pretend she threatened them? What was it that excommunicated her?" (p. 72).
Gilda never finds the answer to these questions, but Jimmie
does find some insight. For Jimmie comes slowly to see that
he has misrepresented the goals that make up beatitude.

Initially he baptizes himself ascetically in the name of property (p. 14). This is confirmed with the adoption of Mrs Healy as his archetypal wife, but even though he recognizes one of her attractive characteristics as her "submissiveness" he fails to realize that possessions alone do not make for the beatitude he seeks. It is possessions and power, and power can only be manifest in its exercise upon someone like himself. So his employers' continual attacks upon his plan for self-improvement are not random and gratuitous, for the dominant are not independent of those they control. Jimmie does not come to this insight directly or suddenly, but it is implicit in his speculations about the necessity to "declare war" which "connoted for him a sweet wide freedom—to hate, discredit, debase as an equal" (p. 52). Although Jimmie has not yet abandoned his economic plan, other considerations are emerging as important to his psychic well-being.

Keneally's treatment of the killings enforces the idea of command as much as it does hate or retaliation. The oppression of the white expectations is seen to climax when Jimmie points the rifle at Newby. But his retaliation is selective. It is Miss Graf's name which has prompted the final suicidal reaction, for she is the "definite release" he requires. "He wished to scare the school mistress apart with his authority, to hear her whimper" (p. 78). As they approach the house, Jimmie is suffused with "a drunken judgmental majesty" (p. 78); the murder axe, "more than a cutting edge was replete with command" (p. 79), and that Miss Graf loses her composure and is "raucous as a beast was more than he had hoped for from her" (pp. 79–80). As they leave, "Jimmie was the master. In him the night was vested, and the gift of swift action." Similarly it is Mrs Healy's self-containment that Jimmie realizes is his object. "Lush Mrs Healy was waiting to be split apart, as Petra Graf had waited" (p. 99). Authority is satisfying in the destruction of Mrs Healy, but not so with Healy. First, as in many a revenge story, Jimmie wants him confronted with the alleged wrongs (or in this case their results) before he is killed— a perverse rendering of the dictum that justice should be seen to be done—secondly, Jimmie wants him to die raucously like Miss Graf and Mrs Healy. Neither happens, and

Jimmie feels "cheated once more" (p. 102) by his failure to destroy Healy's self-containment.

The remainder of Jimmie's career continues his quest to find ways of maintaining the control and authority which is continually sapped from him. The abstract power of anonymously shooting an equally anonymous farmer is rejected as "too fanciful a gesture" (p. 99). Although Keneally himself is much given to abstract formulations of that sort, such as the genetic symmetry of the double copulation earlier, Jimmie has little use for abstractions which he cannot convert into an immediate sense of authority. But Jimmie's problem is that as soon as he does enter into specific human situations he finds he becomes subject because he lacks the certitude which underpins the irony or easy superiority he sees behind other men's eyes. Jimmie cannot help revealing himself as victim. From his point of view the world is peopled with men who refuse to demonstrate a weakness which allows him to gain a psychological foothold. "His great fear was suddenly that when the high moment of encounter came, how could you depend on a white to be ugly or to blunder?" (p. 121). This axiomatic deprivation is imaged throughout the novel in vignettes which show Jimmie on foot confronted by a horesman. Whether it is Healy randomly checking Jimmie's fence-posts, Farrell insulting him with the offer of employment, Newby riding up to expose himself to Gilda, or Jimmie watching the well-mounted Newby boys through the sweat in his eyelashes, the motif stands for their respective stations. The Governor brothers stole horses a number of times in their flight, but Keneally carefully changes that to show them always on foot except for the much less dignified portage by a cow.

There is, however, one scene in which we do see a Blacksmith mounted (apart from Mort's insouciant horse-breaking). This is Jimmie's raid on Verona with Farrell in search of the killer of Jack Fisher. It is an important incident, for it demonstrates the effect that power has. It was argued above that in Keneally's novels the dominant continually exercise their dominance. A corollary of this is that the powerless seek out their punishment, at least when seen from the point of view of the powerful. Man's psychic vulnerability is every bit as manifest as his physical vulnerability, and the only defence against one's own sense of threat is to impose upon others. Hence Jimmie's attempt to align himself with power demands a furious attack on weakness in others.

> Jimmie himself was in a vindictive state of mind. The Verona people were to be punished for their vulnerability. There was a lust in him to punish the race through the man who had done the knifing. [P. 38]

> Sublimely hating them for the wounds they so childishly contracted, Jimmie aligned himself by Farrell's side. [P. 41]

Thus it is, too, that Harry Edwards is killed for his weakness —for "not understanding" (p. 44). The alignment with or exercise of power is an immoral act but an exhilarating one which Keneally associates with sexuality. Paradoxically, like sexual experience it involves vulnerability. One gives oneself up to the power. Thus when Jack Fisher's body is exhumed, its corruption is a comment on Jimmie's soul. He feels "justified" in the punishment he has helped mete out but knows that the emotion is "indecent and one that might run beyond his control" (p. 42). With Harry Edwards "he knew he was being exquisitely cruel and that it was bad for his soul" (p. 43), while the desire to "scare [Miss Graf] apart with his authority" (p. 78) is the greatest "indecency" of all. From this last self-indulgence Jimmie knows he has become "an incurable" (p. 81), a moral bankrupt half of whose mind is aware of the bankruptcy while the other half pursues further indecencies. This in itself is a form of suicide, which is an essential element in the power psychology Keneally draws. Newby's apparent exulting when Jimmie "proves his malice" at last and points the rifle at him (p. 77), Jimmie's need to re-establish contact with the search parties (pp. 132–33), and his satisfaction at "the absolute nature of outlawry" (p. 128) all point to something of a death-wish implicit in the consciousness depicted. This is strong in other Keneally protagonists such as Halloran or Maitland. Keneally is most explicit on this at the death of Mort, who, reassured of Jimmie's love by his desertion, and having disposed safely of McCreadie, waits patiently to be shot.

He lay as Healy or a rabbit, forehead down, worried for breath, appalled more by the force than the pain.

Life, he sensed, was cast in certain jagged rhythms and there was some sort of lasting merit if a person gave himself up willingly to them. [P. 160]

Characters in Keneally often record a sense of impact rather than pain, just as Jimmie does earlier when struck by Healy. The fatalism of Mort's final thoughts, though, suggest that Keneally sees the imposition of man on man as an eternal verity which goes far beyond whatever social remedies may be initiated to right particular types of deprivation. Nor has he any solution for or even distraction from it. It can, I think, be argued that a sort of macabre cosmic power-psychology is what serves Keneally for a religious centre. Certainly, considering the interest in religious scenes and situations in the novels, he is a surprisingly a-religious writer. Even in the seminary novels the role of religion is almost as casual and applied as the laconic unorthodoxy of Healy.

"Yer have any religion? Other than nigger?"

"Methodist, boss."

"Then I give yer me Christian promise that I'll cut yore bloody black balls out if yer mess this job." [P. 15]

While white religion in Keneally is usually a misnomer for humanism or a rationale for bureaucracy, he does give considerable treatment to the parallel truths of the Mungindi and Christian. Typically, the outcome of this is an ethical demonstration rather than a theological one. Jimmie's need to establish dominance to achieve beatitude does not extend to his half-brother Mort. He needs Mort, but sets against his need for him the consciousness of Mort's values, even though they are values to which Jimmie himself can no longer subscribe. The focus of this tension is on Jimmie's desire to retain Mort's company and assistance even though he, Jimmie, in slaying women has become "incurable". "Mort must either be incriminated for fear of losing him or lost for fear of incriminating him" (p. 88). In loyalty and in heat-of-the-moment instinct Mort too becomes a killer, first shooting (but not killing) the nurse at Healy's and then deliberately killing the already disabled Toban. "Then, all his old moralities jangled by the events at Healy's, Mort reloaded. Jimmie, seeing in it Mort's loss of innocence, was indecently pleased" (p. 116). Mort, however, retains "his nearly intact black soul" (p. 148) which Jimmie is required to relinquish if he is to regain any sort of moral standing. It is significant that an act of renunciation is called for to balance the renunciation of tribe which takes place in Jimmie's frosty baptism at the gaol-house pump. Mort, in tribal integrity, loves in an active way; Jimmie, in the ethic of thou-shalt-not, can love only by renunciation.

Jimmie's aim at setting out had been to become "Mr Blacksmith". He is called that by the Newby women, but not out of respect or acceptance in the way he craves. Far more important, though, is the authorial use of the title. Keneally never calls him "Mr Blacksmith" as the characters do, but varies the usual "Jimmie" or "Jimmie Blacksmith" at significant moments of the story, by calling him "Mr Jimmie Blacksmith". There are only five uses of the full title, and they provide ironical comments on Jimmie's initial hopes of status, and the manner in which the status is ultimately earned. The first accession to the title comes in the midst of the mayhem at Newbys, not simply as a result of Jimmie's wielding the axe "replete with command", but as a result also of the possession of Tabidgi, who has gone berserk at Jimmie's example. He is "Mr Jimmie Blacksmith" again as he shoots Healy, and a third time when the territory of his flight seems to turn against him. All these uses are ironical in view of Jimmie's earlier expectations of beatitude through possessions. "Mr Jimmie Blacksmith" emerges not as possessor but as destructive (and self-destructive) wielder of power who realizes his own corruption in the exercise of that power. His equality is not, as he had expected, guaranteed by his "declaring war" (p. 52). He is "still the victim" (p. 114), but he has, like Matthew Arnold's Empedocles, made the one assertion available to the victim, that of setting in motion his own irrevocable destruction. But the final two uses, both at the Aboriginal initiation site, mark his rehabilitation. McCreadie is the catalyst to effect his salvation.

Jimmie sang nothing and was afraid. Gasping McCreadie could see the fear and perhaps confusion. Mr Jimmie Blacksmith, mighty terrorizer, lost beyond repair somewhere between the Lord God of Hosts and the sunken cosmogony of his people. Mort Blacksmith, however, still had his nearly intact black soul. Surely his brother saw it, McCreadie hoped.
[P. 148]

McCreadie's task of separating the brothers has both the practical dimension of ending their flight, for he sees they depend upon each other (and on him) to keep going, and the underlying one of providing each with salvation, Mort's negatively by removing the source of corruption, and Jimmie's positively by requiring of him a loving renunciation. McCreadie puts this to Jimmie, and in his acceptance of it he is termed "Mr Jimmie Blacksmith" for the last time. Ironically, he gains his title finally not through accession of power over another, but through surrendering it.

The Chant of Jimmie Blacksmith, then, continues the analysis of the mind of oppressed victims, aspects of which were explored in *The Fear, Bring Larks and Heroes, Three Cheers for the Paraclete*, and *A Dutiful Daughter*, and since in *Blood Red, Sister Rose*. Keneally's victims manifest a sensitivity which makes them more susceptible to the inevitable attacks. They recognize their oppressors, whether individuals or systems, but cannot understand the malignant assault on their unprovocative weakness, not realizing that weakness itself is always provocative to power. If they come to any such realization, and not all do, they precipitate their own destruction through an act that simplifies the tensions and ambiguities of their existence at the expense of existence itself. Jimmie Blacksmith the victim is every bit as important as Jimmie Blacksmith the half-caste, for human vulnerability and its immoral exorcism through the wielding of power is a theme that extends far beyond the specific example of Australian racism. Jimmie is vulnerable because he is coloured in a white society, but fundamentally he is vulnerable simply because he is human. As always in Keneally, to be human is to maintain a tenuous and temporary hold on physical existence and psychic wholeness. Moreover, the most proximate enemy to one's stability is one's fellow man.

Jimmie and Gilda may be at the bottom of the pile, but those further up, like Healy and Newby and the sarcastic cook, are in the same continuum, and like Jimmie can defend their own vulnerability only by attacking weakness in others. If *undermining* is one of the recurrent words in the book, another is *blunt*. For Keneally, personalities do not interact so much as bludgeon.

NOTES

1. The fullest analysis from this point of view, and in fact the best discussion of the novel to date is Terry Sturm's "Thomas Keneally and Australian Racism", *Southerly* 33 (1973): 261–74.
2. "Doing Research for Historical Novels", *Australian Author* 7 (January 1975): 28.
3. Frank Clune, *Jimmy Governor* (Sydney: Horwitz, 1959).
4. Page references are to the Angus and Robertson edition, (Sydney, 1972).
5. *"The Chant of Jimmie Blacksmith:* taking cognisance of Keneally", in *The Australian Experience"*, ed. W.S. Ramson (Canberra: Australian National University Press, 1974), p. 329.
6. Clune, *Jimmy Governor*, p. 119.
7. Ibid., pp. 96–97.
8. To maintain the Easter/initiation parallel he also delays the executions from January to April.
9. Clune, *Jimmy Governor*, p. 86.
10. "Doing Research for Historical Novels", p. 27.
11. Clune, *Jimmy Governor*, p. 130.
12. Ibid., pp. 78, 84.
13. Ibid., p. 88.
14. Perhaps unfairly, but in the suggested view of Australian society only the underprivileged are allowed to have mates.
15. *Mudgee Guardian*, 23 July 1900, p. [2].
16. John B. Beston, "Keneally's Violence", *Journal of Commonwealth Literature* 9 (1974): 71. The evidence adduced is that they have the same initials.
17. *The Place at Whitton* (London: Cassell, 1964), p. 6.
18. *Bring Larks and Heroes* (Melbourne: Cassell, 1967), p. 151.
19. *The Place at Whitton*, p. 27.
20. *Bulletin*, 14 September 1965, p. 30.
21. *Three Cheers for the Paraclete* (Sydney: Angus and Robertson, 1968), p. 205.

Two Difficult Young Men

Martin Boyd's *A Difficult Young Man* and Christina Stead's *The People with the Dogs*

K. G. HAMILTON

Christina Stead is, I believe, a more important novelist than Martin Boyd. And yet there is little doubt that Boyd's novels, or at least those from *Lucinda Brayford* onwards, are, and will continue to be, more widely read than Stead's; or that Stead's reputation will continue to rest on perhaps two of her relatively early novels—*For Love Alone* and *The Man Who Loved Children*. There may, of course, be a simple reason for this difference in popularity—Stead's novels are almost all long, some verging on the monumental, whereas Boyd, after *Lucinda Brayford*, learned to ration himself to a careful two-hundred odd pages per volume. And, at least for Australian readers, there may be the fact that after *For Love Alone* Stead found her settings in Europe and America, while Boyd in all but two of his later novels returned to this country for at least part of his inspiration, although like Stead he had early in life left Australia to live abroad.

This latter difference between two expatriate novelists may, however, be of more importance than a mere matter of giving rise to Australian chauvinism among their respective readers. In *Lucinda Brayford* and the "Langton" novels, Boyd is portraying a way of life for which he had a great deal of sympathy and understanding—the way of life of Melbourne society, of the Melbourne "establishment", at a time when it still retained strong ties with its English background; the way of life, in fact, of his own family. The focus of interest in his novels is on this way of life, and his characters serve above all to live it out, whether by conformity or rebellion. Boyd writes from within the world of his novels, a world of which he, as narrator, is always felt to be part, whether or not he actually intrudes himself as an auto-biographical character. But whereas this interest in a way of life keeps Boyd firmly tied in part to an Australian setting, Stead has no such pervasive interest in place, or social group, or community, and so is free, and obliged, to find her characters and settings where she will or can. There is no ready-made pattern for her characters to conform to or rebel against as there is for Boyd's. Against Boyd's involvement, Stead, though she seems always to draw on her own direct experience and, at least in some of her earlier novels, may herself be more or less deeply involved in the problems facing her characters, writes rather as an investigator, probing and recording their behaviour.

This difference of approach to their work is, I believe, a major source not only of the kind of novels they write but also of the basic strengths and weaknesses of their respective work. The way of life that Boyd's novels portray provides an underlying unity, a pervasive pattern of which character and action can become an integral part; the pull between the old life of England on the one hand and the new demands of Australia on the other, symbolized by the eternal shuttling backwards and forwards of the characters, provides a basic tension felt by almost all characters; and the very strength of the underlying pattern of life gives effectiveness both to the occasional rebellion from within and intrusion from without. Boyd in these novels, unlike the earlier more melodramatic works like *The Lemon Farm* and *Nuns in Jeopardy*, is not much concerned with the intricacies of plot. Indeed he has no need to be, since the world in which his characters live imposes its own structure, its own inevitability, on the events that happen within it. At the same time this concern with a way of life may lead to a sameness, a limitation of creativeness, in the characters who live it, a fact that may have led Boyd in his last novel, *The Tea Time of Love*, to turn not only to a different setting but to an entirely different concept of character and action. Boyd's family certainly served him well as a novelist, but the evidence of this last novel might suggest that his concern with it may also have served to limit his creative imagination.

Stead's novels, by contrast, have no such constant under-lying pattern. Some of her earlier novels—*Seven Poor Men of Sydney, For Love Alone,* and *The Man Who Loved Children*—may suggest a strong involvement as a novelist in her own experience. But on the evidence of her total work I am inclined to doubt this, to see the obvious points of contact between her own life and her novels as no more than incidental, as evidence of her tendency to use her own immediate experience as material for the creation of a novel rather than to use the novel to explore and express that experience. There are some areas of life or society in which as a novelist she has a recurring interest—those of the socialist Left, of banking and finance, of the business of commodity dealing, for instance—but these interests tend not to develop into a definite theme, but rather to be incidental to her work and only occasionally—as does the banking world of Paris in *House of All Nations*—to provide the kind of all-pervasive unity on which Boyd can rely. Her tendency towards the bizarre, the grotesque, above all her ability to see these things in the apparently ordinary, provide us with some of her most memorable passages—the scene of the wedding attended by Teresa early in *For Love Alone*, for example—which far surpass anything that Boyd has done. But this tendency can also work against any easy, ready-made plot structure or pattern, and since she like Boyd has little interest in the mechanics of plot, seeming rather to allow the characters to form their own story, as a novelist she is much at their mercy, as it were. The result is frequently the real or apparent disunity of life without an artistic unity being either drawn from or imposed on it.

When such unity does emerge, as it does completely in *The Man Who Loved Children*, the result is a superb novel which tightens its grip on the reader as it marches with increasing inevitability towards its tragi-comic conclusion. Where the unity fails to become apparent, where it becomes a simple linear progress towards an end which only seems to be imposed by the limits of endurance of the author, the grip on the reader begins to lessen rather than tighten. *For Love Alone* I see as a special case here. For at least half its length there is an increasingly strong feeling of unity, but somewhere the novel loses its sense of direction, or rather of pattern—or perhaps it retains its direction but loses its imaginative drive. *Letty Fox* on the other hand begins diffusely but gradually begins to fall into some sort of shape without, however, I think ever quite achieving it. *A Little Tea, A Little Chat*, with its extraordinarily despicable anti-hero, is in its detail as fascinating as anything that Stead ever wrote, but none the less, as the expectation that this detail will ever come together in any sort of significant way begins to evaporate, the reader is likely to feel increasingly that what he is reading is just more of the same and that he has had enough. It is perhaps significant that the only novel in which Stead seems to have made a conscious attempt to impose a unified structure is *The Little Hotel*, by far her shortest novel. The three novellas, as she herself styled them, in *The Puzzleheaded Girl*, also, have each an organic unity lacking in some of her full-length novels.

The purpose of this chapter will be to look at this basic difference in structure in two novels written at about the same stage in the career of their respective authors—Martin Boyd's *A Difficult Young Man* (1955) and Christina Stead's *The People with the Dogs* (1952). Before beginning, however, it might be useful to place these particular novels in a bare outline of the two writers' work.

Despite what was said earlier, not all Boyd's novels are set in or indeed related in any way to Australia. They can in fact be divided conveniently into two groups. In the first group would be a heterogeneous collection of works with a variety of settings, all non-Australian. Most of these lie well outside our period and are not likely to arouse much interest today—*Love Gods* (1925), *Brangane: A Memoir* (1926), *Scandal of Spring* (1934), *The Lemon Farm* (1935), *The Painted Princess: A Fairy Story* (1936), *The Picnic* (1937), *Night of the Party* (1938), and *Nuns in Jeopardy* (1940). Of this first group only *Such Pleasure* (1949), and Boyd's last novel *The Tea-time of Love* (1969), the former set mainly in London, and the latter mainly in Rome, are within the period of this study. The second group would consist of the so-called "Langton" novels—*The Cardboard Crown* (1952), *A Difficult Young Man* (1955), *Outbreak of Love* (1957), and

When Blackbirds Sing (1962)—together with *The Montforts* (1928) and *Lucinda Brayford* (1946). Of these *The Montforts* stands apart because of its early date, but is included here because of its relationship to the later works. Like *The Montforts*, all the works in this group have as their setting English county or upper middle class life in the sometimes painful process of metamorphosis into the Melbourne establishment of the late nineteenth and early twentieth centuries —a process in which Boyd's own family had been intimately involved, thereby providing a good deal of material for his novels.

Christina Stead has thus far published eleven novels, as well as, among other things, a book of short stories—*The Salzburg Tales* (1934)—and a volume of three novellas—*The Puzzleheaded Girl* (1968). She left Australia in 1928 at the age of twenty-six, and only her first novel, *Seven Poor Men of Sydney* (1934) has a wholly Australian setting. *For Love Alone* (1944) begins in Sydney as it was in her youth, but later moves to London. Of the others, *The Beauties and the Furies* (1936) is set among the hotels and street cafés of Paris, while *House of All Nations* (1938) uses the banking and financial world of the same city as its background. *The Man Who Loved Children* (1940) is set mainly in Washington, though it retains strong overtones of Stead's girlhood in Australia; while *Letty Fox: Her Luck* (1946), *A Little Tea, A Little Chat* (1948), and *The People with the Dogs* (1952) all have New York as their centre, but move to other settings in various parts of the United States and Europe. *The Little Hotel* (apparently written around 1948, though not published until 1974) takes us to a tourist hotel on the Lake of Geneva, while *Cotter's England* (1967)[3] alternates between London and the industrial north of England. *Miss Herbert*, Stead's latest novel published in 1976, is again set in London.

A Difficult Young Man has been chosen for this study on the ground that it is probably more successful as well as more central to the "Langton" series than the later *Outbreak of Love* and *When Blackbirds Sing*. The still later *Tea Time of Love* has been disregarded because it lies outside the "Langton" series and in most other respects as well is outside what most readers would regard as the mainstream of Boyd's work. *The People with the Dogs* is perhaps a more arbitrary choice, based primarily on the fact that it comes at the end of a fairly continuous run of publication after *Seven Poor Men*—there is no gap between novels of more than four years —and a period of some fifteen years before the publication of her next full-length novel. Added to this, it has some interesting parallels with *A Difficult Young Man*[4].

The dominance of influences which I have referred to generally as a way of life is made apparent in *A Difficult Young Man* from the opening sentences:

> When I told Julian that I would write this book, the first intention was that it should be about my grandparents, but we agreed that it should also be an exploration of Dominic's immediate forbears to discover what influences had made him what he was, and above all to discover what in fact he was. We realized that to do this it might be necessary to empty all the cupboards to see which of the skeletons were worth reclothing, if possible, with flesh. This may bring an accusation of ancestor-worship, or at least of family obsession, but if one has been brought up in the thick of a large clan of slightly eccentric habits, it is difficult not to be obsessed with it. [P. 9][5]

And, too, we are at once introduced to the double and often competing influences of England and Australia: "After this brief glimpse of his English childhood we have to follow Dominic to Australia" (p. 9). The grandfather's mansion at Brighton, itself almost a character in the story, is introduced as a not altogether genuine manifestation in this country of the family's continuing link with England:

> In Australia we lived at Westhill, the one-storied family house in the hills, about thirty miles from Melbourne, but we were very often at Beaumanoir, our grandfather's house at Brighton, one of the suburbs on Port Phillip Bay. It is this house which may have suggested the Spanish galleon. It was bogus Elizabethan, and when on summer evenings the hot sun, slanting across the bay and over the parterres of red geranium, flashed in the oriel windows, and flooded with rosy light the red brick façade and the little green copper cupolas with their gilded tin flags, it did resemble some great

ship on fire, about to sink in sunset splendour. Inside the elaborate plaster ceilings and the baronial staircase were given, by the old portraits and furniture brought out from Waterpark, a more authentic appearance than they deserved. The occasional remarks of our parents made us feel that we lived only in a kind of demi-mode of civilization, but this house corrected the impression, as it was for us the very hub of culture and rich living. As Dominic imagined that he was the heir to all this, the partly imitation but partly genuine dynastic atmosphere of the house may have affected his character. [P. 10]

The sense of a clan, of a closed circle, is emphasized by the almost immediate arrival of an outsider, Miss Barbara Stanger of Moonee Ponds, who was about to become Aunt Baba, married to Uncle George on the rebound from one of his own kind, Miss Dolly Potts, of County Mayo, Ireland, and who "appeared on the scene shortly after our grandparents had settled at Beaumanoir after returning from Europe" (p. 11). There was a good deal of talk about Miss Stanger "before she arrived in our circle".

The name Moonee Ponds amused them, and they thought it ridiculous of her to call herself Baba. They made jokes about black sheep, and mutton dressed as lamb.
   At last she was invited to Sunday luncheon, but, it was said, they would have to leave early, as George was taking her to the Zoo, and Austin, who was then still alive, growled: "I hope they'll accept her." [P. 11]

Baba's own sense of herself as an outsider is made clear through an image which also reveals that the clan could have its own brand of madness, so long as it was kept within the circle:

   One of our English cousins was left a lunatic asylum, patronized exclusively by the aristocracy. He gave a garden party to which he invited a snobbish aunt who was delighted to meet so many peers, but when she found they were all mad she was very angry. Baba must have had something of the same feelings on this occasion. She had imagined that it would be very formal, and that the correct social usages would be followed as a religious duty. When she arrived the place was swarming with grandchildren. Those who had spoken of her with facetious contempt welcomed her with the greatest display of friendliness. [P. 12]

Aunt Baba, and with an equally significant influence for the destinies of Dominic, Uncle Bertie, are among the few outsiders who penetrate the circle. Another is Wolfie, the eccentric German musician married to Aunt Diana. The disasters he brings on the clan by his outlandish behaviour —outlandish in a quite precise sense from their point of view —are the subject of the later *Outbreak of Love*, but here in the opening scenes of *A Difficult Young Man* his influence is seen through its effect on Aunt Diana. By marrying Wolfie she has at best put herself on the fringe of the circle:

> In the dining-room the children were seated, except Dominic, at a separate table in the oriel window. Aunt Diana stood disconsolately in the doorway. She lived in a cottage nearby, to which she was returning to Sunday dinner with her husband and her children.
> "Oh, I would like to go to Tasmania," she said. "I have the hottest house of anyone, and I'm the only one who can't get away."
> "If you're staying to luncheon," said Alice, "do come in and sit down and they'll lay a place for you. But if you're not, please don't stand in the doorway."
> "I must get back to Wolfie and the children," said Diana, but she still stood in the doorway, and stopped the servants bringing in the vegetables. When she noticed this, she stood aside with a martyred air, as if all domestic activity was tiresome. Alice then told her that she might come to Tasmania, if she wished, and she said: "Oh, thank you, mama," but still with a slight note of injury. With a regretful glance at the long sparkling table, where she knew that the food and the fun would be so much better than in her little wooden cottage, she shut the door and went home. [P. 13]

This theme of the intruder, thus introduced from the beginning, persists throughout the novel until the final scenes when Guy meets Wentworth Macleish, about to marry Helena: "I looked at him with envy and admiration of his wealth, but at the same time with a kind of repelled wonder and the conviction that he was a different kind of species. . . . I knew the intruder on my ancient home" (p. 179).

The same theme, too, is significantly widened in the first chapter to include Dominic himself, though in a different way. The "difficult young man" reveals an attitude to the intruder different from that of the rest of the clan. He had "compassionate feelings for anyone who was outside the herd, feeling himself to be so different from the bright, kind, frivolous group in which he moved" (p. 12). A little later, when Dominic is to be left behind when the family go to Tasmania, because of a broken ankle, "tears filled his eyes. It might only have been from pain in his head and in his ankle, but I think it was that he could not bear any further exclusion from his fellows, beyond that which he already knew arose from his nature" (p. 17).

By the end of the first chapter, then, the pattern of the family being disturbed both by the intruder from without and the misfit within has already been established. However, while the disruptive influence of such outsiders to the clan as Baba is straightforward enough, this is not the case with Dominic. There is no doubt of his disruptiveness. When his behaviour is the immediate cause of the family's removal to England, Guy remarks that "owing to him I had to leave my school at Kew, so admirably suited to my temperament, and I have had to live, split between two hemispheres" (pp. 90–91). At times the gap between him and the family is a very real one. "He always imagined that his elders understood perfectly the motives of his behaviour, and then punished him. He did not know that their minds moved almost in different centuries" (p. 24). And of Dominic's climactic act, his elopement with Helena, Guy says that he "saw that what I had dreaded all my life had at last happened, that one day Dominic would deal an irreparable blow at those whom I most loved" (p. 188).

None the less, the conflict was not continuous nor the break complete. "When Dominic was satisfied and happy it was as if a spanner were removed from the works of our domestic life" (p. 20). And again: "In one mood he was an outcast, a black, lonely, religious boy; in another the responsible heir to the throne, quite ready to carry out the responsibilities of his position" (p. 51). In some respects he is completely one of the clan. Laura "in considering a profession for

Dominic did not look beyond the horizons of the family, and in this she was quite right, as they had impressed their limitations so strongly upon him" (p. 86). It is said of him that "perhaps he was the only one of the grandchildren who really loved Alice" (p. 59); and when instructed by his new headmaster (very much an outsider) to kiss his mother, he was "shocked at this intrusion by a stranger into family intimacies" (p. 35). His tendency to become "separated from the world" (p. 48) is in the end a reflection of the plight of the family itself. "There was a sense in which our whole family, and even our whole group . . . were becoming divorced from the world" (p. 49).

Thus though Dominic feels himself to be, and to some extent is, an outsider, he is also a real and especially vulnerable member of the clan; so the pattern suggested previously can become complicated by the role of the true outsiders in the successive crises of his life. This complication is suggested in the first chapter, when he tries unsuccessfully to be kind to Baba on her departure for the Zoo. And it is one of the Dells who is the immediate cause of the first occasion when Dominic makes an outcaste of himself—the lemonade throwing and subsequent unpleasantness of his birthday party at Beaumanoir—and though "no one except Austin, Alice and two or three of their generation knew at this time of the origin of the Dells, it is possible we had an instinct against them, not that they could be blamed for it, caused by a feeling that they were somehow intruders into our group" (p. 30). Perhaps the most traumatic of Dominic's boyhood crises, the killing of Tamburlaine, was the immediate result of Wolfie's bumbling interference, and he too was in a sense an outsider. But it was Aunt Baba, and Uncle Bertie ("who was different from us, rich and strange") who were "the centre of opposition to Dominic, those who thought something should be done about him. . . . They were like patches of strong tweed on a piece of beautiful but tarnished brocade" (p. 62).

Bertie's main contribution to Dominic's destiny was, of course, the introduction of Helena into the situation; but he also made his more immediate contributions by, for instance, being the one to discover Dominic "worshipping" his daughter. Baba's influence was a more continuous affair. She is to blame, at least indirectly, for Dominic's seduction of (or by) her farm girls, and for the escapade of his leap after Helena from the drag during the holiday in Tasmania. And after the "worshipping" incident with Helena had made his parents think of returning to England, it is Baba who actually tips the scales:

> Steven, walking down Collins Street, met Aunt Baba in a "striking rig-out" as he called it, made possible by Alice's death, for which she had already come out of mourning as she thought any sign of family feeling was not "smart," and . . . she said to him, with an insolence as new as her financial securtiy and her hat: "Is Dominic *still* loafing up at Westhill? Why don't you send him to a station in Queensland, or somewhere at a distance?" At this jibe, he went straight on to the shipping office and returned to Westhill with a sailing-list, which he discussed with Laura that evening. [P. 91]

When Sylvia was at a stalemate in her relations with Dominic, "ultimately Aunt Baba released her" (p. 164), by means of her tactlessness. As Guy says, "one was sorry for Baba at this time because of her terrible stupidity. My relatives were often silly, but they were never stupid" (p. 165). Similarly it was Baba's stupidity that led to the climax of the novel, when it causes her to speak to Helena of the "rotten Spanish blood" in the Langton boys which allows them "to kill horses and carry on with the servant girls":

> I was outraged at this reference to my brother and indirectly to myself. Baba saw this and said carelessly: "You're all right. It doesn't show in you."
> My anger was nothing to Helena's. Baba had roused her heroic loyalty to her own kind, that quality she shared with Dominic. Baba, ignoring the look in Helena's eyes, went on with heated stupidity, imagining that she was hammering the last nails into the coffin which held the love between the two cousins, whereas she was splitting the fragile wood and allowing it to break free and spread its wings in new life.
> Helena suddenly turned and left the room. [P. 182]

Dominic, by being an outsider who at the same time reflects to an extent the condition of the clan, points the way to another major element in the pattern already briefly mentioned, the internal tensions of the family itself. But first it may be useful to look at the relationship between Dominic and the first-person narrator, his brother Guy. The whole Langton clan has, of course, a more or less close relationship with Boyd's own family, though the novels are not simply disguised autobiography, the closeness of fiction to fact varying from place to place. Guy's eldest brother, Bobby, provides a direct parallel with Boyd's own brother Gilbert, in that like him he was, when a boy, killed in a fall from a horse outside his parents' home. Dominic is to some extent made the fictional counterpart of another brother, Merric—by, for instance, such explicit links as his short-lived sojourn at an agricultural college. These parallels are, however, irrelevant to a consideration of the work as a novel. What in the novel is stressed is the closeness of the tie which Guy feels with his brother. Again it is irrelevant whether or not this is true to life; what it does in the novel is to provide Boyd as an author with a dual point of view.

The tie between the brothers is not one based on love. After one of Dominic's escapades Guy says, "It may seem odd that I should have joined with Helena in encouraging Dominic's resistance, as I did not really like him" (p. 29). Rather it is a "fixation". Describing how he stood by Dominic after the latter's fall from a bicycle, Guy says, "I think it possible that the emotions I had for that minute while I stood by Dominic, believing him to be dead, caused the 'fixation', if that is the word, the concern I felt for Dominic all my life, the inability to escape from the thought of the processes to which life subjected him" (p. 17). Somewhat later, again as a result of Guy's distress at another of Dominic's accidents, the boys' grandmother describes Guy in her diary as "an odd little boy", who "seems to reflect more other peoples' feelings than to have any of his own" (p. 45). By developing the relationship in this way, Boyd is able to sustain the role of Guy as the uninvolved observer—uninvolved, para-doxically, because he is so much at home in his world, largely free, except vicariously through Dominic, of its strains and tensions—while his deeper feelings are involved with the fortunes of Dominic, feelings which might otherwise have interfered with his essential detachment as narrator. It is interesting that half-way through the novel Boyd, or rather Guy, finds it necessary "to obtrude myself into the story more than I have done hitherto, and ask the reader to put Dominic out of his mind, or rather at the back of his mind for a while", and to insist, "I am one of the characters of this book" (p. 97).

At this point in the story Guy goes on to tell of his own experiences at school, as a result of which he "began to have some of the feelings which so often possessed Dominic, that the human race was hostile to me" (p. 98). This is a restatement of the close affinity of his feelings with those of his brother, but coming from such a "safe", central member of the group it is an indication of the fragile state of the group itself, deriving partly from the extent to which it was becoming "divorced from the world", but mainly from the increasing loss of its inner cohesion. The family suffered, as Guy said, from "geographical schizophrenia" (p. 95), as a result of its never having completely made the transfer from England to Australia. It was "rather like a man with two banking accounts, who, when one is overdrawn to its limit, uses the other and allows his account to lie fallow until it has recovered its credit" (p. 92). Thus when Dominic reached his limit in the incident with Helena, it was natural that the family should react by packing and returning to Waterpark, whence they had departed some fifteen years earlier with "a vague feeling that they had disgraced themselves" (p. 92). Not that this tendency to retreat from difficulty was the only reason for moving, or even the main one. Basically it seems to have been an innate restlessness, mirrored in Dominic's "inability to stay anywhere" (p. 60): "That original restless impulse which made our great-grandparents come to Australia, must have passed on to their descendants, as they could never stay long in one place. When they lived at Waterpark they spent half their time wandering about the Continent, and one sometimes imagines their spiritual home would have been a wagon-lit" (p. 36). Within Australia this "congenital restlessness" (p. 36) was expressed through "yet another summer holiday in Tasmania", attractive partly because it was somehow more "English" than Victoria, but mainly because it was somewhere else to go.

One result of this restlessness was to perpetuate in the children the feeling of living in a double world. Thus the return to Waterpark in 1907 fits the pattern of the family's behaviour, but it also resulted in Guy, as he has already been quoted as saying, having subsequently "to live split between two hemispheres". But for Guy's generation this kind of movement had other and more far-reaching overtones. Hitherto the family had moved as they did on their holidays in Tasmania, *en masse*. At the centre of the family was Alice and, in Australia, Beaumanoir. But with the death of Alice and dispersal from Beaumanoir their "life lost its focus" (p. 89):

> Beaumanoir was like a castle which children throughout a long summer's day have proudly built on the sands, walled and moated and with a garden laid out and planted with sprigs of tamarisk for trees. Then the tide is rising and it is time to go home. The children run and jump gleefully on the thing they have created. During the month following Alice's death, her children and grandchildren were like those on the sands. We did not realize as we swarmed over the place, gathering our fallen crumbs, that we were ending the kind of existence we had known hitherto. . . .
>
> Hitherto Alice's grandchildren had been like one family, and our cousins were as familiar to us as our brothers. Where she was we collected like bees, or flies, round a honeypot. Now, in a last swarm we buzzed round the emptying pot, not realizing that when it was gone there would be little to keep us together. . . . When we lived or travelled *en masse,* our oddities did not worry us, as we were surrounded by a sufficient number of people with our own habits and idiom to keep at bay the disdain of the bourgeois world. On Alice's death we were like the Jews after the dispersion. [Pp. 77–78]

Not that this was really a new element in the pattern, for as Guy goes on to say, "Anyhow we were always a little like this, through our homelessness on either side of the world."

I have tried in this brief look at *A Difficult Young Man* to give not so much a general account of the novel as some idea of its all-pervasive pattern, to show it as a thoroughly "well made" work, in which Boyd's concept of hereditary and social influences and of interpersonal relationships dominates every aspect of the novel. But even within this limited aim it is desirable to say something about Boyd's prose style. Guy says at one time in the novel that "even the more muddleheaded of the family sprinkled their chatter with phrases which were gems of concise and vivid expression" (p. 37). Boyd's own style does not often have this quality; at times, indeed, it can be rather flat. It is a style that one tends to define by negatives—never crude, forced, harsh or awkward, never boorish or ill-mannered. None the less—perhaps because of this—he is the perfect spokesman of the particular world he seeks to recreate. He never raises his voice, is always the "gentleman who writes with ease". Thus for all the careful interweaving of character and events, what as much as anything gives the pattern of the novel its unity, its real existence as a pattern, what finally gives the novel its imaginative truth, is its style, the convincing voice of the narrator.

The neat pattern of relationships that chacterizes Boyd's novel is not to be found in the second work we are concerned with in this chapter, Christina Stead's *The People with the Dogs*. Stead is more involved in the rich variety of her world than in its pattern:

> In lower Manhattan, between 17th and 15th Streets, Second Avenue, running north and south, cuts through Stuyvesant Park; and at this point Second Avenue enters upon the old Lower East Side. The island here is broad between the two rivers and heavily trafficked, north–south, east–west. Here, Third Avenue up to 18th Street is still the Old Bowery, with small rented bedrooms and apartments like ratholes, cheap overnight hotels, flophouses, ginmills, fish places, bowling alleys, instant shoe repairers, money-lenders, secondhand clothing stores, struggling cleaning and tailors' places, barber schools, cellars where some old man or woman sells flowers and ice in summer, coal in winter, dance academies up crumbling stairs, accordion and saxophone schools and such businesses as are carried on for very poor people by very poor people. [P. 3][6]

Such pattern as there may be in Stead's novel is no more than a loose framework into which this variety can be fitted; whereas for Boyd it is of the essence of his work. Events do not have the kind of significance expected of them in Boyd's world. The murder described in some detail in the first few pages is scarcely referred to again, nor is Miss Waldemeyer, the character who witnesses it. Both are simply part of the New York scene, vaguely connected perhaps to the occasional theme of houses and housing. There is a danger which must be kept in mind, then, in any discussion of Stead's work, of giving an exaggerated impression of the importance or pervasiveness of any pattern that may seem to emerge.

Dominic, in Boyd's novel, is seen as struggling to find an identity. Edward the "difficult young man" of *The People with the Dogs*, has an identity that he is determined to hang on to. He has no desire to become involved in the post-war boom:

> It's only because there's full employment I know that I'm so worried about working. Flora and Mark want me to go into a radio show with them. Why? Every cluck in New York is in some little show business now. Al Burrows who comes here to flop wants to save his feet, get out of pharmacy and get into the black market! Electric goods for South America. Comes the crack-up everyone flat on his back and can't get up, like a black beetle. Have I got to be one of them? [P. 30]

Painting a picture of the "good guy in civilian life" who had become "a desk major", he declares, "That would be me . I wouldn't be an American, I wouldn't be a New Yorker, I wouldn't be a Massine, I'd be a heel" (p. 31). An American, a New Yorker, a Massine—we are not much concerned with the first, but rather with the claims, sometimes conflicting, sometimes complementary, of the fact of Edward's being the other two.

For Edward, New York is a tiny area of lower Manhattan in the immediate vicinity of the couple of houses where he lives and on which his livelihood depends. He "walks everywhere" and "has never been in the Bronx in his life". Asked, after turning down a proposed fishing trip, whether his girl "doesn't like the water", he replies, "I don't know.

We never go out. We just go from one apartment to the other and sometimes to the theater. Once, about ten years ago, when we first met, we went to Staten Island to see what it was like" (p. 64). To an inquiry whether he saw the murder in his street, he answers, "Naw, was in bed." He is completely at home in his environment: "People got to feel they had known him a very long time; and he was one of those everyone called by his first name. Strangers talked about Edward long before they met him, and would even retell his tales and recount what he had said, without ever having met him. What he said got round town, in some circles. It was almost as if people were his friends for years and at last managed to meet him" (p. 59).

This side of Edward's character, the "New Yorker", allows for the introduction of a rich gallery of characters, some with a definitely Runyanesque touch. There is big Al Burrows, the pharmacist; Sam Innings, the oculist; Vera Sarine, the cosmopolitan singer; the Barbours—tenants so intent on their rights that they would have their home condemned and demolished around their ears; Waldemar, the German toymaker who ate so much when he did eat that he could only afford to do so every third day. These and many others who come and go in Edward's life have no essential role in any plot; they do not affect the course of the narrative in any specific way. They are part of the scenery, rather than the action; yet they are vital to the imaginative life of the novel.

Just as are, too, the vignettes of New York life—the extraordinary description, for instance, of the women at the Turkish bath:

> The women wore light wrappers open in front, or slipping from their shoulder, or bras and drawers both pushed down as far as possible on account of the heat. Some heads were wrapped up in bandannas, some were unwrapped with wild black and reddish and dyed blond hair, naturally curled or freshly permanented, writhing in fresh tendrils in the damp hot air. Alongside the women on chairs or on the tables were huge shopping bags gaping, collapsed, with loaves of bread, packages of cooked meats, pickles, Kraft-paper cones of mustard, dried fish and other delicacies pouring from them,

each bag a cornucopia. On the tables beside the women, on
bits of cloth brought for the purpose or sheets of paper, were
hunks of bread, mostly rye or black; but some machine-cut
white bread pouring from waxed paper, and beside this slabs
of fresh butter, pots of sour and fresh cream, with Italian,
Hungarian and German kinds of sausage-meats, galantines
and sausage-links beside them, with bits of lettuce and little
cardboard boats of potato salad, Russian salad and mixed
sour pickles, slices of smoked salmon and "whitefish," little
curls of anchovies, sweet-and-sour herrings, their handsome
blue and silver-white showing through the milky white of
the cream sauce, with onion rings, peppers and capers. The
women chewed and laughed and fought holding up their
cards in their fat ringed hands, chuckling, roaring with
laughter, shaking their huge fallen bellies and breasts, circling
on their immense bottoms, wet and pink through the damp
wrappers or drawers; and telling, in a language partly
American and partly a composite of many foreign languages,
the most horribly indecent and ordurous tales that Edward
had ever heard. [Pp. 239-240]

Or the strange night encounter between the old dog, Musty,
and a Negro:

Musty fluttered along, excited by his customary night walk,
by the figures which appeared in and out of the dark—he
would start, snuff, give an excited bark—by people talking
in doorways. They were coming down Amsterdam Avenue.
About 90th Street, a Negro taking a stroll appeared suddenly
in the darkness. Musty jumped nearly out of his skin and
began to bark nervously. The Negro, a tall angular man,
made a bogey gesture at the dog as if to pick him up: bent
down, he splayed his fingers at him. Yelping hopelessly,
Musty took to his heels and fled down the side street, Edward
was startled, somewhat frightened, for the man took after
Musty, running fast. Edward gave chase. Edward knew this
part of town very well, but the man might have been a
newcomer, a dope-taker, might simply hate dogs. The dog
fled before them, yelping, scrambling, running for his life.
At the corner, the Negro caught him and held him struggling
against his coat. When Edward arrived, so breathless that
he could not speak, the man handed him the dog, saying,
"You don't want him to bark at folks, brother."
    He went off into the dark. Edward, holding Musty, came
back up the side street, so winded it seemed like a steep hill

to him. He could feel the dog's heart pounding too. Presently
he dropped the dog on the sidewalk.

"Dumb little mutt!" [P. 61]

Set against his role as a New Yorker is Edward's role as
a Massine, as a member of the family; and this provides a
main part of such conflict, of such tension, as the novel
contains. Just as New York is represented by Edward's
particular part of Manhattan, so the family is represented
by Whitehouse, its decaying summer retreat in the Catskill
Mountains. Early in the novel Edward says, "I dread the
thought of going to Whitehouse this summer" (p. 30). Later
on, when the Solways and other Massines begin "to re-
arrange their furniture, their clothes and to telephone each
other about their plans for going to Whitehouse", Edward
wants to stay in town. "He did not want to go back to the
idle gossip of family life. . . . he now spent his time in a
delightful way, by himself, without Margot and without
Musty, calling on friends, dining out" (p. 101). It may be,
indeed, that he is most completely a New Yorker when he
abandons the family, and their dogs, to lose himself for a
time in the city, as he does when he goes to stay with Philip
Christie in the "Flop":

> In Edward's boredom, loneliness, aimlessness, when his
> family and old habits were repugnant to him, the mysterious
> pleasures of Philip's life, these pleasures, affections and lives
> which cost nothing, were worth nothing, and took place in
> an even stranger setting than that at Whitehouse, appealed
> to him. Here he was acceptable, as acceptable as in his family,
> but an unknown. He was not "that man Edward we have
> heard about all our lives." In that circle they spoke about
> no one. . . . He was surprised to see that he did not care
> to take walks. He had lost his dog and he had no interest
> in the people he used to meet with their dogs. He no longer
> recognized them and they, since he was without his dog, and
> they had never looked into his face, did not recognize him.
> Once he had to explain, "I am the man who used to have
> the Scotty." [P. 264]

But even so the family is part of his New York life, and
escape from it can leave only emptiness. After Margot's
marriage he asks himself:

Where could he go? He knew two hundred people at least who could put him up for that is the way in New York, people become friends overnight and are at once and forever ready to offer bed and board. New York is one of those villages. But all of these friends would mean the old life. At one time, the family had meant everything to him, he had been sulkily, greedily happy in it. Now he had lost Margot—and even Musty—since he had been left alone without Musty, a perpetual daily ache in his heart had come to reinforce the irregular pain of Margot's indifference. The little foolish dog that he hated to see now, for his aged imbecility, still recalled to him his old-time days. Since the departure of this little foolish dog, coming after Margot's marriage, he had felt a hunger in his heart and when he got up in the morning, he wanted to sleep again, for fear of facing the empty day.

"I have too little to do, but nothing attracts me." [P. 258)

But Whitehouse is the real centre of the family, where its full influence is to be felt. In a rare excursion into overt symbolism, Stead depicts the overpowering, strangling, yet somehow benign influence of the family through the great wild hops vine that had grown over the house:

It held, embraced, but did not crush the ground, the house, and all there brought by dogs and men: bones, sheathed copper wire needed for watering the cows, old leather shoes hidden by a predecessor of the Abbot, a sadiron, and all the things lost by this fertile careless family, and all the things loved by this productive, abundant family for seventy years; the deep ineradicable cables plunging into the hill soil and sending up at great distance their wires and threads; and the whole family and house and barns and the home-acres, in the great throttling of the twining vine. It tore away easily, leaving all the growing roots there. In a few days, the injured roots completed their repairs and sent up a new line of roots and leaves and the work of monopoly went on. [P. 151]

Edward finally goes to Whitehouse because he belongs there, even more completely than he belongs in New York. "For many miles around he was known; or he would be at once if he said his name, Edward Massine. By saying Edward Massine, he could get food, lodging, friends, get his bus fare paid, his shoes mended, get provisions if he had forgotten his purse. The dogs and cats were descendants of other Massine dogs and cats" (p. 133). To a girl on a bus he says, "I lived here all my life; this is my home":

> In France, in Cairo, in Rome, he had hated Whitehouse and thought of it as stifling his talents. In the deep sweet summer cold, sluggish and healthy, like a pool that never stagnates under pinewoods, healing, with this cloud on the orchard, the open air and the bear they said was still on the mountain, and the strong black-eyed women of the family up at dawn and active, people of a gaiety and love he had not met elsewhere, he thought; I am wrong, a modern restless nervous man: this is right, and what is wrong? I am wrong. [P. 118]

For Margot's cousin, Walt, what he shares with his family is what keeps him from marrying. "You run a lodging house, you run a community. You're married to many. . . . You only understand the communal life. . . . You don't see the reason for crawling into a corner with one woman and having one child. You need abundant multiple life around you like Whitehouse, like the Massines" (p. 94).

No consideration of the family is, of course, complete without the inclusion of their dogs. "All Massines have to have their dogs," declares Ollie on the first occasion we meet the family, gathered at the vet's office for an operation on the ancient Madame X; and it is significant that Edward's partial emancipation from the family follows the death of his old cat, Westfourth, and the handing over to Oneida of the ailing Musty. It was on Oneida that the family cult of dogs centred:

> She was not unhappy, as other women, such as Irene and Ollie, and she had no ambitions, she was not dissatisfied. Why? It was merely candor to say that it was because of her dear doggies. She was still a lonely child, hordes of friends had evaporated, from those that remained, like Victor-Alexander, this love had gone, the dogs had been her only friends. She did not care for furniture or clothes as such, only for affections: and what alone was faithful? But she hardly thought these things: she only thought them out in dogs as mothers think them out in children. She had her family, the farm, her town house, Victor-Alexander, Lou, Big Jenny, Edward of course, Thais and all such people; and

the sweet close honeying ones who were her intimate life, her perpetual joys—her dogs. [P. 200]

This concentration of emotion on their dogs symbolizes, if it does not actually provide the basis for, the sense of community, the impregnability of the family. "Yes", says Margot, "you can't bear a dog howling, but you can bear a soul howling" (p. 100). And Oneida, fondling Musty's ears, tells her that no one "shall ever beat us, no one will ever get the better of us because we don't want anything, do we, we only want each other" (p. 100). For Oneida it was "the plenitude of this one love, her dogs, which had given this life to her small thick-set frame, which had no noticeable dwindling and spindling like other women. Wherever she was, with a glance, a tone, she could call her soft bodied, anxious, scolding toadies to her" (pp. 178–79).

Edward might grow occasionally restless against the "holy shiftlessness", the "admirable human sloth" (p. 111) represented by Whitehouse; he might think "half in anger" of the "sloth that stretches back into my childhood and had its foot in my cradle" (p. 152), but he also "luxuriated in the thought that this life could go on like this for a long, long time 'centuries of Massine time' " (p. 253). The real attack on the family comes from without; first, unsuccessfully from Margot, in her attempts to marry Edward:

"I have no chance against you", said Margot. She looked down at the seated family, Lou, Oneida, Edward, and behind them Lady and Leander who had their backs turned and were examining the prints hung along the wall. She spoke again with bitterness, "The family is an army surrounding this house and this house is filled with allies and all is a fortress to keep Edward safe from me."
Oneida laughed heartily. "You are always attacking from the outside and we surround Edward like a regiment." [P. 99]

The full bitterness of Margot's defeat is expressed in her remark "When it comes to getting a dressing for a dog, Edward is a good boy" (p. 99).

More successful, at least in marrying Edward, is Lydia —though her success in defeating the family is perhaps at best uncertain. This conversation takes place between the couple at their wedding:

> "Have we got a house then?" asked the bride smiling.
> "Yes. This morning I made up my mind to take Solitude off their hands. We won't call it Solitude. You can write plays there all summer; and we'll have people up."
> When they were alone, Lydia said, "But in summer we'll be in Cape Cod, or on the road. I'll have no time for Whitehouse."
> "Yeah—we'll have to cut that scene. That's out of an old play I used to be in."
> "Imagine being born into your own company. I have to recruit mine," said Lydia pondering. "Handy, in a way."
> "Yes, it's a pity about Solitude. I thought I'd give you a country estate."
> "*A month in the Country!* No–o," said Lydia, walking up and down smoking. "How could you make a life out of just a backdrop?" [Pp. 338–39]

The imagery is to be expected, since Lydia is an actress; but it is also appropriate. Edward has indeed made his life out of the backdrop of his family, of Whitehouse, of New York. But now he is prepared to break away. When he and Lydia go to give news of the marriage, after receiving the congratulations of the family they "stood aside by the bookcases that covered one entire wall, beside a pot plant on a glass and wrought iron table. Edward talked to his new wife" (p. 341). And to Leander's hope that they would come to an arrangement "to keep the family together and things on the right footing", Edward responds: "Yes, but the summer's far off and Whitehouse isn't in the picture for Lydia and me at present. I'll lend you an axe to cut down the great vine, that'll be my contribution" (p. 341).

But when Leander suggests that he will sell the Little Farm and bring Mrs Mustbrook up to turn the Big Farm into a self-supporting institution:

> "Ah, no," said Edward swiftly, with pain. "Let's us have the Comedians on the Hill. What harm do we do? We're creative sloth: what life ought to give but it doesn't. The right to be lazy."
> "What," said Lou, "but aren't you coming back to us: or

are you going to change us? Maybe you're going to turn us
into a socialist colony, a summer camp?"

"I can't bear to see the Massine Republic change," said
Edward with tears in his eyes. "The mere idea is a real agony
to me. . . . My soul! Must we be efficient too? I would rather
have the vine. [Pp. 342-43]

And the novel ends with the family very much in control
of their world:

At this moment, the family, not especially arranged, but in
natural order, stood about, at the door, in the lobby, and
on the two flights of stairs, as well as in the room, and round
the long table, waiting for the toasts. There was no silence
or constraint, no impatience and no flurry. In this moment,
as in all others, their long habit and innocent, unquestioning
and strong, binding, family love, the rule of their family,
made all things natural and sociable with them.

Dr. Sam looked at the flight of people standing on the
inner staircase, a broad pretty wooden one leading up through
a cast bronze ceiling to the upper floor. This ceiling was cast
in the shape of a sunburst through clouds with cherubs and
female figures. It was gilded, with cream walls round it. The
family, lightly, naturally, moving like birds, seemed to roll
up through this ceiling. Others pressed against the faintly
colored pebbled panes of the windows which shone in the
kitchen. Others stood against the garden in the backyard; an
affair with plants, a tree in a tub and a stone coping, all
of which did not measure more than ten feet by five. Others
stood against the bookcases and under the handsome portrait
of Lady done by Dr. Edward. Some had come up the blue
carpeted staircase leading into a cellar. Others stood round
the long table with glasses in their hands, and Oneida stood
with Lou, who was in a blue shirt, near the grand piano
which was open. Dr. Sam looked for a long time and then
turned to Edward. He smiled childishly. "Edward, I did not
think there was anything like this left in New York."
[Pp. 344-45]

Because it is so shadowy, so intangible, it is difficult to do
justice to the pattern of a novel like *The People with the
Dogs*—much harder than it is with *A Difficult Young Man*
—and there is much that has been left out of this analysis.
More serious, however, is the danger that by selecting

passages for attention in this way one is doing just what the author may have deliberately declined to do—that is, imposing a pattern on material whose real interest, real truth, lies in its rich variety. Against the precision of Boyd's novel, in which every event has its place in an overall pattern of development, *The People with the Dogs*, in the decisiveness of its action, is to be measured not so much by the murder with which it begins as by the staying on of the remnants of the family into the chilly autumn of Whitehouse until it is time for old Westfourth, who was "after all only a barn cat", to be put to sleep.

Some points of similarity between the two novels do emerge. At the centre of each is a family threatened both by something of a misfit within and by intruders from without. But the differences remain much more important than the similarities. As Lydia charged Edward with having made his life "just out of a backdrop", so Stead might be charged with having made a novel out of the same thing; of having relied on the backdrop to hold the novel together, rather than on the action which takes place—or should take place—in front of it. Boyd, too, has his backdrop which perhaps as much as for Stead contributes to the unity of his novel; but he does not rely wholly or even mainly on this, but rather on the foreground interaction of characters and events.

It would appear that for Boyd the task of the novelist is to impose a pattern on the flux of life; or, if this seems unfair, at least by conscious selection to reveal the pattern inherent in life that can give art its necessary unity. Stead seems rather to seek to portray life as she depicts the family in the closing scene of her novel (from which I have already quoted) "not especially arranged but in natural order". Perhaps the cause of this difference is a fundamental difference in their respective outlooks on life; but the result is two novels which in this respect at least tend towards opposite ends of a continuum—at the one end the neat, carefully patterned structure of *A Difficult Young Man* and at the other the rich, disordered profusion of *The People with the Dogs*; the one pared down, restricted to what is explicitly relevant to its pattern, the other seemingly unable to leave anything out;

the one tending towards the precisely integrated structure of the detective novel, the other towards what has been termed "the loose baggy monster".

I would not suggest that one rather than the other of these two attitudes towards the novel is intrinsically "correct". But a consideration of the full range of work of these two novelists would indicate, I think, that while Boyd's method is the safer, Stead's offers the greater possibility of reward, as well as the greater danger. I suggested earlier that *A Difficult Young Man* is perhaps the most successful of the four "Langton" novels, but in fact there is not a great deal to choose between them. Stead's work, however is far more uneven. *The People with the Dogs*, perhaps, lies somewhere in the middle, between the comparative failures of *The Beauties and the Furies* and *A Little Tea, A Little Chat* and the magnificent success of *The Man Who Loved Children*. If one uses life in its "natural order", or in the full richness of its variety, as a basis for art, it perhaps inevitably means that even if an order exists it will not always become apparent within the limited scope of the novel. Either what appears will be a "partial disorder" within an order whose scope lies beyond that of the work, or the novelist will fail to realize any real order and present only the disorder. But where order does emerge, as in *The Man Who Loved Children*, and less consistently in others of Stead's novels, the result is likely to be richer, more convincing than when life is "especially arranged" to accommodate it to the demands of art, as one may feel is happening in the "Langton" novels. It is this difference in their art which I believe determines that Boyd will stand as a successful but minor novelist, Stead as a major but not always successful one.

NOTES
1. The extent of knowledge of Stead's novels is perhaps indicated by the fact that the most recent account of her work claims that *The Beauties and the Furies* is set among student life in London and Paris (*The Literature of Australia*, ed. Geoffrey Dutton, Penguin, 1976 p. 490). This is simply incorrect. It is set wholly in Paris, and though one of the main characters is a student, there is virtually no reference to student life. In extenuation it might

be said that copies of *The Beauties and the Furies*, as of some others of Stead's novels, are very difficult to come by.

2. Published in America under the title *The Aristocrat: A Memoir* (1927).

3. Published in America under the title *Dark Places of the Heart* (1967).

4. The fact that *The People with the Dogs* is little known and difficult to obtain may be a disadvantage; on the other hand there may be good reasons for making an interesting novel better known.

5. All references to *A Difficult Young Man* are to what is probably the most easily obtainable edition, that published in paperback by Lansdowne in 1965.

6. All references to *The People with the Dogs* are to the first, and only, edition, published by Little, Brown and Company in 1952.

"Where a Man Belongs"

Hal Porter's *The Paper Chase* and
George Johnston's *Clean Straw for Nothing*

ALAN LAWSON

In 1971 a parody competition in the *Australian* invited
readers to contribute an episode for a book entitled *The
Education of My Brother Jack in the Carr–Stein Academy*.
Introducing this competition, Max Harris commented that
"we are becoming a Proustian nation, busily trying to regain
time rather than experience it in the moment".[1] It has often
been observed that the autobiography and the autobiographical novel are significant phenomena in modern
Australian literature. Indeed in *The Extra*, the third volume
of one of the most remarkable of these autobiographical
sequences, Hal Porter lists (characteristically) the names of
some fourteen Australian writers who yielded to the autobiographical impulse in the 1960s. He offers the comment
that "each can only interpret an age in terms of his or her
own limitations. Trite enough statement".[2] Trite it may be,
but it nevertheless points to an exceptionally important
common feature. These books *are* generally concerned to offer
an interpretation of a society in terms of an individual's
experience and an individual's perception, so strikingly so
that one critic[3] has urged the adoption of Donald Horne's
term "sociography" to describe many of them. This suggests
a difference between these books and the "portrait of the
artist" genre familiar to readers of twentieth-century European and English literature, especially of the modernist
period. With these Australian works of the 1960s we are
firmly in the field of national literature.

A point is reached, it seems, in the literary development
of a nation when the objective world is no longer so pressingly

important for its own sake, nor is the nation's past yet so convincingly acceptable as a way of explaining the essential experience of being in a particular place and time, nor are the conventions and values of contemporary society felt to be sufficiently sustaining to provide an aesthetic basis for an ambitious fiction. Then the quest for self-knowledge and the customary modes of self-exploration become more literal, and the autobiography, the autobiography-as-novel, and the novel-as-autobiography become more attractive literary forms. Not only is the concept of self-knowledge literalized to the extent of utilizing the author's own biographical self, but so also is the metaphor of the quest literalized in the use of journeys and exploration in another important Australian literary genre, the so-called voyager poem or novel. The second volume of George Johnston's trilogy, *Clean Straw for Nothing*, is both autobiography and voyager novel. In it, as in most of the other modern Australian autobiographies, one of the most important subjects is clearly the essence of being Australian.

Other critics have discussed some of the general outlines of this genre in Australian literature, and some have considered the relationship between fact and fiction in particular books: the concern here, though, is with the implications of the autobiographical form for two books which seem to me to be singularly and self-consciously aware of those implications. The themes of these two books, Hal Porter's *The Paper Chase* (1966) and George Johnston's *Clean Straw for Nothing* (1969), are each radically related to some fundamental aspects of the autobiographical impulse.

Both of these books are the middle volumes of trilogies; both are concerned with the writer's years as a writer; both, in their strikingly different ways, depict the search for material, describing the period that produced the book; in both, the writer leaves Australia and returns at the end; both show a concern with the cultural changes to Australia in their absence; both are concerned with the significance of the apparently trivial, and this has evoked praise for the value of their social observation. But in each case the personal issues, as might be expected from works in this genre, are of considerable importance. Between the two books there is a further connection, of a different kind, for Porter reports in *The Extra* (p. 115) Johnston's testimony that the writing of *My Brother Jack* (1964) was inspired by his reading of *The Watcher on the Cast-Iron Balcony* (1963).

It is useful, in this context, to consider with these two books another interesting contemporary variation on the form, David Martin's *Where a Man Belongs* (1969). (Perhaps it might be suggested that if Porter's book is acknowledged autobiography and Johnston's is autobiography-as-novel, then Martin's is novel-as-autobiography.) Although in Martin's novel an autobiographical element is apparent, it is the significance of its title that is most important here. It refers in the novel, primarily but not solely, to Max, a German-Jewish writer now living in Australia who, having discovered that his literary energies are exhausted, decides to make a journey back to such of his past as is still recoverable in London and Germany with the ostensible purpose of sorting out a complicated, and ultimately symbolic, inheritance. He takes with him an Australian book-keeper, Paul Burtle, an ex-soldier who hopes to marry a German widow with whom he has been corresponding. For Burtle, too, the trip is a way of matching self and past. But for Max the autobiographical journey, the search for his sources, and the attempt to discover where he belongs yield a predictably complicated answer. A symbolic resolution, though, of this theme is provided when his ability to write is restored as he produces (on the voyage back to Australia) "a poem of some two hundred lines in which both languages (German and English) mingled, a strange hybrid, but one which did not displease me, unpublishable though it was".[4] The need to find a place, a pattern, a self-concept, is satisfied through the symbolic journey of the writer who tells his own story.

For Hal Porter, too, the issue of where a man belongs is a governing motif. His three volumes of autobiography are concerned with the attempt to place himself, to claim a piece of personal territory and, through an almost obsessively verbalizing memory, to annexe it. To assert, by the accretion of details (personalized by his memory and his literary style), that this is where a man belongs is Porter's special version of the autobiographical impulse. When we turn to George

Johnston, though, we find that the phrase *where a man belongs* is to be read in its interrogatory form. To simplify, for the moment, the relationship between the approaches of Porter and Johnston it might be said that where Porter tries to assert his rights to a past, to a place that belongs to him, Johnston seeks to find a past, a pattern, a place to which he can belong. It is only an apparent paradox then, I think, that one finishes Johnston's trilogy of (autobiographical) novels with a much more pressing and intimate sense of a personality than one does after reading three volumes of Porter's autobiography. What one does know about Porter is what has been inferred from his depiction of, and apparent attitude to, the place that belongs to him.

One of the temptations autobiography tantalizingly offers to readers is the opportunity to judge the quality of the subject's experience. Not only is this a temptation for the reader: it is a temptation also for the author, and one that Hal Porter confronts directly on the very first page of *The Paper Chase*. There Porter reconsiders his reaction to the death of his mother, which was described in such a different context in the predecessor to this book, *The Watcher on the Cast-Iron Balcony*. He reflects now: "My death-side agony may not be authentic agony at all. . . . Does one—does a writer with his eyes in his heart, and his heart in his brain —ever really get to know?"[5] We are, it seems, invited to judge by Porter, and with Porter, the quality of the experience, the quality of the life in the art: how "to put down what is felt *then* even if *now* has changed the feeling" (p. 275). Memory is the medium for the autobiographical writer, and its reliability is naturally to be judged, its reflection in the style to be considered, and its influence on the material to be accounted for. George Johnston too is acutely aware of this problem and raises it in the context of the anxious attempt by David Meredith, the narrator of *Clean Straw for Nothing*, to recall the flavour of his earlier experiences with his wife, Cressida. He acknowledges that ". . . there is the danger that we try to preserve something false and spurious as if it has the appearance of uninterrupted identity. . . . We can never really know what is true recollection and what has been implanted there to *seem* true".[6]

Johnston's response is to keep trying to get at the experience by diverse means, principally by changing his vantage-point, and without abandoning the *Angst*-producing doubt. Porter's response is somewhat different. Early in *Where a Man Belongs*, David Martin's first-person narrator, Max, considers the reasons for *his* marriage break-up and suggests that "marriages . . . are broken not by attitudes, which are not fixed, but by events" (p. 8). Porter does not dismiss attitudes quite so summarily, but for what are clearly aesthetic reasons arising out of the autobiographical form, he too settles for events rather than attitudes.

Perhaps the most obvious aesthetic issue inherent in autobiography is the dichotomy between art and life. Autobiography is arguably more concerned with this problem than other art-forms, and an autobiography, like *The Paper Chase*, which is about an autobiographical writer's deliberate search for material, must be concerned with the problem in a uniquely concentrated way. Not surprisingly then, this art/life dichotomy is, in several guises, a governing motif in *The Paper Chase*. The most familiar is Porter's device of distinguishing between Porter-the-writer and Porter-the-man, but on the first page he confronts the issue in an even more basic form: "Mother's death and the unromantic form of it affront me deeply. No Lady of Shalott she. Writers with their aesthetic inventions about death and death-beds—*I am dying, Egypt, dying* and so on and so on—are, it is too clear to one wading heart-deep in fruitless tears, charlatans" (p. 1). The book's opening strategy then is to juxtapose the experience of art and the experience of life and to question the influence of one upon the other. The "life-experience" of his mother's death allows him to judge the "art-experience" of his reading of Tennyson and Shakespeare; it also moves him to wonder whether his "death-side agony may not be authentic agony at all". Another part of this episode was quoted earlier to illustrate one of the directions from which Porter approached the problem of the memory of emotions and attitudes, but it is clear that that is not all he is questioning here. It is the nature of the experience itself which is being scrutinized in this art/life context. Ultimately he is approaching the central aesthetic problem of the process by which we impute words and descriptions to feelings and experiences, for in Porter's highly verbalized art-form it is this particular aesthetic awareness which gives the familiar character to his writing. He is less interested, I think, in character, emotion, or even event than in the problem of how to describe them.

Perhaps as a deliberate test of this aesthetic awareness, perhaps as a reflection of the theatrical aspect of his personality, Porter further confronts the two sides of the art/life dichotomy. The experience of his "death-side agony" is followed about six lines and as many weeks later by a piece of pure literary convention, his midnight walk, dressed in black, on a fog-bound pier. This walk, so self-consciously described, produces for the eighteen-year-old Hal the revelation (transformed by the fifty-five-year-old Porter's prose into an epigram) "that eternity is what goes on behind one's back, that living is what goes on behind the backs of the dead" (p. 2). The process by which life and its perceptions are turned into art is, for Porter, a fascinating one. In his hands the old question then has subtly, but significantly, changed from How do you make art out of life? to How do you make life into art? *The Paper Chase* is avowedly about the experience of the chase for copy, for material for books (including this one). It is the autobiography of a man gathering material to write his autobiography. Small wonder then that the relationship between art and life in it is an intricate and close one. Porter's own image to describe this curiously circular activity is "ride a horse to catch a horse" (p. 90). Certainly some of the material he catches is used in the short stories, and much of it appears here in the autobiography, but nevertheless one has a final impression that it is the chase itself rather than the paper which has received the most fascinated attention.

If Porter's has often been a life lived for art's sake then the writer who produces the art and the man who lives the life will have had an odd, and obviously very close, relationship. Porter, indeed, frequently uses the device of discussing "the writer" as a being separate from "I" in a sort of Siamese-twins way to acknowledge another of autobiography's dualities. "The writer certainly has stronger views than I, but is always willing to let me sweat out a situation on his behalf, long after I have found the situation not only offensive but intolerable" (p. 248).

On this particular occasion, in fact, "the writer" lets him stand for six hours, without food or drink, at the Filipino consulate in Sydney, apparently the butt of a petty act of diplomatic retaliation. But the relationship between the writer and the man is not always of the same kind. Two days before the Second World War begins, Porter is knocked down by a car (outside St Vincent's Hospital) and rendered unfit for military service by a hip injury. Then too his reaction is in the characteristic terms of the dichotomy. "As a writer more than as a man, but also as a man, I regret losing the opportunity to experience war directly" (p. 151). The image is repeated in one form or another so often that it becomes a motif, but it is in any case a device, and an ingenuous one, I think, for an autobiography, the form of art perhaps most obviously concerned with life. But the most telling versions of this device of Porter's occur when the writer's quest for paper comes to seem the preoccupation of the autobiography. Even here, though, his phrase is a pointed one. War, for Porter (the writer?, the man?), is an "*opportunity*" for direct experience.

The chase makes the writer segment of Porter rather a single-minded, not to say bloody-minded, character, and the ruthlessness with which he pursues his goal challenges *our* tolerance no less, certainly, than it challenges the tolerance of Porter, the man. His half-hearted reasons for leaving Adelaide, for instance, at the end of 1945 are substantially augmented by those of the writer, who "having picked up all the copy he can in Adelaide, prods me" (p. 181). The candour with which the artist confesses his attitude to the life about him is no doubt part of the rather stagy honesty which critics and reviewers have so often praised. His rapacious pillaging of life is rather like that of Hurtle Duffield in *The Vivisector*, though without most of the double-edged *angst* with which White's artist struggles. But the artist is not always the sole scapegoat, for the man sometimes accepts joint responsibility. Much of the book's energy derives from the fact that the artist's quest for material is also the man's search for knowledge. Together (it is to be assumed) they "pick the pockets of those who have hard-earned a handful of wisdom or a shillings-worth of nobility" (p. 12). Typically, he describes his education and his chase in terms of an acquisitive misdemeanour. Of this sort of honesty we can say, in Porter's own phrase, we "nearly respect yet do not wholly admire" (p. 12).

For an image, though, which captures not only the artist's ruthless acquisitiveness but also his particular concern with minutiae, one turns to his reaction to the conclusion of his record-breaking ten years as a junior teacher at North Williamstown State School 1409.

> So, recording and learning, I advance on the day of departure, having piecemeal discerned that an addition of years, information and experiences, while making me older, more informed and experienced, certainly does not make me wiser. Suddenly, in July 1937, it seems to me that, after ten years of peering and partaking, all that needs to be known about Williamstown is known, stored away, and that the time has arrived for the storehouse packed hugger-mugger to the rafters to be tidied up. I must leave Williamstown so that this tidying up can be done without the danger of my being tempted into acquiring more Williamstown bric-à-brac.
>
> I shall tidy the decade into a novel. [P. 69]

Here too we have the artist and the man working side-by-side but, as always, separable, "peering and partaking", "recording and learning" the art and the life, with the writer at the end of it resolving to "tidy the decade into a novel", to adjust life into art. As usual, the verb Porter chooses is revealing—*tidy*. Readers who remember his fascination with landladies will not be surprised by it, nor will those who remember his propensity for cataloguing words, songs, events, objects, for tidying the materials of life into a list, for picking things out of time and giving them an apparent aesthetic order. But it is not only the aesthetic principle that is interesting here. One inevitably notices the quality of his descriptions of the life too, "Williamstown bric-à-brac". I will return to the idea of life as a collection of "bric-à-brac", but for the moment it is still more pertinent to consider further the nature of this aesthetic consciousness.

Porter, from time to time, indicates that he is alert to the limitations imposed on his art by life, to the conditions under which he must (in a memorable phrase) "commit an act of lucidity" (p. 5). This act of lucidity, he goes on to admit, "is limited by one's own nature, one's own short-sightedness, one's own conviction that, while a form of compassion is seemly, life is too short for the exercise of outright pity or unpruned tolerance" (p. 5). This too is a kind of honesty about the art, and it is an honesty that arises from a contemplation of the essential aesthetic qualifications—How can we know?, How can we allow for the personal observer? (the "eye/I" problem), and How can we eliminate or compensate for the present perspective? Indeed, immediately after this passage, and as if by way of honouring an obligation, he describes the circumstances in which he is writing it and offers a present (that is, 1966) artist's reflection on it. "As a writer it occurs to me, right here and now in the country kitchen where this is being written . . . " (p. 5). So the double-focus, the "then and now" referred to earlier, are built into the structure of perceptions and the assumptions about them which Porter shares with us. He has, at least so he would have us believe (for this kind of honesty is part of the artefact), eschewed the significance which he can no longer confidently ascribe—"what it is for is now arcane" (p. 26). This too helps to explain, I think, the apparently random nature of his ubiquitous lists: he will not pretend to know now the significance of the events, names, or objects but will insist that as much of them as can survive in verbal form be preserved.

In a book in which, as I have suggested, Porter is particularly interested in the implications of the form he has chosen, it is not surprising to find him returning with fascination to images of his own method (the writer of the autobiography writing about the autobiographical writer). To my mind the most striking of all these is one that is concerned with the self-image through which the life is refracted. "I am not the panted-after crystal able to be seen through by myself, but a grime-clouded pane of glass—the pawn-shop window!—on which my own reflection intrudes, with the grime, to defile the glowing images, and make them secondhand. Secondhand objects may be valuable, second-hand people are valueless" (pp. 60-1). It is the intrusive self-image, the observing, recording eye, which makes the images second-hand. This accords, I believe, with the strong sense many readers have of Porter as an ever-present but always unmaterialized observing personality. The personality is almost never there *per se*: it is *always* there though as the inferred perceiver and recorder. The feeling that the artist's self-image defiles the images of life presumably evokes the strategy of eliminating it as far as possible. This explains, or begins to, Porter's preoccupation with objects and external experience and hence the apparent absence, or near absence, of the solipsism so often inherent in autobiography as a form. The objective details are, to be sure, recorded by this personality whose shadowy image intrudes on them, but the focus of attention is almost exclusively on the "bric-à-brac" and seldom on the self which, for many other auto-biographical authors, gives the objective world its existence, and the autobiography its principal *raison d'être*.

Certainly one of the most striking features of *The Paper Chase* is its concentration on objects, words, things, events; all impersonal except for the ubiquitous verbalized and verbalizing personality of the observer. Indeed, considering the prevalence throughout the trilogy of the concept of the watcher, one is surprised to have to wait until the third volume for Porter to at last make the "eye/I" pun (p. 1). The things observed and especially the connections between the objects and the people who come into their orbit are of central significance. "As much as the plot and characters are interesting, the background, the 'local colour', the incidental details, are even more so."[7] This comment, made by Porter in the introduction to an anthology of Australian writing which he edited, could be applied to his own writing. But there the incidental details do not remain merely incidental. Trivia, in Porter's world, has its function. It allows him to describe people and experience in terms of the nature of the contiguous reality. This empirical materialism counters the potential solipsism and attracts some of Porter's most loving and spectacular verbal energies. The empiricism also leads to a preoccupation with "what" and "how", which only very infrequently lead directly to "why". "What and how people eat in the privacy of their own boxes, and how they behave within those boxes, are the sharpest pointers to what they are" (p. 28). This behaviouristic view of life conditions the aesthetic modes he adopts. Underpinning both method and style of this autobiography is the belief that observed behaviour, social customs, habits, and products are the essential focus, and the inevitable limit, of our attempts to understand both human personality and the past. People, in Porter's world, are known by the titles of the books on their shelves, by the brand of toothpaste which they use, or by the names of their favourite drinks. But, for Porter, this is neither a limitation to be regretted nor a labour-saving device to be indulged. It is rather a matter of constant fascination.

His relationship, for instance, with the portrait-painter William Dargie is described for four and a half pages by the clothes he and Dargie wear, their literary tastes, their artistic enthusiasms, and the way they each cut their fingernails. The relationship begins in 1934 when they are both junior teachers at Williamstown, and they meet again twice in 1965 (once when Dargie paints Porter and once while Dargie is painting the Queen and her horse). Throughout these three periods Dargie is never described by his conversation or his paintings or even recollections of these, nor, except for the slightest and most incidental details, by features or appearances, but mostly by surroundings, apparent choices, by contiguous reality. For example, his London flat is "within a few blocks of . . . the Wallace Collection, Madame Tussaud's, his favourite Greek restaurant, Queen Mary's Garden, and *le cinéma bleu*" (p. 25): the Keeler/Profumo and Barrett/Browning assignation places are even closer. We seem to learn, then, more about the environs of 9 Wimpole Mews (Dargie's temporary London flat) than about Dargie himself. All of these details, though, are only apparently incidental. To the selecting and tidying mind of the artist they have a significant connection with the man in the middle of them. But of all the details, the two that strike Porter most tellingly are that his London hotel room has a Belgian marble chimney-piece identical with the one in Dargie's Melbourne studio of thirty-two years ago, and that he is wearing a trench-coat very similar to the one in which he sat for Dargie in Melbourne thirty-two years ago.

> I find both trench-coat and chimney-piece apposite elements in the Williamstown-London-Dargie-me relationship. Their accidental duplication—another trench-coat, another chimney-piece—does not, of course, affect the relationship but does intensify my conception of the relationship. No matter how invisibly fine is the thread strung from, say, coat A to coat B, it is a straight, a dead-straight, thread passing through thousands of miles and thousands of hours, and connects the centre of my consciousness directly to yet another dimension of the world I am composed of. The quality of one's connection with people through their relation with things, tunes, scents, sounds, and so on is a subject of great allure, its existence a great blessing. [P. 25]

That such connections exist testifies for Porter to the existence of continuity and significance in the world he inhabits. They are the means by which the writer confirms where a man belongs, and they are clearly what enable him to survive in a world that is otherwise fragmentary in the extreme. Though the connections are neither inevitable nor absolute, they do provide a focus for the residual meaningfulness of life. Life (and time) in this trilogy seems to be composed of bits, of small, discrete units which fortunately, because they can be extracted and catalogued, have the power to indicate the lineaments of experience. This is an indirect and severely limited way of suggesting life and attitudes, but it is, Porter insists, all we can have. For example, his 1966 recollection of his 1939 ignorance of the imminence of the Second World War provokes this catalogue to suggest his 1939 feelings about war:

> The Civil War is as remote and romantic as any remote and romantic war, be it Pelopennesian [sic], Hundred Years, Opium, Maori, Jacobite, Ashantee, or Boer. Certainly I have read *All Quiet on the Western Front*, and Siegfried Sassoon and Stephen Crane and Henri Barbusse and Guy de Maupassant and *Vanity Fair*, and have seen *The Birth of a Nation*, *The Big Parade*, *What Price Glory?*, *A Kiss for Cinderella*, and *Cavalcade* on films, and Frank Lawton in

Journey's End at the Athanaeum [sic] Theatre in Melbourne. The war shelf of the littered shelves of my mind is pretty full—Napoleon in a funny hat, Nelson saying "Kiss me, Hardy!" dolls dressed as Red Cross nurses, Karl Dane and George K. Arthur, popguns, Horatius on the bridge, the Black Hole of Calcutta, Lady Butler's and Grandfather Porter's paintings, "When Did You Last See Your Father?" Florence Nightingale, Boadicea, the Wars of the Roses, the Massacre at Glencoe, Tobler cards of *Navires de Guerre*, wooden swords, tin soldiers, the Relief of Mafeking, the Motherly and Auspicious Dowager-Empress and her Boxers, *The Burial of Sir John Moore at Corunna*, *The Charge of the Light Brigade*, and the photographs of dead uncles and cousins, wearing puttees or leather leggings, in special frames on top of which are the crossed Australian flag and the Union Jack, and a wriggly ribbon, two-fanged at each end, on which is printed FOR GOD, KING, AND COUNTRY. Among the first songs I am taught at school in 1917 are "Anzac" and "Men of Harlech"; they lie at the back of the shelf with "Just as the Sun Went Down"; "Goodbye, Dolly Grey"; "Just Before the Battle, Mother"; "Roses of Picardy"; "Over There"; "The Rose of No Man's Land"; and "Mademoiselle from Armentieres". I know every word of the Harfleur speech and the St Crispin's Day one. They too are on the shelf with Mata Hari, Wolfe, Kitchener, Lord Bobs, Bonnie Prince Charlie, Old Bill, Lord Cardigan, and all the Philistines and Huns, galleons and Spartans, submarines and Medes and Persians, all the losers, all the winners, all remote, all romantic. So many skulls glinting like infinitesimal beads in the embroidery that weighs down the dirty and glorious cloak of history. [Pp. 130–31]

It is not surprising then to read: "The writer segment of my nature . . . seems to need to find its fodder in places as chock-a-block with objects and human beings as a Brueghel painting" (p. 56), or to notice, often, that the objects are more prominent than the human beings.

This is the mental bric-à-brac which now gives aesthetic existence to a personality long since lost. One critic has written of Porter's "triumph over time":[8] if there is a triumph it is of a precarious kind. The memory provides the bits and pieces which, of themselves (and because there is a memory to provide them), imply a life and a connection between it and the present. "I am composed of what hangs on the millions of hooks" (p. 110). The accretion of memories of experiences (the catalogues) are a way of finding one's self and one's place. He records elsewhere that he picked up Cyrillic script "in the same way as one picks up and puts aside pieces of string . . . in a this-might-come-in-handy-one-day manner" (p. 94). The Cyrillic script earns the man his dinner at the Café Petrushka: the lists of new words, songs, films, people's mannerisms, the records of first and last appearances and experiences, acquired, one presumes, with more purpose than the Cyrillic script, earn for the paper-chasing artist the survival of the man's earlier personality, and a book.

Dorothy Van Ghent, in *The English Novel: Form and Function*, suggests that the autobiographical novel is the artist's attempt, in response to a society that no longer provides values and sanctions for art or even life, "to test out in the materials of his own experience the possibility of a new conceptual and aesthetic form which will give him imaginative grasp of his world.[9] Hal Porter certainly has a vision of the "cultural crisis" which, Van Ghent claims, is the "historical compulsion" under which most auto-biographical artists write, but his almost immediate defence is "a nickel-plated belief in myself" (p. 5), a confidence in his own values even if those of the society in which he lives are untrustworthy. He finds that confidence in "the materials of his own experience". George Johnston does not have that confidence. It was fleetingly present in *My Brother Jack* when David Meredith became, briefly and with a savage final irony, "Jack's brother Dave"; it is part of what is sought vainly in *Clean Straw for Nothing*; it is impossible in *A Cartload of Clay*. But in the middle volume the attempt to make sense of reality by making sense of the self first (another variation of the art/life dichotomy) is integral to both theme and method. I mention method too because Johnston's sense of alienation, of cultural uncertainty, is so profound as to demand of the artist "a new conceptual and aesthetic form".

Johnston, within the novel, canvasses the several kinds of pattern which could give him, or David Meredith, an "imaginative grasp of his world". There is the pattern of history, the pattern of nationality, the pattern of sociology, the pattern of mythology, the pattern of nature, the pattern of narrative. None of these will, for Meredith, provide any more than a temporary basis for the recollection of experience. Almost obsessed with his failure to find a pattern in the life, and without the creative confidence or perhaps the fundamental belief in the possibility of finding it in the art, he finally has to settle for the pattern inherent in the memory itself and to allow this to determine the aesthetic pattern for his book. The pattern is found in his search for a pattern. Like *The Paper Chase*, though in ways as different as the personalities that energize the two books, *Clean Straw for Nothing* is concerned with the relationship between art and life. The book itself is, by way of the literary convention embodied in the first line (" 'I'll tell you why I'm not writing' "), a means of testifying to some meaning in the life. Its impulse, though not so literally the results, is as obviously derived from "the materials of his own experience" as Porter's was. In the long run, David Meredith's life has been a kind of paper chase too. It is only the long, frustrating, often empty years, and more immediately the difficulty of recollecting them authentically, which have enabled him to write this magnificent novel. That which causes the anguish has, to appropriate the words of Cavafy's poem, "given [him] the beautiful voyage" (p. 282). This voyage is one kind of structure for the book, and an image of its thematic conclusion.

The Cavafy poem, the experience of life, and the experience of writing the book (for this is the illusion engendered by its first line) teach him that "it is what happened in between that is important, but this is something that will dry up and vanish very quickly, like water splashed on a hot pavement" (p. 275). The book is an attempt to "get it down" before it dries up, leaving only the record of beginnings and endings, those "markers" of experience in which Hal Porter was so interested and which David Meredith has learned to distrust so strenuously. He cannot believe, for instance, in the passage just quoted, that the goal of his actor-friend Archie Calverton's journey was "a striving towards spectacular obituary" (p. 274). Although Meredith spends a considerable amount of time pondering the significance of beginnings and endings, of going away and coming back, the book is finally a triumphant testimony to "what happened in between". Even in this, as in so much else, the structure parallels the meaning, for the first and last episodes (both "Sydney 1968") serve to enclose and frame the "texture of reality", the "what happened in between". Acknowledging early in the book that "you . . . traded in experience for the memory of experience" (p. 10), Meredith tries to reproduce, not the experience, but rather the memory of it. The sequence which *Clean Straw for Nothing* has is not the sequence of events but the sequence of memory: the dates and places heading each chapter do not indicate a past experience but locate the source of a present recollected one.

The form that resulted from Hal Porter's autobiographical impulse was a reconstruction of a sequential narrative, despite his occasional insistence that the connections he now felt to be significant were seldom sequential ones. The form that Johnston has adopted seems more faithful to the experience of memory. "For whatever *did* happen has now an imaginary existence; it is no longer what it was, it has become only an image we are able to manipulate" (p. 219). Certainly the structure of *Clean Straw* is explicable in terms of the manipulation of images, but even more interesting, I think, is the concept that the past life enters the province of the imagination and hence, presumably, the province of art. Memory then is the means by which, in Johnston's case, life becomes art. This may well explain why George Johnston chose the form of the autobiographical novel rather than that of the "straight" autobiography. In addition, though, Meredith is aware of "the danger that we try to preserve something false and spurious as if it had the appearance of *uninterrupted identity*" (p. 215, my italics). To avoid "the appearance of uninterrupted identity" and because he can no longer believe in the continuity of his own life, David Meredith abandons altogether the form of the processive novel which seems to guarantee, or at least to impose, a continuity. For the autobiographical novelist (and this is as true for David Meredith as for George Johnston) this semblance of uninterrupted identity is even harder to avoid because of the further risk that "the 'and then, and then' of biography will intrude on the more complex 'because' of the novel, allowing chronology to shape it rather than the internal necessities of a central idea".[10]

In *The Paper Chase* some of those shaping, causal connections were discoverable in the realm of details and objects—"the quality of one's connection with people through their relation with things" (p. 25). Meredith, under an even greater compulsion than Porter to find a significant connection, a pattern, and having eschewed the ordinary chronological narrative pattern, also tries to find it in what he (perhaps portentously) calls "the texture of reality" (p. 20). In a sense, Meredith's episodes, the chunks of recollected experience, have a similar function to that of Porter's lists: they assert that reality has been encountered and (unlike Porter's lists) they provide a way, tentative though David Meredith is about this, of experiencing the recollection. The significance of it, however, is sometimes, as Porter observed of his experience, "now arcane" (p. 26). In Tokyo in 1945 Meredith is given a collection of stamps from the conquered and now lost Japanese empire. (The motif of surrender, of advance and retreat is present even in this detail.) His reaction is "What do I do with a thing like that?" (p. 20) and he does not mean the stamp collection, he means the experience. This event, and even the surrender ceremony on board the *Missouri* which he witnesses, is part of "the texture of reality", but it seems not to be part of a pattern.

In pain in a Sydney hospital in 1966 Meredith has a revelation that the past was "composed entirely of fragmented things he didn't have to go through any more" (p. 25). That his life, experience, and past are fragmentary he is prepared to accept, even to find some consolation in, but that the past "turned into something that no longer had to be experienced" (p. 25) he can accept only while confined by pain and by the timeless, featureless world of the hospital ward. This is one of a series of false discoveries scattered throughout the book, tempting Meredith with the comforting possibilities of disburdening himself. " 'How *can* you bloody well go back as if nothing had happened?' " (p. 24) is his response to

Gavin Turley's platitudinous quotation from Kafka (" 'and then he went back to his work as if nothing had happened' "). "Going back" becomes a governing motif, and it is one with such frequent and diverse resonances that it will be discussed in some detail later, but it should be observed that "going back" is a central problem for the autobiographical writer and a central problem for the expatriate. The "going back" of autobiography (and memory) is objectified in the "going back" of repatriation. The way in which these historical and geographical senses of "going back" are played off against one another as a structuring principle throughout the book is fascinating. Time and place are the details we are always offered first, and the operation of the recalling mind is constantly set before us. Finding "where a man belongs" by combining the figure of the returning expatriate (the man trying to regain his place) and that of the autobiographical writer (the man trying to regain his past) is one of the aesthetic devices employed by Johnston to put into effect his autobiographical impulse. Carefully built into the structure of the book, and underlying all of the searching and journeying, is the awareness given to us explicitly only on the last page, that alienation or belonging are conditions not of geography or history but of personality—"alienation is something you carry inside yourself" (p. 288), or as Max is told in *Where a Man Belongs*, "you are your own country" (p. 168). But having learned that just as his plane is about to touch down after twenty years of exile, Meredith is, understandably, even more urgently pressed, perhaps masochistically as he admits at least once, to find out what it was all about, "what *was* the meaning of experience" (p. 286). The voyage leads to no convincingly significant conclusion: the significance then must be in the journey.

I suggested, when discussing *The Paper Chase*, that some notion of double-focus, indeed a general duality, was inherent in the form of autobiography. The duality of perception (then/now), the duality of form (art/life), the duality of mode (memory/experience) are all present in *Clean Straw for Nothing*, and they are augmented by the duality of self-concept (alienation/belonging) and the duality of impulse (going away/going back). Each of the latter is character-istically shown by Johnston to be ambiguous.

My Brother Jack begins with the return of troops (and nurses) to Melbourne at the end of World War I; it ends with the return of troops (and war correspondents) to Melbourne at the end of World War II. The earliest events in *Clean Straw for Nothing* are of that same 1945 return; the latest, Meredith's return to Australia from his expatriate experience. It is, of course, fitting that the motif of return, going back, should be this novel's particular narrative and autobiographical impulse. It is also interesting that Meredith should, in 1945, ascribe most of his personal problems to the effect of the war, the result of responding "to this call towards the distant adventure [which] is repeated to gener-ation after generation of my countrymen".[11] But if this is the cause, it may also be the solution; Meredith's impulse is again "to look elsewhere for the great adventures, the necessary challenges to the flesh and spirit".[12] The "distant adventure" has created "the new nomadism" (p. 22) as Gavin Turley calls it in *Clean Straw*. But the war seems to have had a further, unacknowledged, effect on David Meredith's unconscious, for two of his continuing problems throughout the book are to dissociate the idea of going away from that of escape and to dissociate the concept of going back from that of retreat, pejorative forms which seem to be a heritage of his experience of describing military manoeuvres. The confusion between going back and retreating, going away and escaping is one of the ambiguities which Johnston finds, and with which Meredith must come to terms in order to make sense of the pattern of his life and the autobiographical impulse of his art.

The second ambiguity is in Meredith's concept of his place in the sociological and historical pattern of post-war Mel-bourne and hence his concept of "where a man belongs". In relation to the breaking-up of his marriage to his first wife, Helen (the significance of whose name to the going away/going back motif and to the Odyssey images is obvious), David repeatedly asserts: " 'We're just parts of a thing that's happened, that's still happening, all over the world, all over this city' " (p. 17). He insists, that is, that he is not unique, not different, but part of a pattern, although it is, paradoxically, a pattern not of belonging, but of alienation. "I must keep my hold on instability. . . . I want to stay identified with a dilemma, because this makes me part of what is unorthodox and unstable; it retains me in a world which is still out of balance" (p. 11). This too, a reaction to one return, prefigures in most of its elements (though not its mood) his reaction to his later return, to Sydney in 1964. While his alienation from Helen is described in terms of belonging to a pattern (albeit an ambiguous one), his new feeling of belonging to Cressida (in whose name the trilogy's theme of betrayal is consciously objectified) is described in terms of antipathy towards belonging—" 'I don't want to fall into these awful dull ruts' " (p. 43). Meredith's response to this particular ambiguity is to revert to the other major motif of the novel. He assents to the call to "the distant adventure", subscribes to "the new nomadism": his second recorded sentence to Cressida in this book is " 'Will you come away with me?' " (p. 42). Incidentally, Meredith's recollection that she was reading *Tristram Shandy* when he first saw her is a further indication of Johnston's predilection, which he shares with Porter, for providing images of his own method: the Lockean association of ideas which motivates that eighteenth-century novel is at least a clue to the structure of this twentieth-century one.

Most of the other patterns to which Meredith attempts to subscribe are also felt to be ambiguously solaces and traps. Life on the Island, being part of an expatriate community, offers a sense of belonging which in the end only emphasizes their alienation, their status as fugitives. They belong only with those who do not belong: "But how *could* they identify with this specific pattern into which, in the final analysis, they could never properly fit; was it not, rather, that he and his wife had reached a point where they had lost, or were losing, their own identity, and were ready to accept any substitution for the loss, however superficial?" (pp. 187–88). Having hoped that, like those who had participated in that last great national "distant adventure" (World War II), "they had a place there" (p. 16) the Merediths come to accept that they simply have to "push on and try to make it to the tape" (p. 259).

Two other patterns seem more successful. In a climactic scene of love-making in the surf at Lebanon Bay after their "escape" from Melbourne in 1946, David and Cressida feel themselves to be "an inextricable part of some absolute congress of nature" (p. 55). But the passage is obtrusively (and self-consciously?) lyrical and, as Meredith observes anyway, "for a long time we forgot about it". Nevertheless it does prefigure the quality of their best experiences on the Island.

The other more amenable pattern is, appropriately, both literary and Greek. The explicit references to the *Odyssey* are few and often qualified,[13] but the parallels are made available, if not often emphasized, by the novelist. In addition to these explicit references, we are invited, I believe, to make further (speculative) connections. For instance, Lebanon Bay is a period of Lotus-eating; Sydney, the Cyclops from which Meredith and some others escape but by whom others (such as Jefferson) are devoured; England is the island of Aeolus to which he is driven back when his winds run out and where he is refused re-entry to journalism; his eight years on the Island correspond with Odysseus's eight years on Ogygia with Calypso. The entire journey takes Meredith, like Odysseus, "nearly twenty years" (p. 51) if we count it as starting from Melbourne in 1946 rather than from Sydney in 1949. The departure from Melbourne either "in panic flight from that constrictive city . . . [or] considering Sydney the better springboard for the jump to somewhere else" (p. 63) is clearly the beginning of his Odyssey. Like the legendary one, it begins with Helen. Other Homeric parallels are, I think, possible, but they would require detailed explication. The general relevance, though, of Odysseus to David Meredith is straightforward enough.[14] The particular version of the Odyssey in which Johnston is interested is that which underlies C.P. Cavafy's poem, "Ithaca". It is the version that Meredith considers in relation to his own life after his return to Sydney. "We are not told what happened to Odysseus after he got back to his Ithaca and ridded himself of the suitors . . . did he plant trees, I wonder, olive and quince, and pistachio and resinous pine, and retreat into reverie behind them?" (p. 160). We have to wait until *A Cartload of Clay* for the "retreat into reverie", but in *Clean Straw*, as in the *Odyssey*, "we are not told what happened . . . after he got back". The significance of the *Odyssey*, as of *Clean Straw for Nothing*, is in the journey.

The particular impulse of this novel is indicated by its frame—it begins and ends in Sydney, 1968. Meredith has returned to Ithaca, but he is not yet certain in those opening episodes if he has "understood by then what Ithaca means" (p. 283). Even in the final episode, his recollection of the plane flight home, there is the paradox central to the theme and form of this book, and it is characteristically expressed in images of geography and time.

> He rested his head against the seat and half dozed. The Cavafy book lay closed on his lap, and perhaps this was why quotations went on drifting through his mind, other quotations, Hemingway's "The people and the places and how the weather was," and Horace's "You can change your skies but not your soul,"[15] and Herder's "We are carried ever forward; the stream never returns to its source.
>
> But here he was, high over the Spice Islands, certainly being carried ever forward, rushingly, at almost six hundred miles an hour, but being returned to his source just as certainly. Yet how far it was away . . . how terribly far away. . . . [p. 286].

The pages in between are an attempt to understand the meaning of Ithaca ("the place we have to get away from" [p. 171] rather than the source to which we return): an attempt to resolve the paradox of time (and life) progressing while memory (and art) regresses.

The first line of the book, "I'll tell you why I'm not writing", is, as I have already remarked, a self-conscious literary device to enable him to start writing, but it is not the real impulse. Two other questions precede that statement, though he has to locate the incident in time and place before he can recollect them. The sequence of these two questions is important. Firstly Jeremy (who "was working and saving towards his first trip abroad") asks " 'Why did you come back?' " and then " 'Why did you go away in the first place?' This was even more difficult" (p. 9). He doesn't answer either question at the party: he writes the book instead and in doing so arrives at Cavafy's other conclusion.

Without her you would never have taken the road.
Ithaca has given you the beautiful voyage.
But she has nothing more to give you.

[P. 282]

So the last two stanzas of Cavafy's "Ithaca", quoted finally on page 282 as he flies over Alexandria on his return to Australia, represent the answers to the two questions " 'Why did you go?' " and " 'Why did you come back?' " (now neatly reversed). He has to answer both, so the novel has to account for his expatriatism, and despite the emphasis on personal alienation, the novel does locate a considerable amount of the significance of "what Ithaca means" in the national experience. The self-consciousness and the propensity of Meredith to see himself as typical (in contrast with Porter) make the personal-national analogy continually illuminating.

The novel's second episode, the brief "Sydney, 1968", containing the resolve "to set it down", is in effect the beginning of the book. As on a number of occasions, an explanation of the artistic method is followed by a long narrative explanation of the life. The third episode then, the much longer "Melbourne 1945", is the beginning of the story and is resonant with images of absence and return. As often in the first third of the book, the narrative vantage point changes rapidly, from 1968 to 1945 to 1959, and so on, as Meredith tries to find a position from which it will begin to make sense. He achieves this once he has dealt in some measure with the experiences of departure and return and settled down to memories of the voyage itself; not the impulses, but the life. After the second episode set on the Island (p. 105), the historical jumps are generally smaller. It is appropriate, though, that the first excursion into the past is to describe the experience of going back, the national experience of returning from the war, "to something that wasn't here when they went away" (p. 16), an experience reflected, Meredith believes, in the collapse of his marriage to Helen. This mood of betrayal is echoed in the next episode ("West China–Japan, 1945") where the images of the journey (the "Great March" of the Chinese) are put alongside images of defeat and surrender. Already the ambiguity of return and defeat is ingrained. Even the moment when Meredith most conclusively leaves Australia—his arrival at Tilbury—is, like Richard Mahony's first arrival in England (in the Proem to *The Way Home*), compromised by the unsatisfying homecomings of other passengers. As Meredith will eventually learn, every homecoming is an arrival. Again, at Calverton's departure from Australia someone quotes the lines from the "Barrington Prologue"— "HE LEAVES HIS COUNTRY FOR HIS COUNTRY'S GOOD" (p. 88). This includes the double focus too, for the lines originally, of course, applied to those making the journey in the opposite direction. As in *The Fortunes of Richard Mahony*, "the way home" is for the colonial a particularly ambiguous one.

Once Australia has been left, once the escape has been effected, there is considerable and often anguished speculation about the meaning of *escape*. Characteristically, the speculation is about goals (what have we escaped to?) and is resolved by recognizing the overwhelming importance of personality. In one of the crucial third-person episodes, "Sydney, 1949" Meredith reflects that "he has removed himself, but he has not escaped" (p. 77). This is the beginning of the attempt to answer Why did you go?, and it is also the beginning of the compulsive questioning of the fundamental significance of the journey. This involves the other question, Why did you come back? For some time return seems impossible. " 'I jumped off the bus and wandered round to pick the daisies. Now they won't let me back aboard' " (p. 221). It also seems dishonourable. " 'I think . . . that going back is a kind of confession of failure' " (p. 127).

But the novel is structured around departures and returns (especially the latter): his unexpected return to London, which embarrasses Calverton and Cressida; the return from England to Greece; his return to the Island from Big Grace's; his return to the Island after trying to leave Cressida. "Going back" becomes a *leitmotif* in the novel investing so many events with the wider significance; going back to Cress, going back to Australia, going back to writing, going back to his past. Indeed his return flight to Australia is a series of returns; to his old wartime experiences—Karachi brothels, Calcutta smells, and so on; to his dead father (a possible shared experience of Cairo); and the brief fantasy, "if one could live backward" (p. 286).

The idea of return then (which is not living backwards, but "being carried ever forward" [p. 286]) is one to which Meredith must adjust. He learns first to go back in time— when he accepts the autobiographical impulse—and then learns that geographical return is possible too. The auto-biographer shows the expatriate how to return. Since you can't go back "as if nothing had happened" (p. 24) no going back is ever a repetition, or, therefore, ever a retreat. Ithaca is not a goal and so not a conclusion. The voyage, like Johnston's trilogy, is unfinished, ended only by his death.

NOTES

1. *The Australian*, 23 January 1971, p. 22. The books alluded to in the prospective title of the parody are *The Education of Young Donald* (Donald Horne, 1967), *My Brother Jack* (George Johnston, 1964), and *The Watcher on the Cast-Iron Balcony* (Hal Porter, 1963).
2. Hal Porter, *The Extra* (Melbourne: Nelson, 1975), p. 189. All references are to this edition.
3. Patrick Morgan, "Keeping It in the Family", *Quadrant* 18, no. 3, (May-June 1974): 10–20.
4. David Martin, *Where a Man Belongs* (London: Cassell, 1969), p. 213. All references are to this edition.
5. Hal Porter, *The Paper Chase* (Sydney: Angus and Robertson, 1966), p. 1. All references are to this edition.
6. George Johnston, *Clean Straw for Nothing* (London: Fontana, 1971), p. 215. All references are to this, the most easily obtainable, edition.
7. Hal Porter, introduction to *It Could Be You*, ed. Hal Porter (Adelaide: Rigby, 1972), p. i.
8. Robert Burns, "A Sort of Triumph over Time: Hal Porter's Prose Narratives", *Meanjin Quarterly* 28, no. 1 (1969): 19–28.
9. Dorothy Van Ghent, *The English Novel: Form and Function* (New York: Rinehart, 1953), pp. 264–65.
10. Barbara Jefferis, *Sydney Morning Herald*, 7 March 1964, p. 10 (review of *My Brother Jack*).
11. George Johnston, *My Brother Jack* (London: Fontana, 1967), p. 271.

12. Ibid.
13. Diana Brydon ("Themes and Preoccupations in the novels of Australian Expatriates" [PhD thesis, Australian National University, 1976], p. 284) points out, for instance, that the three explicit references to the *Odyssey* are each followed by one to Kafka. This is another manifestation, I think, of the double perspective which I have been discussing.
14. See, for example, Brydon, "Themes and Preoccupations", pp. 265-90 and A.E. Goodwin, "Voyage and Kaleidoscope in George Johnston's Trilogy", *Australian Literary Studies* 6, no. 2 (1973): 143-51.
15. This quotation from Horace, "Coelum, non animum, mutant, qui trans mare currunt", is applied by Richard Mahony to *his* situation as he decides to "return" to England. It is one of several echoes of *The Fortunes of Richard Mahony* in Johnston's novel.

Indulgence

David Martin's *The Hero of Too,* Frank Dalby
Davidson's *The White Thorntree,* Dal Stivens's
A Horse of Air, David Malouf's *Johnno,* and
Frank Hardy's *But the Dead are Many*

CECIL HADGRAFT

H.G. Wells once confessed that he occasionally had in mind
a minor character or incident of which he was enamoured,
so much so that in the novel he contemplated he was
determined that it should find a place—or, rather, that it
should be found, even though it had no place. It was, he
acknowledged, a small self-indulgence that, come what may,
he was going to permit himself.

If Wells's oddity were removed we should hardly guess
that the alien from outer space had ever been among us. But
other indulgences are not to be removed by omission. These
are personal motivations, the particular reasons for expression, without which some novels would not have been
written. They are personal in a sense other than the literary
or professional. It is not that the author wants to write a
particular novel, but that he has a particular reason, and
acting on it is in a way his indulgence. This affords a
satisfaction different from those that usually result—money,
reputation, release, fulfilment. He does not start with a theme
but an impulse perhaps only half-confessed, and this determines the theme. It does not mean that the novel will be
the better or the worse for it. But for a reader it tends to
make the writer himself bulk larger, as himself. Such reasons
vary—to express joy at homecoming, to vent an obsession,
to indulge and deny a daydream, to do what is expected,
to gratify an ambition. The five novels that are discussed in
this chapter have their own importance as novels; perhaps
they may have an added interest because—possibly? probably?—they spring from such sources.

If a Hungarian Jew, whose native tongue is German, comes to Australia, then nobody is surprised if he finds oddities and anomalies. (Many have done this, among them Australians returning after a few years' absence. The latter, indeed, can tend to become enraged.) But it is most unlikely that such a stranger should acutely see and sensitively feel what makes us tick, should digest the lingo that we use about our inner mechanism, should be kindly, amused, tolerant, and satiric about it all, and then produce a small comic classic of a kind that nobody else, native or foreign, has managed to approach. This is what David Martin has done in *The Hero of Too*.[1] We can only repeat what a critic remarked some years back, that he is the most improbable Australian author ever.

A troubadour, Martin has moved through many lands, and his verse and prose have accompanied his passage. But his conquest was delayed until this novel. He set out to possess, in sympathy and humour, some of Australia—myths and *mores* that beset, delight, deceive, and mould us. The process is not of course in any sense complete. But, to cover one country town, it needed many persons and events, and the result is a rich and complicated novel that is intricately knit together.

The core or focus is Dick Grogan, a bushranger with the usual accompaniment of legend. To his memory all characters are directly or indirectly linked: Steve Turner, appointed to his first school, who is going to research the legend; Jack Bollman, the wealthiest man in Tooramit, with political aspirations; Norma his wife, George his son, and Alison his sister; Captain Horváth, the Hungarian hairdresser, both prey and pursuer of Alison; Henry Lovelett the doctor and his daughter Clare; Rufus Jamieson the lawyer; the members of the Quinn family—Peter, aged ninety-four, Alfred his son, the sanitary man, and Lacy, daughter of Alfred. On the outskirts: Sylvie, later Lady Moira Levine, nearly thirty years earlier Jack Bollman's love; Delaney, a member of the federal parliament; and Lam, the old Chinese herbalist, years ago the masked off-sider of Grogan.

To have woven all these into a pattern made of smaller patterns is a feat of literary virtuosity. One pattern, for instance, is the relation of the rich and respectable Bollmans and the poor and disreputable Quinns, revealed at last as a connection through a common ancestor, Peter Quinn. And all the characters are carried along in the preparations for the town's seventh-fifth anniversary festival.

The chief flaw in this carefully built novel occurs, oddly enough, in that very field—structure. Grogan, the mysterious hero, is linked to the present by myth, practically all of it misleading or sheer fabrication, and by memory. This memory is that of Lam and Peter Quinn. One might think that either, under certain conditions, would tell his story, or part of it, to Steve Turner, the dedicated researcher. Or, if this disclosure should seem to be out ot character, at least clues might be made available to him. Instead of this a clumsy and unnatural device is employed for our benefit: Lam in a muse imagines he hears the ghost of Grogan telling him of the past, or else Lam's thoughts become articulate. It is difficult to say which of the alternatives is employed, except that we are told quite often of actions done and words spoken when Lam was not on the scene—so then the first applies. On other occasions the author simply tells of Grogan without any intermediary. When we think of the dextrous handling of the story elsewhere, we feel this clumsiness all the more acutely.

All that a reader could cavil at apart from this structural oddity is the emotional see-sawing of George, Lacy, and Clare, the eternal triangle perhaps, but a most unstable one. George favours Clare, then Lacy, then Clare, then Lacy. And the two girls, though not as volatile, change in temperature towards George with his changing glances. One almost feels that Martin had not made up his mind, and then found himself constrained by the demands of a happy ending: like George, he bowed to circumstances. But unlike the structural fault, this depiction of emotional vagaries, however unlikely and however coincidental, does not offend so much: it is comical, even farcical, and fits easily enough into the background of events. Absurdity has a good digestion.

Martin's concern, though, is not essentially with plot. He casts a whimsical and comprehensive eye over Australian characteristics—our dealing with names, for instance: abbreviations, where Alfred Quinn is known as Klep (for kleptomaniac); or nicknames, where Peter is called Pongo (from his habit of breaking wind very profusely); or contraries (Snowy, of course, is an Aboriginal half-caste). Or he comments on the relations between country parents and the schoolmaster; or the Australian press and Australian figures such as Lady Moira: "The press had hailed her with the obsequiousness proper for returning celebrities. Perhaps even more obsequiously than usual, on account of her being the widow of Sir Nathan Levine, one of Sydney's most far-sighted Real Estate operators and art patrons" (p. 279). The dunnies in country towns receive loving attention from him as well as from Klep on his weekly rounds. These edifices have no locks and in an emergency the door cannot be reached and held shut. This is one of the few occasions where Martin's comment betrays imperfect insight: "It requires strong nerves to sit in an unlocked, unlockable structure of this kind" (p. 10). It doesn't.

Then there is the theme of inter-tribal jealousy. The Sydney Harbour Bridge collapsed, runs the folk saying, so Melbourne declared a public holiday. But large cities and their feuds are too generalized for treatment; a couple of small outback townships, within a few miles of each other, are quite a different proposition. Tooramit is predominantly Protestant, Boobyalla Catholic; one is fairly prosperous, the other scrapes a living from stingy soil; one thinks of itself as fairly sophisticated, the other has no such decadent pretensions. The inhabitants of one even differ in facial contours from those of the other. It is richly latent in possibilities—for example, in a football match between the towns, or in the celebration that concerns both, the anniversary.

But these are lesser objects of satire. The main object is the legendary bushranger, with his invariable traits of independence, revolt, and masculinity. Bit by bit these are dissolved away: Martin is elaborately complete in his treatment of this perennial humbug—his rebellious youth (Grogan was timid, except with horses), his daring (he had to be pushed and bullied into action), his faithful followers (he had only one, who unhesitatingly decamped in an emergency on Grogan's horse), his masculinity (only a determined woman could get him to bed), his heroic and defiant end (he was shot in the left buttock and captured), his aspirations for glory, best seen in his musings: "What was it Father O'Brien had said? A poor boy. He was so young, so young. . . . They would grieve for him a while, his parents, his brother and his sisters. Maybe, Fat Mary. Mag even. And that charming boy, McKenzie, whom he had given his watch to. Some would burn candles. Perhaps God, who was merciful, would let him come back as a girl" (p. 304).

The satire finds one of its most entertaining outlets in parody. One is in verse, a skit on bushranging songs. Anyone who has had anything to do with Australian literature of last century inevitably meets with such songs, still valued by some for their "folk" quality, which expresses the real Australian ethos, the independence of spirit, the sense of adventure, the hostility to authority, and so on through the list of virtues hopefully attributed to our ancestors. Not all readers are convinced that there is any real "folk", or that the imputed virtues are derivable or demonstrable. Rather, it is asserted by some, it is a worn cult embraced by romantics and those in search of proletarian values.

Such aspects of the songs do not, except incidentally, concern Martin. He simply has read them, parodies them as a class, and entitles the result "Dauntless Dick Grogan". He has caught the traits admirably, from the pseudo-literary inversions and *Come all you* . . ., the sorrowing parents, the judge that swore to hang him, to the metrical ineptitudes.

It is not only the songs that he parodies. Prose, that of the biographers of bushrangers, comes in for its appropriate treatment. As good an example as any is the account of Lam and Grogan riding "to keep the rendezvous", where "the black angel was waiting for him". Grogan ruminates as he rides in front, his Tranter rifle "athwart his pommel, death sleeping in its magazine".

The living do not escape Martin's eye any more than the dead, for almost all the characters are shown with their comic or harmless weakness. Even Captain Horváth, hailing from the same country as the author, is revealed with his foibles and frailties. An exile, with one precious stone preserved,

as the fruit of a theft, not at home in the raw materialistic
new land, only slowly prospering in his hairdressing salon,
seeking a licence so he can open a bistro, in love with Alison
but hoping to profit from her, he is both charming and fickle,
and always with an eye to the main chance. Embracing her
in her lounge, he surveys the room over her shoulder: "the
tinted window, the expensive curtains, the multi-coloured
cushions, the three Van-Goghs and the percolator. He knew
that he would not go to Sydney. He sniffed her perfume and,
from old experience, estimated that it must have cost at least
ten guineas" (p. 147).

The story ends happily in Dickensian harmony. George
and Lacy are united, Steve and Clare, Alison and her
Captain. Jack Bollman, driven by an access of memory, goes
to Sylvie–Moira in her hotel room. His wife Norma, bitter,
frustrated, jealous, remains in the house with their guest
Delaney, the federal politician. With an understanding
perhaps born of his campaigning he senses the situation and
the need, and takes the chill fortress by storm. For both, it
is almost love. Bollman is to be offered a seat in parliament.
Klep Quinn is assured of a position in the Sewerage
Department to replace his humbler job on the nightcart.
There is only one death: old Lam dies—in the grave and
seemly phrase he used of others: "Time took him away."

There are only two overtly serious passages. The Captain
at the gala dance asks Clare what she is going to do:

> "This is where I belong."
> "Here? My dear Mademoiselle!" He nodded towards the
> garish decorations, and all at once she could see how he saw
> them: the too-showy banks of flowers, the dingy row of
> portraits of dead and retired Shire Presidents, the tawdry
> silver stars on the curtain of the stage . . . [P. 348]

This, we may conclude, is Martin viewing things through
the eyes of "Captain de Mántoky–Horváth, nobleman and
one-time officer in the Royal Hungarian *Honvéd*." The other
passage is contained in the brooding of Steve Turner over
the collapse of the Grogan legend: "He was sick of myths,
sick of bushrangers and sick of his own juvenile idealism.
What was now left of heroism? He might spend his days

debunking phoney legends. It would be a profitable trade. . . . Australia was a country like any other. Everything was a ring-in: from now on he would take nothing for granted" (p. 335). Almost like an afterthought, this casts a long retrospective glance over the book. Is it possible that not all our absurdities are comically harmless?

Martin has, it seems, accepted this country; it is his and he is its, and he can allow himself to laugh at its absurdities. Coming upon them fresh, he is sensitively alert to them. We, living here since childhood, have assimilated them like bread. We know that these things are funny, even hilarious, but we sometimes need to have our attention directed to them before we are aware that they exist at all.

There is a qualification to all this. Behind the author quietly stands a sort of other self, sardonic, mature, judicial. It is not only this land that has its absurdities: put that *alter ego* anywhere, and the maturity would have its unspoken comment. The novel is so funny, the leavening of the serious so light, that it is easy to forget this quality in Martin. He is essentially adult, and yet has not forgotten youth. Few of our writers are such sophisticated people. This novel is so much more a confirmation of citizenship, of belonging, than any naturalization papers could be. It is in its way a tempered love letter to this country where, to our good fortune, he has decided to remain.

Not to be content with seven books, two of them acclaimed in their time as almost models of their kind, and a couple of others containing short stories inevitably anthologized— this might indicate restless ambition. At the age of seventy-five to see in addition one's longest book appear—this might confirm the verdict. Yet it seems probable that Frank Dalby Davison's *The White Thorntree*[2] is not, and was not intended as, the crown of his ambition.

This enormous novel, running to almost half a million words, invites statistical treatment. To inhabit this territory many characters are needed. If we include the twenty-two relatives of two of the chief characters, the number is nearly seventy. It may be remarked that the twenty-two relatives play almost no part at all in the rest of the narrative. But the other forty to fifty characters make their solitary or repeated entries later, each serving to illustrate some part of the thesis that is the substance of the novel. Their interactions or intertwinings are mostly sexual. It is difficult to give an accurate estimate of these encounters. Three of the characters, promiscuous at certain periods and popular among their acquaintances, run up a tally that must be formidable but is at the same time indefinite. One male, for instance, is recorded as sleeping at one period with three or four of his acquaintances every week; but we are not told if they are the same three or four women or if his tastes are more diversified. Those beddings and layings that can be approximately listed number nearly fifty. Even the most expectant reader can hardly complain.

The theme, then, is a basic concern, sexuality, but the stress laid upon it incurs a possible danger—boredom. To obviate this, Davison varies time, place, persons, and types of encounter. This last is especially notable: we are shown most of the more or less normal varieties in profusion, ranging from masturbation, fetishism, rape, homosexuality, lesbianism, exhibitionism, erotic reverie, obsession, adultery, to everyday marital coitus. And even within these sub-species there are seldom two examples alike, except perhaps for the last named. The reasons that move the characters to stray in these directions from suburban orthodoxy are equally varied—ennui, jealousy, doubt, malice, unsatisfied desire, revenge, and all the obscure and ineffable promptings that even the victim can give no name to.

Anyone who should come upon such a summary as this, not having read the book, would be tempted to classify it without more ado. By its obsessive theme and its preoccupation with the physical manifestations of it, the novel must surely be pornographic. No verdict could be more mistaken. The treatment of the individual acts of sex, for example, is seldom if ever stimulating, and some readers indeed may find it positively anti-erotic. There are no four-letter words; indeed Davison goes to almost comic lengths in his diverse labelling of the various genitalia. This circumlocution, then, is never coarse. Nor is it, on the other hand, clinical. It may even verge on the romantic when the feelings of the participants are tender and responsive. Davison's attitude is that sex is essentially healthy, and he imbues certain of his characters with the appropriate sentiments.

From such attitudes, salacity is very unlikely to emerge. And the style, the overt expression of Davison's tone, reinforces the edification. It is for the most part a formal style; it can even be prim, the pursed mouth utterance of a maiden aunt, and then it is irresistibly reminiscent of last century. A reader frequently enough may encounter such incredible locutions as: "Each waking hour was filled with pleasurable diversion"; and, equally unbelievable: "It quickly became their object to arrive simultaneously at the culmination of their tender exertions and, being well suited to each other, they rapidly became adept at this, though they failed to observe that they were never further lost from each other than in yielding to the convulsive seizure with which nature crowned their efforts" (p. 13).

The novel is, then, an unusual work, and any reader must ask himself what intention lay behind it. Davison's foreword may go some little way towards providing an answer. The novel, he says, deals with the difficulties of some persons in a society where "there is no generally approved and openly arranged outlet for sexuality" before marriage and "no endorsed and socially viable outlet for romantic proclivities" after it. Some people rebel against the restraints; others, perplexed in the extreme, flounder miserably; and members of both classes often enough end up in law court or asylum or morgue. Despite all this, Davison disclaims any intention of advocating particular social changes or of drawing a moral —"your fictioneer is limited to exposition". The theme to be expounded is the inadequacy of any past, present, and indeed future society in satisfying "the complex and changing needs of every individual". Even the changing economic status of women and the availability of contraceptive devices have introduced as many new problems as they have solved old ones.

This foreword reads like a notation prefixed to some sociological thesis, and is couched in prose as little exhilarating. Its confident assertion that no society can cater for the needs of every person is hardly a revelation. It needs no ghost come from the grave to tell us that. But the foreword is unusual in that it exists at all—a preface to a novel, defensive in its way, overtly frank, but guarded in its terms. And it really does not tell us why the particular theme was chosen. All men and women find themselves in some ways inadequate to society and society in turn inadequate to them. The reasons are very many—complexes of envy, egoism, credulity, ambition, and so on through the gamut of our frailties. But why concentrate almost completely on sex? It is not that a reader objects to such a choice; but he wonders why it was made. Possibly the story may help us.

It is a very long, not very complicated, mostly episodic, and often repetitive narrative, set in Sydney and its suburbs in the twenty years of the inter-war period. The characters who are seen most often are four, two married couples—Jeff and Norma Mitchell, and Tom and Pam Gillespie. Each marriage gradually stales. Tom turns to Norma, who is in turn attracted to him. But whereas she is seeking reassurance, Tom finds himself more deeply committed. This is something of a recurrent pattern in the book: it is nearly always a case of *l'un qui aime, et l'autre qui se laisse aimer*. Finally, in a confusion of exasperation and calculation and compassion, she yields to him. The next time he comes to her house she closes the door in his face with a deliberated finality. Tortured and frustrated, he gradually sinks into a condition of drink and idleness. His slow recovery is aided by women, whom he uses as surrogates or refuges. This theme also is recurrent: men and women nearly always use one another, Davison writes, even when they think they are devotedly in love. The ironical conclusion to Tom's career is a second marriage. He falls in love with a widow, who, like him, is recovering from an unhappy affair. With backward glances unobserved by the other, each feels sure that this is a happy match.

Jeff Mitchell is less fortunate. At a party he accompanies Margaret Tesdale to her home to bring back more liquor. There, alcoholically amorous, he kisses her. He finds his mild advances so ardently returned that there is only one thing for a gentleman to do. The situation is the opposite of the last: this time it is the woman who loves. When at long last

Jeff finds that he is more drawn to Margaret than he had thought, he resumes the relationship; but, discovering he is not the only suitor, he rejects her. From then on his course is like that of Tom Gillespie: bitterness, drink, and a succession of women. At length he encounters Lyn Sheridan, who like him has had her share of unhappiness but is now, as she thinks, proof against life. " 'Falling in love' ", she says to him, " 'is simply letting it make an idiot of you.' " They agree to marry, when a woman he has deserted, neurotic and jealous, shoots him. Lyn kills herself with chloral. The prospect of at least one happy union in the long train of griefs in the book is summarily aborted.

These two men, Tom Gillespie and Jeff Mitchell, are the main focus of attention. But there are dozens of other characters who are in various fashions similar victims. Roger Tesdale, Margaret's husband, who had become impotent, is confident that he may be cured if a woman is frightened or resistant. So he approaches Margaret, but without success. Madly jealous, he keeps watch upon her and, while she and a lover are engaged, enters the room and batters the man to death with a piece of iron piping. He anticipates punishment by jumping over a cliff.

A very different variety of sexuality is provided by Leo Taunton, intelligent, considerate, charming, almost the professional seducer. Suddenly, to his own and the reader's surprise, he discovers he is really homosexual. He becomes infatuated with a young man who, unexpectedly finding himself to be now no longer homosexual but heterosexual, marries secretly and goes off. Leo seeks news from a lesbian who bears him a grudge. With malicious relish she taunts him, and Leo, beside himself with rage, strangles her. He is later condemned to death.

These are but selected examples, though admittedly the most notable, for it would be impossible to detail the permutations and combinations of the long list of victims. Indeed, it is difficult to keep the characters and connections in mind without notations. So this summary gives hardly any indication of the vast irregular pattern that is the book. Only a reading could be expected to give the reader what the foreword does not provide—a reason for the writing. It hardly does that; in fact it does not accord with the foreword. It is not merely the defects of society that cause sexual relations to be unhappy. In the novel we find parents, good and well-meaning, to blame for ill advice and bad training; aberrations of taste and behaviour that are peculiarly individual and seemingly innate; accidents of time and place and opportunity; and normal instincts that suddenly are erased or modified or inverted. In this black recountal there are very few gleams of light. There are the occasional terse cynical comments, but only one or two scraps of humour remain in a reader's memory, as for instance the sidelong glance at the ambitious wife of a professional politician: "She granted him sex relief as if, on her side, at any rate, it were a shared experience only to the extent that it was a duty to the electorate" (p. 378).

No marriage is seen to have prospects of being happy for long except two, and one of these is only half happy, a compromise. The other is perhaps ironical, a cautionary tale, the marriage of two celibates, Wilfred Packer (aged seventy-two) and Margaret Fallon (aged sixty-eight). This is a withered idyll. Sex, it seems, is harmless only when you are too old for it. But those who perforce devote their hearts and souls to love and their bodies to sex have no choices. Only two of Dorothy Parker's four lines apply to them:

Whose love is given overwell
Shall look on Helen's face in hell,
Whilst they whose love is thin and wise
May view John Knox in paradise.

The relentless dwelling on the one theme is underlined by the woodenness of the characters and the sometimes drab formality of the style. The grim Depression years receive no treatment. Even the milieu is barely sketched. These men and women are observed as it were *in vacuo*. And as *in vacuo* no sounds are heard, so there is hardly any dialogue.

It would have taken a more gifted writer than Davison to transform this huge mass of experiences into a comely work. It is tempting, as perhaps the opening paragraphs of this analysis witness, to make fun of the novel. Nothing would be easier than to guy its frequent absurdities. Yet, as one reads, these cease to be so obtrusive. The iterated calamities begin to seem self-subsistent, as though they had little need of style or structure in their presentation, or of any comment but their own mute presence. There broods over them an exhalation of their very multitude, a sense almost of fatality. As readers, we know that life, however selectively illustrated, can hardly be like this. But, though unwilling to believe and even reluctant to continue, we find our resistance abraded. Unless we are impatient enough, we can succumb to this unshaken disbelief in happiness. It is, so to speak, the author and not his book that overcomes us. The novel, we know, meant much to Davison, what with the long years of writing, the unsuccessful search for a publisher willing to accept its bulk and its contentious material, until at last the costly limited edition. It was of enormous importance to the man. It is an obsessional book. And that is perhaps its significance. In it lies still hidden the reason for its composition—some deep-seated trauma? some deepening despair? some irrational *idée fixe* that had to find expression? The course of the story suggests a developing malaise: the movement is labouredly slow in the early parts and the misfortunes slighter; and then the characters under the flail of their recurrent desires grow less attractive, their unhappiness more insistent; the last sections are more pressing and crowded and the deaths more frequent.

This mounting urgency can have a queer effect on a reader. You may come to feel that you have been accosted by some stranger who has a tale to tell or a revelation to deliver. It is sex, he insists, sex. As the spate of words continues, however, you may feel that there is something more being meant, perhaps the general dottiness of life, the inescapable calamity of being human. He does not convey this with any great skill or vividness, having but two resources, volubility and sincerity. But a painful intensity is evident. It is a strangely disturbing performance. You experience a perverse fascination, not so much with what is being said as with the tortured speaker. From a reader you have changed to a listener. And then it may be borne in upon you that you are perhaps not a listener, but an eavesdropper. The grotesque monologue beats at your ears. In all decency you ought to turn away. But you do not, perhaps you cannot.

Before the publication of *A Horse of Air*[3] in 1970 the reputation of Dal Stivens, in spite of a few novels, depended mainly—some would say almost totally—upon his short stories. Most were highly individual, tentative even when quite successful, for they were exercises in fantasy and nuance. Some fifteen appeared between 1954 and 1958 in three American science fiction magazines. Some of them were odd in the extreme; others trembled often on the edge of non-existence, their elements being evanescences and hints and dubieties. Stivens seemed to be seeking the nature of reality in the untypical or the peripheral: the fantastic momentarily crystallized, a sigh the equivalent of a sentence.

If he sought reality in the short stories, he attempted even more in *A Horse of Air*. Here it is not a case of trying to ensnare reality, but of trying to analyse what has not been ensnared. The instrument in this paradoxical attempt is a device long known and used, the first-person narrative.

It has in general as many obvious dangers as obvious advantages. In this novel, for instance, it is characteristic, or is made to seem characteristic, of the narrator, Harold Craddock: he is such a person, situated as he is, as would be likely to tear off such a mixture of analysis and story. The composition serves as therapy, for he is in a mental home when he writes it—though it is not the therapy that the psychiatrist thinks he is using.

While in the institution he declares that he shot a man. But we are not told why he made such a confession. Anyhow, it is false, for the real murderer goes to the police; Craddock withdraws his statement, and is later released. It is deliberately left incomplete, we must assume, for it does not seem part of the man as we come to know him. It may have arisen from a guilt complex; but we are not told the genesis of that either. So it remains an indefinite and unsatisfactory item in the novel, which appears to be the condensed auto-biography of an unusual and gifted man.

He filters through as an oddly attractive figure, anything but ordinary. He has a considerable background of training, he is by taste a naturalist, and he has more than adequate means to indulge himself. This he does—often to his own subsequent shame and the immediate embarrassment of those near by. He can become a clown when drink and the mood are upon him. He can afford to. *Richesse oblige?* Sometimes he forgets that. It is the most serious charge we can bring against him.

Perhaps his most engaging features are his likes and loves, which can be extreme. An amiable eccentric? The words are not quite strong enough, for the phrase suggests a balance, while underneath all Craddock's overt behaviour wavers a basic instability. His is a precarious personality, which he recognizes and maintains, as it were, by an effort of will. When we have finished reading the book, we are not surprised that he should—for a period at least—have found himself needing psychiatric treatment. A doctor would probably call him a mild type of manic depressive: Craddock himself writes of his alternations of inertness and euphoria.

That is one level on which the book may be read, the level of autobiography. But this is an over-simplification. In such novels the narrator by convention is automatically accepted; and he starts, he tells, he finishes. Here it is not so. There are four characters, each with a contribution to make—an editor, a psychiatrist, Craddock the chief figure, and Joanna his wife. It is the editor who opens the account. He vouches, as it were, for Craddock, who to his way of thinking is sane. The psychiatrist is vouched for by Craddock, and in turn he vouches for Craddock. So far as he is concerned, Craddock is insane. Craddock, in other words, is to be created before he starts his story. We have a convention within a convention, and the effect is not a reinforcement but a rarefaction. To be vouched for implies a need, and here it is the need for an identity, a personality.

This ambivalent Craddock, the ghost who is to cast a shadow, does little to help definition. He has an odd gift of truth—he tells us when he is lying. After that, truth necessarily becomes an ambiguity. Unlike Pilate, we wait for an answer; like Pilate, we are sceptical of receiving one. Did Leo, his mistress's rejected lover, really shadow them in Sydney? Was Leo the mysterious figure on the fringe of their expedition to the Centre? Who disabled the Land-Rover—Leo in revenge? Craddock in one of his abortive attempts at suicide? Or was it an accident or a delusion? Within the fiction there are fictions. Stivens, confronting the difficult, has converted it to the impossible.

It is a quite deliberate act of art. And the tremulous outlines of human identity are rendered vaporous by the solidities of nature. These are found in Joanna's account of the expedition to the Centre and the search for the night parrot. Interwoven into Craddock's real or fictitious accounts of his movements and motives, pages from her diary offer us vivid vignettes, filled with the heat, the rain, the mud, the flies, the spinifex, the food, and the earthy presence of members of the expedition. So the enigma of Craddock becomes the more insistent by contrast. If he can hardly be said to dominate the book, he certainly is our main concern.

Despite him, however, two minor characters manifest a spiky insistent presence. One is Dr Sullivan, the psychiatrist at the mental hospital where Craddock is for a time confined. He talks with a professional patience to this no doubt exasperating inmate, doing what is protrayed as his misguided and absurd best to dig down to the roots of delusion. Craddock does not like him at all; he finds the closest approximation to his tormentor in the natural kingdom— the short-necked swamp tortoise of Western Australia (*Pseudemydura umbrina* Siebenrock)— and so he concocts fictitious stories of his childhood, at the same time concealing the memoirs that make up the novel. In the preface the editor in apparent naivety states that Sullivan later objected to publication of the memoirs—very naturally, we may think, in view of the way in which they present him. But the reason he gives is that they form "a tangled complex of falsehood, truth, half-truth and phantasy, which only a psychiatrist such as himself could unravel". The editor concludes with the statement that Sullivan "requested that I should make clear in this preface that he was not as ignorant of German and other literature as Harry Craddock claimed." And last there is his note: that Sullivan insisted on the insertion of the analysis of a dream of Craddock's. This analysis of sexual symbolism reads to a layman rather like a parody, which

is the very term the doctor applies to Craddock's version of
his dream. (The doctor is not altogether a fool.) But the
analysis is entertaining, and is reminiscent of some modern
explications of literary works—for instance, Christopher
Caudwell's hilariously serious treatment of society as found
in *The Tempest*, removed "from the rottenness of bourgeois
society. . . . there is an exploited class—Caliban, the bestial
serf—and a "free" spirit who serves only for a time—Ariel,
apotheosis of the free wage-labourer."

The other character, the editor, shrouded in vague
anonymity, is even more subtly sketched in. He is, he tells
us in his preface, a naturalist, and has been acquainted with
Craddock for some years, but was not a close friend. As
trustee of the text, he speaks dutifully of the man who has
entrusted this autobiography to him. But his most rewarding
contributions are his conscientious footnotes. He notes dis-
parities between the narrative and statements made by others;
he checks doubtful points; he clarifies doubts; he annotates
what the reader may not know; he gives the dates of birth
and death if he thinks a name requires them. In short, he
adds footnotes, and most of them have a sort of idiotic charm.
When Craddock quotes from Ernest Giles the explorer, who
writes that he called a green oasis in the ranges the Vale
of Tempe, the editor's footnote runs: "The Vale of Tempe,
renowned from ancient times, lies between Mt Olympus and
Mt Ossa in Thessaly. It was sacred to Apollo." One can
almost see his spectacles shining with scholarly enthusiasm.
He has gone dutifully to his Lempriere.* All this may be
a sort of mock-serious device to buttress the pretence of
autobiography, or perhaps it is meant to throw further light
on Craddock. At all events it has the additional advantage
of providing us with this editorial wiseacre, a miniature
miniature we should not wish to be without.

The novel is told in a style of apparently unstudied ease,
which has the immediate capacity to engage a reader's

---

* John Lempriere (1765–1824), classical scholar whose *Classical
  Dictionary*, first published in 1788, has been frequently revised since
  then. The English poet John Keats (1795–1821) used an early
  edition of it.

attention even in things not obviously inviting. This power to fishhook the reader is of course no mere accident; it seems natural, but it has been moulded and polished by years of writing. In this novel it is most effectively exhibited, dealing as it does with recalcitrant material, in the middle sections. Here the characters move about in the desert west of Alice Springs in search of the night parrot (*Geopsittacus occidentalis*). Neither the search nor the quarry is calculated to provide universal delight. No man, said the grim American humorist W.C. Fields in one of his more abrasive sessions, no man who hates children and dogs can be wholly bad. Though some may consider this rather too sweeping an assertion, the point is well taken. And Fields might profitably have added nature to his list. Not all of us love to distraction the romantic chasm or the deserts from which the prophets come. Nor are all enamoured of the denizens.

There is of course a savour of guilt in this. We may smile at letters to English newspapers or notations in the monthlies where bird-watchers and bird-listeners announce the advent of the great booming bittern in some remote marshland; but we feel, conditioned as we are by childhood training and reading in Wordsworth, that we ought to respond with some measure of spiritual joy to such news. The black truth is, however, that many do not. And such people, likewise, are not basically concerned with Craddock's search for his parrot. But the style will carry them where they have no intention of going. Indeed, were it not for the adjectives, which are both effective and just a little sought-for, Stivens's writing might well be thought to fulfil Conrad's criterion—an almost transparent medium that hardly comes between the reader and the reality. It is also the medium of a writer soaked in other writers. It draws on Shakespeare, Donne, Joyce, and Eliot, to mention a few, and perhaps *Prufrock* is a favourite. All this is something of a bonus for some readers—how satisfactory to pick up the brief allusions so casually dropped in! (And at the same time how alarming to feel that one may be passing over others all unrecognized!)

A further bonus is esoteric information. Anyone who wishes to know may learn the method of curing a dog of the habit of chasing cars; or what attitude is adopted by a *beta* mouse when confronted by an *alpha*; or what coloured lights to use on captive birds so that they think it is moonlight; or what to do in a jeep in a spinifex fire.

The novel, then, has its varied interests. But there still are only two main themes—the character Craddock, and Craddock's expedition. What led Stivens to this? One reason for writing must have been the reluctance to waste good material (Thrift, thrift, Horatio). How Stivens came by it is not stated. It seems likely enough that he himself went on some such trip to the Centre. If he did not, but gained the information at second hand, then the novel is a tiny miracle or, if that is too portentous, a substantial conjuring trick. For the expedition and what goes with it are described in detail. It tastes, smells, looks, and sounds like actuality. It is a pervasive and vivid experience. If a writer has such accumulated material at his disposal, then it would be a literary crime to discard it. So it is assimilated into a novel. It is only after reading the book, and not feeling aware of all this during the reading, that one thinks of looking back at the nature of the expedition and its significance in the narrative. And then one admires the transformations that have been effected, the assimilations of factual matter into the plausible form of fiction.

Another motive was perhaps the wish to be Craddock. If God made man in His own image, the novelist, a lesser god, often makes a man greater than himself, but still basically in his own image. Craddock is like his creator Stivens: he is a fifth generation Australian, is something of an expert on azaleas, is interested in music and the theatre, has studied animal behaviour and has published his findings in overseas journals. And Craddock (Stivens?) tells his own story in the first person.

But if Craddock were only Stivens he would not be Craddock. He is more than Stivens, more indeed than practically any one of us. And Stivens, as if to challenge us, perhaps as a double bluff, quotes William James's comment on the roles that most of us dream of playing, the people we should like to be but know we cannot—"handsome and fat and well dressed, and a great athlete, and make a million a year, be a wit, a *bon-vivant*, and a lady-killer, as well as a philosopher; a philanthropist, statesman, warrior, and African explorer, as well as a 'tone-poet' and saint." Craddock goes some way towards fulfilling these desires. He is a millionaire; he got firsts at Oxford and a science degree at Sydney; he is independent, has had three wives and numerous mistresses, is proficient in more than one tongue, and can devote himself to the most recondite researches if the fancy takes him. Of course, the mere possession of millions may not ensure happiness; but, as the modern addendum runs, if you have millions, who needs happiness? So that it might be pleasant to be a Craddock.

Was Stivens tempted? Probably. He half yields, half renounces. It's nonsenee . . . let's be sensible. . . . The fable of the sour grapes is thereupon exemplified once more, and so he puts Craddock in a mental hospital, where nobody would wish to follow him. Still . . . on the other hand. . . . And so he finds he has not the heart to keep him there. Craddock is released, goes off on another expedition, returns, and meets the editor for a talk and a drink. He is unaware that he has less than a page to live. He steps into the road and is killed by a truck. It is a very summary dismissal of a daydream. And the ironical thing is that it is quite gratuitous; while Stivens is capable of writing novels like this, he does not need to envy Craddock.

In one of Compton Mackenzie's novels an elderly character talks to a young friend about some youthful first novels. These may or may not begin with family life, but certainly schooldays are a *sine qua non*, where the author-hero may be misunderstood or he may not, but is at least noticeable. He invariably encounters sex in some form or other, and this can be a disturbing experience. At the university the thwarted spirit comes more into his own and encounters people interested in literature (or music, or mysticism, or). There he can find belated fulfilment in sex embraced, religion discarded, and political beliefs transmogrified. When he graduates he writes a novel about all this, and it is occasionally successful.

The young man blushes as he listens, for he too has just written a first novel and the pattern conforms to what he is hearing.

Such first novels are less frequent now. But if you are committed to literature and have written poems, which are shorter and do not require the persistent physical effort— among other efforts—that a novel does, then it may seem that a novel is next in the natural order of things. But a saving sophistication makes you wary of the thinly veiled autobiography. A decent camouflage of interests and themes is advisable. Instead of yourself, an acquaintance may serve as a focus. And if he is in the novel, then you yourself are naturally, even necessarily, present as well, so that you may introduce him, accompany him, and possibly farewell him. A further device should add the last touch to the disguise: enclose it as it were in a frame. If you are seen, at the opening of the novel, in process of doing something, then a mere triviality can serve to remind you of the friend. The flashback is effected, the novel starts, with other flashbacks *en route,* and at the end you shake your head in wonderment at where your fancy has so naturally led you. And you are back in the process of doing the something you were doing at the start.

You can even introduce an additional refinement. To underline the fact that it is the friend, not yourself, who is the main attraction, you note some inexplicable trifle that stresses the oddity of the friend. That, indeed, that was characteristic of him, it was part of the fascination that induced you, almost in despite, to take up a reluctant pen to tell his story. As David Malouf puts it in *Johnno*[4]: "The book I always meant to write about Johnno will get written after all . . . he had me hooked. As he had, of course, from the beginning. I had been writing my book about Johnno from the moment we met" (pp. 11-12). To say we don't believe Malouf is to pay him a compliment, to enter the conspiracy, to join with him in the literary jape.

The jape, however, has taken charge of the author. Johnno, the narrator's friend, is to be the lure, distracting our attention while the author enters unnoticed. But a third contestant has slipped in and occupies at frequent intervals those parts of the stage where the spotlight rests. This intruder is Brisbane. It turns out to be the book's real concern, a background against which people move and things happen. It is brought before us by appeals to sight and hearing, touch and even smell: pubs and brothels, corners and alleys, the river and its banks, gardens and backyards, wooden walls and iron roofs—the whole range of dubious items that make up an old-fashioned entirety that as child and adolescent and young man the author carries off as indelible memories. In even greater particularity there are the individual details of rooms and their contents. Indeed, furniture and food have a special place. The most lyrical passage in the book, for instance, is on lollies:

> Lift the tissue, take a deep breath, and there they were. A jar of boiled lollies, glistening pink and yellow, and in every conceivable shape: scallop-shells, ovals, little barber-pole cylinders with pinched ends, medallions with roses in their depths, even some bite-sized candy-striped pillows that smelled (I could actually smell them) of a medicinal spice like the ambulance tent at Scarborough. [P. 168]

For any reader familiar with the reality evoked, such parts of the book are extremely effective in their nostalgic savour. They are authentic and unromanticized except for the haze of the years between, which gives them the charm that mist confers upon even an unromantic scene. This really is how it was.

Even the misspellings look like a faithful adherence to old memories—*paroxism, Cooparoo, Grammer, fulfillment, Jeu de Paumes*. We can almost imagine them deliberate, for they are the forms which as youngsters we continued to spell that way for a few—or many—years. If only Malouf had intended them so, we could readily find it in our hearts to applaud the subtle deceit.

Malouf's reactions to past and present are not those of other personages who have returned to our shores after years in other lands. They will talk of changes; they want to. Malouf is under no such constraint: his heart is given to the buildings and food he once knew, and refuses to be comforted by substitutes. Here at any rate he is like Charles Lamb, who was also interested in furniture and food: "Any alteration, on this earth of mine, in diet or in lodging, puzzles and discomposes me. My household-gods plant a terrible fixed foot, and are not rooted up without blood."

Charming as the book is in style and vignette, and however
evocative, one has to be careful not to overestimate it on this
last score. Anyone who knows the period and place cannot
but respond to Malouf's re-creation of parts of the overgrown
country town. A name is given, of street or suburb or
building, and, conjured up with a phrase, the old and
sometimes vanished reality rises before the reader. Momentarily he is back where he once was, and he perforce feels
a sort of gratitude for this rejuvenation. The same thing
occurs in, say, poetry, where an untutored reader finds a
poem effective in one way and therefore good in all ways.
An example as apposite as any is Dylan Thomas's elegy on
the death of his aunt. Many Australians of a certain age
who have been at the funeral of some aged relative must find
the poem bizarre in its immediacy, as though the scene of
their childhood were recovered, for furniture and customs
must have been much the same then as in smaller English
or Welsh towns. But what is unconsciously being made on
such occasions is not an evaluation of novel or poem but an
evaluation of memories.

If Brisbane, then, is the hero or heroine of the novel, what
of Johnno, the overt eponym? He need not worry any reader.
Malouf has been saying: Bear with me a little, and join with
me in seeing how we can ring the changes on a rather trite
theme—Looking Backwards. A variation here and there, an
elaboration, an omission, an altered stress, and we almost
have a new genre. . . . It would be an unresponsive reader
who would not collaborate. In doing so, he comes to recognize
that Johnno is of little consequence. Johnno appears most
frequently in the schooldays, less frequently at the university,
and sporadically after that. He dies at the end of the novel,
whether by suicide or accident does not matter. So he bulks
large when he is small, but when he grows up—if he ever
does—he is minor. And this is how he should be. Malouf
does his best for him, but nobody adult could find him of
much attraction.

At school he fascinates the others by his apparent re-
belliousness. But he is a rebel without a cause—except
himself. What lies behind it nobody knows. The only passage
to suggest complexity or subtlety in the boy deals with a visit

the narrator pays to Johnno. To impress Johnno, an expert in shop-lifting, he pinches two articles and takes them with him. This does not impress Johnno: "His embarrassment was for *me*. What I had done was utterly out of character—all I had revealed was my low opinion of *him*. . . . He was quieter and more generous than I would have thought possible" (p. 44). This is well said. It may even be too well said, for the boys at the time are twelve or thirteen years old, and many readers may find these emotional nuances a little unnatural at that age.

As he grows older, Johnno becomes, for the reader at any rate, more and more unpleasant. He can behave outrageously in public—provided he can arrange for the blame to fall on somebody else; he is brazen and even arrogant if there is no real danger, but he is obsequious in a situation if real discomfort is likely to come his way; he is not a man for a friend to trust, for he will eat when hungry the share his companion needs; and in the face of all this he expects friends —if there are any who haven't found him out by this time—to come to his help: indeed, a friend is merely a man to be used.

The only quality he has is his honesty to himself. Hypocrisy being, as the adage goes, the tribute that vice pays to virtue, we all of us try to justify or hide our failings— we may even try to cure them. Johnno will have none of this: he is not so much shameless as indifferent. He is as he is—let them do what they like about that.

This is not endearing: it is merely surprising. We are not shocked at the natural behaviour of a leech or a scorpion, but we are shocked that a human being should resemble both and apparently think this natural. So any fascination Johnno may have for us at the start evaporates as the novel progresses. We come to find him distasteful. Then we lose interest. This is a probability that Malouf must have foreseen, for he attributes to Johnno an element of mystery. He is spoken of as having some inner life, as though he concealed an enigma that would be worth solving. And near the end of the book this mystery, we are told, still resides in that fascinating figure—even his death is a mystery. Most of us will remain cheerfully unconvinced. That mystery, if ever it existed, is a bagatelle.

But perhaps there remains for us a further mystery—the puzzle why anyone in real life should have found Johnno of any great interest at all. If we feel this, it is because we are readers: we did not know Johnno in our youth. Malouf did, and has remained his captive ever since. (My old headmaster, remarked a venerable bishop, was a martinet and a man of impressive personality. When I recall him, I still think of myself as a boy. If he were suddenly to appear before me in the street, and order me to bend over, I should obey without a moment's hesitation.) To be puzzled is to pay momentary tribute to Malouf's legerdemain. Then we return to our senses and recall what we have recognized all along, the role designed for Johnno. For Johnno, of course (how in keeping to end with food!), is only a red herring.

Thirty years ago Frank Hardy hacked out of Australian private and political life his savage representation of violence and corruption—*Power Without Glory*. The charge of libel unsuccessfully brought against him deepened the impact of the book. Since then he has had to wear the title as a sort of label, for despite other works he has been known primarily as the author of that volume. To produce a rival out of the same material was impossible; to offset the memory, to become a novelist of a different quality, would be to leaven political material with something else. It is conceivable that *But the Dead Are Many*[5] had some such genesis.

Comment on the novel varies according to a reader's knowledge and interests. It is for one thing a novel of ideologies. The scene is Sydney, with Moscow a parallel and contrast. The active figures are John Morel, a Communist intellectual; his friend Jack, half participant, half observer; Trevor Duncan, chairman of the Party Industrial Committee; and Claude Redpath, secretary of the Party Control Commission. The period is indefinite, since names are not necessarily intended to fix dates; Buratakov, the main Russian character in the book, is presumably the historical Bukarin, who was shot in 1938; Stalin died in 1953; the

Russian invasion of Hungary occurred in 1956, the invasion of Czechoslovakia in 1968.

This indefiniteness is of minor consequence for a novel; it is minor even for this book as a documentary, since it is not intended as a history of Communism in the USSR or an outline of the movement in Australia. The political moves themselves are of importance for those readers interested in such themes, for those who want to see Hardy's changing views since *Power Without Glory*, and for those who have enough background knowledge to recognize characters and incidents under their disguises. Other concerns are the Party manoeuvres in Australia, such as the divisions between Moscow-orientated hard-liners and those who are presented as anti-bureaucratic sociological idealists.

Whether the picture is objectively accurate or personally biased is a matter for political historians. The point is that here is one field where we might have expected Hardy to do what no other Australian novelist has managed—to illuminate political infighting. It is surprising, indeed, that more has not been written on this theme, for Australian history has been social, political, and economic in its essence. Vance Palmer's trilogy—*Golconda, Seedtime, The Big Fellow* —was wide enough and long enough to have encompassed this. And Palmer surely had enough contacts and access to enough sources to have given us revelations. There is indeed a general outline of a man rising to political power; but the bones and gristle are not there. Palmer was probably too kind as man and as author: he does not afford us insights into the thuggery of the committee room, the promises and bargains made, the influence of word and gesture and report, the treachery and envy and jealousy, the commitments and hypocrisy that provide the hierarchical pattern in party and group. The nearest Hardy gets to this is the vivid glimpse of the German Communist arrested in a Russian apartment building, the subdued life of self-imprisonment of a political victim's widow, the watchful hag by the door. But these are the fictional clichés of the intrigue novel, not the inner workings of power politics. This still remains to be done in our literature. Hardy's *Power Without Glory* gave us intrigue and corruption, but that bristly monster is too eccentric to be compared with this more sophisticated and more sinister novel. The nearest we have to the stew with the lid off is found in articles written by sardonic and irreverent journalists. But these explain, they tell us, they do not show us; dialogue, for example, is almost invariably—and understandably—absent. So the vividness of actuality is also absent.

On the other hand, though Hardy's novel gives little detailed insight into what goes on behind the scenes in a particular political party, except for a brief mention of rigged votes in an election, it has a certain unintended spread of application. Being general, all it needs is to have names changed, and the outline of jealousies and anxieties and resentments is one that most Australians, with a healthy distrust of politicians, would be willing to apply to any political party of left or right or centre. Here Hardy has wrought better than he knew.

It is not so sure that he has done so in the main theme of the novel. Here the aim is overt—to meld politics and psychology, to trace the movement to suicide of John Morel. The work is done by his friend Jack, who is shown as encountering, in his investigations, some of the obscurities of the human spirit. We learn, bit by bit, the sources of Morel's disturbed personality. His father commits suicide when Morel is thirteen, leaving behind his dominating wife. Morel later enters a Catholic seminary, but is converted to Communism. The pressure of his mother leads, seemingly, to a mother-fixation, and with his wife he becomes impotent. In practical affairs he is a mixture of incompetence—he cannot even manage a shopping errand—and unconscious dishonesty. His hunger strike during an industrial dispute provides an injection of self-reliance, but he lives on that reputation for years. It is all he has, except the Party, which is life and mother for him. This may seem enough to bear, in all conscience, especially when stresses within the Party and mingled kindness and accusations from colleagues (mother turning against him) are added to the emotional burdens. But Hardy wants something more. Using parallels from the Russian trials, he presents Morel as a deliberate suicide: if a failure in life, he is to be a success in death. He leaves, tucked behind the hotel notice in the room where he dies, a testament of explanation and exculpation. This and his death, he hopes, will influence Party ideology: Communist bureaucracy is to see that human love and compassion and understanding are of primary import. This change of motivation, from emotional disturbance to deliberate rational intention, may seem to some readers rather implausible.

Hardy takes one further step. The tortured Morel is no commonplace cipher in a system, but a man of intellectual stature. This is, we can assume, one of the main justifications for Jack's long commitment to his task, for the object of a search must have an importance. So Morel is often spoken of as something akin to a genius. To make us believe that he is lies beyond Hardy's power. If a great poet is to be portrayed, then we should be satisfied with some of his verse, and this is never likely to be provided. If it is not, then we depend on assertion or the opinions of other characters, and are likely to remain incredulous. A good modern example is found in Lawrence Durrell, who almost persuades us in *Mountolive* that Pursewarden is a man of exceptional talent. Henry Handel Richardson in *Maurice Guest* offers us Schilsky, a musical prodigy. The accompanying description of his composition and his rendition of it, elaborated with not too many technicalities, very nearly carries conviction. But the burden of demonstration weighs very heavy on any writer who makes such an attempt.

Hardy's task is less demanding than either of these, for Morel is a spokesman for some of the Communist doctrines, and it should have been possible to provide, say, a paraphrase of some of the classical texts in the field as evidence. Instead, characters affirm, without illustration or reference to possible effects, that Morel is a shining light in propaganda. We do not believe them. Nor do Morel's visionary meanderings at the close of the novel convince us, however well they convey in their voluble confusion the spiritual turmoil that he is trying to transform.

One affiliation of Hardy's novel, oddly enough, is with the spy thriller. The psychological analyses, however artless, and the biographical threads, however confused, are woven with the political and doctrinal elements. The two countries concerned are Australia and the USSR, and the influence of one on the other and the changing reactions of characters form a considerable part of the book. In a novel of such a kind the form and pressure are best shown in individuals, but except for the account of Buratakov and his trial, and the lingering effects on his widow and daughters, we are given theory and comment rather than personal action. Here the conventional novels of this type are superior, such as the popular fiction of Deighton, Le Carré, and Forsyth. However slick, they are highly professional, and they provide almost unremitting tension and violence. They present a problem, with a solution that is often unexpected. This tightness gives a unity to such works that is lacking in Hardy. But though in this respect he is their inferior, his spread, almost his diffuseness, allows him other effects. This novel, as was suggested earlier, is vaguely sinister, for both characters and readers are often denied explanations. With his stress on the psychological, Hardy has managed to invest politics and persons with a sense of threat. Things are said and done that seem to have more than one motivation; something is left to be guessed, or feared, and the unknown is disturbing.

It seems reasonable enough to think that Hardy attempted in this novel to do what he did not do in *Power Without Glory*—what indeed he would probably admit readily enough —and that is to write a novel of literary merit. That early documentary novel had its own strength, but few would claim it had many pretensions to style. It is very different with *But the Dead Are Many*. The very first sentence strikes a new note: "I drove through the city as if in flight." Hardy could not have written that in his first novel; indeed he probably would not have wanted to. But this latest novel is a study in human reactions and relations that demands a less blunt pen. The danger, however, has been one of overwriting, of being formal where such tones are out of place or obtrusive or pretentious. Examples are numerous enough; one may suffice: "I resolved to depart quickly." This would be just possible in the third person: in the first person it is too much on its best grammatical behaviour. And the figures, especially similes, are sometimes strained—pressed to yield implications that are not naturally present, or inflated as though they were a comment on the portentous.

The chief devices are the narrative modes. The title page
tells the reader that this is a novel in fugue form. As a method
it has its value as a means of indicating stresses or contrasts
or reviews. But it also has its danger as distraction, so that
the reader deliberates or puzzles over significance in the
device instead of significance in the prose. Then there are
the alternations of the first-person narrators—John Morel,
with his suicide and its causes, and Jack his friend, who is
concerned to trace the last days, especially, of Morel's life.
These do not make for easy reading: narrative and statement
and comment change places abruptly and even confusingly.
An additional complication is that third-person narrative is
intermingled with these two others. Then it almost becomes
a guess who is writing—the author, or the character standing
outside himself, or another character. The overall effect of
the obliquity is a mild sort of obfuscation, a slight blurring,
as of our difficulty in understanding one another. Added to
these variations from usual narrative, there are flashbacks.
Combined with the events, which are not told in chronological
sequence, they give a sense of the haphazard. Occasionally
the sensation is that of watching actions on a stage under
strobe lights—movement momentarily frozen, darkness per-
petually flickering.

All this experimentation is of course quite deliberate. Few
who have any acquaintance with fiction since the appearance
of *Ulysses* are likely to find it very surprising or confusing.
It is a move into complex modern structure. Hardy has
changed much since *Power Without Glory*.

One cruel comment runs that he is the most improved
novelist in Australian fiction. That irony condescends to the
efforts made and the directions taken. But it does not allow
for the unexpected. It is true that, in spite of the ostensible
fugue pattern, and because of the vagaries in narrative
structure, the book can appear disorderly, even chaotic; and
it is true that Morel as a character does not have a convincing
substantiality. Yet these flaws reflect, as it were, upon a
confused period and a complicated man. (To say this not to
fall into the old fallacy of forgiving, say, an insane book
because it deals with insanity or of accepting a boring one
because it describes a bore.) One might go so far as to claim,

reversing the trite phrase, that the book has the qualities of its defects.

There is something more, an effect that Hardy presumably did not have in mind. What we are looking at is two books and two authors. One is Jack, whom we follow in his long dedicated search for anything that bears on Morel and his suicide. It is a research project erratically conducted. And as in a research project, when the pieces are gathered they are mentally assembled into a pattern that satisfies; they explain, for Jack, the mystery. But the book he envisages is yet to come. He is fortunate, for he himself is the jury. The other author is Hardy, who has written his best book, one that will gain literary recognition of a sort not previously given him. He has his book, the physical container of his patterned material. But he is less fortunate than his creature, for the jury considering the pattern is composed of all except him. It is an ironic parallel and contrast—the character, with his satisfying pattern but no book, and the creator of the character, with his book but not yet a completely satisfying pattern.

NOTES
1. David Martin, *The Hero of Too* (Melbourne: Cassell, 1965). Page references are to this edition.
2. Frank Dalby Davison, *The White Thorntreee* (Melbourne: The National Press, 1968). Page references are to this edition.
3. Dal Stivens, *A Horse of Air* (Sydney: Angus and Robertson, 1970).
4. David Malouf, *Johnno* (St Lucia: University of Queensland Press, 1975). Page references are to this edition.
5. Frank Hardy, *But the Dead Are Many* (London: Bodley Head, 1975).

The New Novel

David Ireland's *The Unknown Industrial Prisoner*,
Michael Wilding's *The Short Story Embassy*, and
Frank Moorhouse's *The Electrical Experience*

LEON CANTRELL

There is no recognized tradition of innovation and experimentation in Australian writing. Those works that drift
outside the mainstream (such as Marcus Clarke's fantasies
or Furphy's speculative novel) form local backwaters, more
often signposted than visited. Like our history, our literature
has tended to be expedient and down-to-earth. We have
preferred to call a spade a spade rather than to question
whether we are digging in the right place. Hence there has
been little theoretical discussion from our writers about the
meaning and purpose of their work and even less discussion
of its aesthetics. The series of interviews with Australian
writers published in *Southerly* over the last ten years has
frequently revealed surprise that anyone would want to ask
questions of a theoretical kind about such a practical,
everyday activity as writing. The *Bulletin* in the 1890s
exemplified this characteristically Australian approach: "Boil
it down!" adjured editor Archibald, whose theories of literature centred on the fact that only 1,360 words could be
squeezed into a column. Such writers' manifestos as we have
had have more often been opposed to modernist trends than
in support of them. One result, for Australian fiction, has
been a reluctance to move outside received concerns and
models. Patrick White, twenty years ago, spoke of the
"dreary, dun-coloured realism" and the "journalistic prose"
of much of our fiction; yet his own work, given the power
of its language and vision, is curiously uncontemporary in
its overriding concern with the sanctified individual in a
hostile society. Indeed, it is arguable that as White has

developed as a great writer his strengths have become increasingly akin to the late nineteenth-century European masters and that he has owed less and less to his earlier models—such later writers as Proust, Woolf, and Joyce. The enormous influence of White in the Australian context can thus be seen as an influence that has reinforced our antipathy to innovative writing, especially of a non-linear, non-representational kind.

Certainly the novel of ideas, the theoretical novel, has never been a central concern of our writers. Those who have recently attempted such a work (I am thinking especially of Frank Hardy's *But the Dead Are Many* and of Xavier Herbert's *Poor Fellow My Country*) have met with much critical consternation, for the *roman à thèse* here has often been confused with the partisan novel, more concerned with expounding than with exploring a particular argument. Indeed, the tradition of Australian criticism as well as of our writing has been one of engagement with practical rather than theoretical or abstract issues. Such writers as have delved in speculative or metaphysical ideas have had their knuckles soundly rapped. The paucity of writing on the history of ideas in Australia could well lead an outsider (or even an insider) to imagine that there weren't any.

Even less have our writers and critics been concerned with our (and their own) concepts of what it is the novel attempts. The continuing debate in France over the nature and status of the *nouveau roman* has no Australian counterpart or parallel. The pronouncements and practice of such writers as Michel Butor and Alain Robbe-Grillet indicate a profound dissatisfaction with conventional novelistic modes and expectations. They both insist upon the necessary complexities and difficulties of novel writing and reading. Butor sees the *roman* as a kind of "puzzle", as a "mythology difficult to unravel". Such traditional features as character and plot are held to be unimportant. Instead, Butor sees his goal as the discovery of the nearly mathematical order which lies behind the world which we have chosen to call reality.[1] The new novelist must search for new forms. "The novelist who refuses to perform this task, who demands no special effort from the reader, who does not upset him in his habits, who does not force him back on himself, making him question his most cherished opinions, certainly enjoys an easier success, but he acts as an accomplice of that profound *malaise*, that night in which we are all struggling." Far from being opposed to realism, the creation of new forms in the novel is seen as "the *sine qua non* of a more far-reaching realism".[2]

Robbe-Grillet has also argued for a new notion of realism, a new method of conceiving the relationship between fiction and life. The tangible world has no morality or meaning, he suggests. It simply *is*. The novel has sought traditionally to break down the resistance of this obstinate reality: to impose a degree of moral order or purpose. Yet "all around us, defying our pack of animistic or domesticating adjectives, things *are there*. Their surface is smooth, clear and intact, without false glamour, without transparency. The whole of our literature has not yet managed even to begin to penetrate them, to alter their slightest curve. "[3] Robbe-Grillet suggests that film, with its immediacy of object or gesture, has significantly altered the nature of our realization of reality in art. Whereas in fiction objects and gestures are important only for their meaning (a vacant chair is an absence or an expectation; a hand on a shoulder is a sign of sympathy), in film meaning becomes just one more attribute: the chair is essentially a chair and the hand a hand. In future novels, he proposes, gestures and objects will similarly be *there*, before they are *something*. And they will still be there afterwards, indifferent to the meaning which has been foisted upon them, which has reduced them to the "precarious role of utensils".[4]

Australian writers are only beginning to explore issues such as these. Very few, for instance, have questioned the relationships between the novel and other forms of artistic expression or have asked what the novel as an art form can achieve. There has been a reluctance, for example, to consider whether the conventional, narrative mode of the novel best suits the needs and interests of our present world. The concept of fiction as necessarily having a linear development emanates from a particular view of society which sees the exposition and resolution of problems as essential to its ethic of progress. If we question that ethic we must also question the continuing centrality of those art forms that reflect it. Yet the makers of Australian fiction, like the makers of Australian politics, have by and large offered the public what it wants: that which it recognizes, that with which it feels at home. The notion of the novel as an agent of social or intellectual change, in other words, presupposes not just a society in need of change but one prepared to recognize the need and strive towards it. Our society has no such reputation.

It is in the face of these unpromising traditions that David Ireland's politically and structurally radical novel, *The Unknown Industrial Prisoner*,[5] has emerged as a major work of contemporary Australian fiction. Unashamedly a thesis novel, it argues from a committed ideology, concerned to explore the very corners of it contentions in great detail. Its principal ordering device, the accretion of image after image, suggests this concern, for the accumulated structure of apparent fragments enables both writer and reader to examine each shred of evidence individually (as if reading a report with numbered paragraphs) while it enacts the view of random disharmony which is the novel's argument. A more conventionally continuous narrative would impose a misleading sense of order and coherence on Ireland's world. Equally, it would tend to preclude that tone of objective reportage the fragments allow. For they are devoted at intervals to analysis on the part of the narrator: direct interpolations challenging us to discover the underlying polemic, the socio-political patterns which the other fragments form. The narrator is more correctly the guide or commentator, speaking over and around his material, as if on the sound-track of a documentary film.

The formal organization of the various parts supports this technique. The novel's 370-odd pages are divided in to twenty-five chapters. Each of these is divided in turn, making over three hundered sections in all. In addition to the chapter headings there are titles to the smaller divisions, directing our attention yet more specifically to their concerns. All of this suggests a much more conscious effort to control the reader's responses that we expect to find in a novel. Indeed, it suggests a textbook or a manual of instruction. But to say this is to say something of the gulf which the traditional novel has carved between us and earlier prose forms. The authors of anatomies, for instance, like David Ireland, were intent on showing us their subject from all points of view, and on guiding us and commenting on our responses. Allegories too were constructed around a series of ideas rather than on the notion of a convincingly self-contained world. The skills required to read such works, as well as to write them, have lain dormant during the hegemony of the novel. In fact, the cast of over a hundred characters in the *Industrial Prisoner* reminds us of the allegory: none of them have "real" names, only such labels as relate to their place in the overall pattern —sobriquets which tell us something of their relationships to each other and to the Puroil (puerile/pure oil?) refinery where the action of the book takes place. Thus the Sumpsucker craves to be a foreman. Luxaflex, in personnel, spies on the workers from behind venetian blinds. Calamity Jane is in first-aid. It is of course Ireland's intention that such names distance us from the characters as human beings. After all, they are industrial prisoners, cogs in a vast machine, who know one another only as cogs, dehumanized and degraded by their daily contact with each other. Even the title of the novel, *The Unknown Industrial Prisoner*, suggests a monument to nameless sufferers and victims, those whose anonymity is their only measure of importance. Throughout the book we learn how people have been stripped of their humanity. Clothes are described more often than faces, cruelty is more common than kindness.

Ireland draws our attention to this aspect of his work, and to some of its broader implications, as early as the second page. The evening shift-workers are waking in the early morning. They have spent the night as usual on the floor of the locker-room, for there is not nearly enough activity to occupy them all. Yet the company insists on their attendance, on their bundying on and off, for this ritual (and their night-time discomfort) is a measure of its control over their lives. They stretch wearily and prepare to leave:"Dust and silverfish dropped from overalls and hair and boots back into the rags from which they came. Look back at the title of this chaper, it has saved me an explanation" (p. 2). The chapter is called "One Day in a Penal Colony", and of course is reminds us of the title of Alexander Solzhenitsyn's *One Day in the Life of Ivan Denisovich*, a novel about a Soviet penal colony in Siberia. The opening sentence of *Denisovich* reads, in the translation published in England and Australia: "As usual, at five o'clock that morning reveille was sounded by the blows of a hammer on a length of rail hanging up near the staff quarters."[6] Ireland's novel begins: "It was the same every morning. At ten to six reveille sounded. Mostly a broom handle was applied to the green dented side of a locker, one of sixty to hold the clothes of the men of the four shifts" (p. 1).

This first section of chapter 1 of *The Unknown Industrial Prisoner* is called "Lower Depths", the title of Maxim Gorky's play about a doss-house for impoverished workers. In relating his own work so explicitly to these earlier Russian accounts of imprisonment and poverty, and in drawing our attention to the relationship, Ireland stresses further literary and moral contexts in which we must read his novel. He wants us to see the life of his prisoners as akin to those who suffer under the worst kinds of tyranny. True, at Puroil they get up fifty minutes later, but the dust, the silverfish and rags which litter the locker-room are straight from Gorky's stage and the hut of Ivan Denisovich. The Russian connection also suggests a political context for the *Industrial Prisoner*. Western concepts of freedom have increasingly based their argument on the nature of advanced capitalist society. Within this framework, we have been told, human beings are free in a way in which they have never been before. The examples of Russian oppression which have had a wide currency in the West, such as the novels of Solzhenitsyn, have been cited as proof of the superiority of our own society and the principles upon which it is based. Ireland forces us to rethink this hypothesis. The "lower depths" of his "penal colony" are in every way as horrific as their Russian counterparts.

The Australian location and yet the wider significance of the *Prisoner's* world is again indicated by the characters we meet in this first chapter. Such figures as the Samurai, Blue Hills, Dutch Treat, and the Volga Boatman suggest that the analysis of one particular society (of which the refinery, as we shall see, is a paradigm) may well reveal truths about others. Indeed, the novel sees itself as a vision of those forces that have gone to shape our modern industrial world—the modern Australian world, specifically, but unknown industrial prisoners, like unknown soldiers, are to be found in every country. The emigrant workers in the Sydney refinery underline this sense of a universal fate as the idea of the penal colony underlines the particular weight of Ireland's local historical argument. Australia was founded by Europeans as a dumping ground for convicts, and the stench and tyranny of its origins hangs heavily over the book. Australia is thus a peculiarly apt country in which to set an account of alientation and industrial oppression. Most of the prisoners show an "inch-wide residual scar of chains" on their ankles (p. 2), the heritage of the earlier penal colony from which they have descended through six generations. Such visible signs of their imprisonment as balls and chains may no longer be seen, but the "residual scars" are both physical and mental. Growing up under the yoke and shadow of authority, these men are ill-equipped to challenge its power over their lives. In fact, the "unknown" of the title intimates their ignorance of imprisonment as it suggests our ignorance of the industrial conditions under which many in our society labour. New prisoners even scoff at the idea of their internment when it is suggested to them, revealing a naïve belief in freedom and their own ability to choose.

ASSEMBLY LINE LOVE   Ambrose turned up, a youth of twenty. Just old enough for adult pay.

"Welcome, prisoner!" said the Great White Father as he stumbled in.

"What prisoner?" asked Ambrose, lost. They passed him a can. His eyes crossed as he watched its rim approach his mouth.

"Us."

"We're not prisoners," he said stoutly. "I go home when the shift ends."

"What do you do tomorrow?"

"Come back here."

"Why not go away somewhere?"

"I'd get the sack."

"What then?"

"I'd have to get another job."
"And you're not a prisoner?"
"I can work some other place."
"Why not just stay home?"
"Cut it out. You've got to have a job."
"Then you're an industrial prisoner."
"Then everyone is."
"What difference does that make?"
"Everyone has to work for a living."
"Do they? Read the social pages."
"Working for a living is the right thing to do."
"You're crazy."
"Work is good for you."
"A good crap's better."
"I'm free to starve."
"Freedom to starve! That's it. The clause they forgot to put in the Atlantic Charter. Declaration of Human Rights. Freedom to starve."
"But if everyone—"
"—Not everyone, son—"
"—Practically everyone has to work, then it all cancels out."
"It doesn't cancel out, it adds up. We're prisoners." He could see Ambrose was excited and confused. He changed the subject. [Pp. 73-74]

Images of prison life, and an awareness of their socio-political significance, surround us from the beginning. As the evening shift-workers stretch from their sleep in the first section, it is to an account of the political realities of their world that we turn. We learn of the unplanned development of the country, of the drift of population to the cities, which have become the ghettos of our civilization. We learn of the illusions of freedom upon which our world is built. These men are free only "to choose their place of detention" (p. 3). Laws about property, loitering, and vagrancy force all but the most recalcitrant into the labour camps of the big cities. The veneer of democracy posits a number of options, but these work only within the context of accepting one of these prison jobs or starving. The bitterly ironical tone of much of the novel points out that the "infinite freedom of choice" which our society boasts for its members is ultimately only the freedom to starve "sitting, standing, asleep or awake". For once he has entered a penal colony, the prisoner finds that his relationship with his employer/ gaoler is the keystone of his life. The employer determines each prisoner's mode of existence: the hours he must keep, the clothes he must wear, the food he can eat. Even his bodily functions (pass-outs are issued for the lavatories to discourage their use during working hours) and the words he can speak (talking on the job is a sure sign of slackness; reading matter is banned for the same reason). The days of five hundred lashes for insubordination belong to the history of the earlier penal colony. The modern one can exact penalties of five hundred dollars a day for strikes. The prisoners have to knuckle under or get out. The only place they can go is to another prison.

The life of the prisoner, in fact, extends to the home. The octopus of industry stretches to every bedroom, where the night-shift prisoners, attempting to sleep by day, are kept awake by the sounds of machines or by the "howl of advertising" from radio and television (p. 31). The prisoners are expected to raise their families within close distance of the refinery so as to be on easy call if they are needed. Their houses are constantly stained with the fall-out of industrial pollution. They are jolted awake night after night by the shriek of sirens and the roar of explosions from the works. Their commitment to even this kind of domesticity further tightens their shackles. Banks and finance companies demand their money as the employer their time. This double bondage becomes a double bind: the more they commit themselves to pleasures in the home, the more they are committed to the refinery: "Hire purchase prisoners will do work a free man won't touch" (p. 324). A further avenue of exploitation is opened up.

The industrial world, in its wisdom, has sanctioned trade unions and courts of arbitration to protect the interests ostensibly of worker and employer alike. Here we see that these institutions are simply part of the prison system. The employer's profit is usually safe in the judge's hands; especially as union officials live off the prisoners' labour, just as the refinery itself does. The unions don't want to rock the boat: all their funds might go over the side. Officials

234 / Leon Cantrell

collaborate with management to end disputes as swiftly as possible. Like those prisoners who become foremen, they have climbed a rung in the hierarchy and come down hard on those who scramble below them. Those who are in positions of power over the refinery prisoners, the white-collar workers of the Termitary, are also inextricably caught in the system. It is their function to drive the prisoners to their seemingly meaningless and endless tasks. The staff taunt the men with threats of retrenchment and punishment. Those who want day work are put on the night-shift. Those who apply for sick leave or accident compensation are confronted with insuperable administrative problems. Prisoners who planned to retire at age sixty are given a week's notice at fifty, and packed off on a lower pension. Yet the white-collars themselves, as their place of work suggests, are caught in the same endless trap. The ability to perform to the company's satisfaction is under constant review. In the name of efficiency they are encouraged to inform on one another's lapses. Young graduates yap at their heels for jobs which are increasingly insecure. Far above even the Wandering Jew at the top of the Termitary is the mysterious board of seven in London, answerable only to the rapacious shareholders. Like the prisoners, we meet neither the board nor the shareholders, but their malevolent presence is felt throughout the novel:

What was Puroil? In Australia it was a few gardens in which distant proprietors planted money and after a while tangled masses of plants grew, though with no fairy princess inside waiting to be wakened with a kiss. Their financial budgets were larger than the States in which they operated. What was Puroil? At Clearwater it was a sprawling refinery, an army of white shirts, a fleet of wagons, a number of apparently separate companies, dozens of monolithic departments protected from each other by an armour of functional difference and jealousy. On the refinery site it was two hundred and fifty shabby prisoners, a heavy overload of foremen, supervisors, plant controllers, shift controllers, up to the giddy height of section-heads (popularly miscalled Suction Heads, a metaphor deriving from pumps) who were clerks for the technologists; project and process engineers and superintendents who were whipping-boys for the—whisper it!—the Old Man himself, the Manager, who was actually only a Branch Manager and a sort of bum-boy for Head Office in Victoria which was a backward colonial outpost in the eyes of the London office, which was a junior partner in British-European Puroil its mighty self, which was the property of anonymous shareholders.

Did these people know their humblest prisoners were asleep on the job? Could they have ridden easily on their magic carpet of dividend cheques if they had known the foundation of their empire was missing? Would they have suffered attacks of vertigo, thinking the whole edifice was tottering? Not at all. For not only was their investment spread over dozens of countries so that whatever tariff barriers were erected Puroil could get underneath them and whatever upheavals occurred Puroil would survive and only people would suffer, but with real ingenuity the humble prisoner was being replaced as the foundation on which the structure was built; machines were to be the foundation. Machines that ran day and night; machines that ran for years. [P. 5]

The transition to this new machine age is the period when the action of the novel takes place. The vast and complicated machinery of the refinery, with its tanks and towers; its pipes and boilers; its ladders stretching to dizzy heights; its stacks and outlet pipes with their eternal flames; its control panels with uncounted buttons to press, dials to read, taps to turn —all of this machinery, surrounded by concrete compounds and an eight-foot barbed wire fence with guards at the gate, forms the tangible structure of the prison. Ireland writes with fury of such conditions, of such foreign ownership and control of Australian resources and lives. He sees organizations such as Puroil, the world's second largest company, "a world-gripping monster" (p. 218), as part of a vast multinational conspiracy to line the pockets of the already rich. In this inhuman milieu, imprisonment is a political rather than an economic consideration. The prisoners are kept behind barbed wire, not because the company needs them, but to keep them off the streets. Out of its vast profits, Puroil and similar companies can afford jobs for even more prisoners than it now employs rather than let them go free to become "the new political menace" (p. 91). Like the inmates of those other prisons where men cannot bundy out each day, Puroil prisoners perform meaningless and repetitive tasks. Instead of crushing stones they push buttons and sweep floors. Their frequent sabotage of the plant's equipment is their only means of protest, the catalyst of hate in the industrial relations process. But this too is cruelly counter-productive. Lungs are destroyed by silica dust after each furnace crash. The more crashes there are, the more men are needed to repair the damage. These contemporary Luddites are continually re-employed to repair the havoc they have caused. Their real enemies, those few who control the whole industrial world, those who are "more powerful than governments" (p. 88), are as safe from the prisoners' fury as the lighthouse from the storm.

I have sketched here at some length the complex social, economic, and political structure of the novel to emphasize the extent to which *The Unknown Industrial Prisoner* is concerned to make a serious assault upon the basic assumptions of our modern capitalist society. For clearly Ireland goes beyond the easy polemic of class politics. In his world there are no obvious answers, no solutions through working class revolution or changes in government. Each individual in the Puroil hierarchy is as much a victim, a prisoner, as the next. The god-like stature of the Board of Seven suggests that the refinery is indeed a microcosm of our modern world. Just as its complexities and inanities overwhelm and contain the prisoners, so too is the reader unable to find any rationale or purpose in its operation. It is an image of a cruelly meaningless universe, one from which delight and fulfilment have fled, to be replaced by subservience, drudgery, and a return to the basic animal instincts of survival: a world where machinery has replaced humanity at the centre, where workers are "replaceable parts of an economy" instead of "individuals and mortal with one life to live" (p. 119).

Certainly the prisoners are dissatisfied with their lot. But they are beyond organized political action. To ease the burden of each working day the Great White Father, the most independent of them, has established the Home Beautiful, a collection of galvanized iron huts in the mangrove swamp across the river from Puroil. Here, unlimited supplies of beer and sex provide "the only bit of heaven" (p. 49) the prisoners know. The prostitutes (with names like Never on

Sunday and the Old Lamplighter) do a roaring cut-price trade, coping with shift-work as regularly as the men. But if this is heaven, it is also perilously close to hell. Among the muddy, steamy mangroves paradise is hard to find. The scenes of drinking and whoring are some of the most unpleasant in the book. Carnal pleasures are seen in terms both bestial and repulsive. The Old Lamplighter refuses to perform her duties in the dark: the light reveals her clearing out lettuce from underneath her dentures. Her tongue encounters further supplies: "Several tomato seeds and half a peanut. She finished the peanut" (p. 111). During the Sumpsucker's allotted half-hour she talks incessantly. The man smells so much she refuses to be helpful.

Sumpy let her talk.

"It's funny. The family knows I do this. Remember the cruiser at Bobbin Head?" She grabbed his ears and shook his head.

"Sure. I remember." She was a big woman, six feet tall and very strong. If she had been a man the Sump would have been afraid of her. "You don't still have fits, do you?"

"No. Only a couple a year, now. Do you really remember Bobbin Head?"

"My back remembers it. We were having a tread below decks and your son David comes looking for you. Where's Mum? he yells and instead of waiting for an answer he jumps down the hatch right in the middle of my back. Hullo, Mum, he says. And you say, Go back, David. Do I remember? Neither of us could get our breath back. 'Go back, David!' " He mimicked her voice.

She was gratified. Her son had been worried she might go into a fit, but the strange thing was the fits had come less often after he had seen her at it. Strange how you feel your children have a hold on you, forcing you to put on a good front.

"I'll have to have a shave soon." She glanced at her legs, black with stubble. Her armpit patch was long. A woman has so much maintenance. Men were lucky. Just their faces. Forgetting the Sumpsucker was there, she eased up one buttock.

"Sorry."

Reflectively she picked her nose with her little finger. The other fingers enlarge your nostrils, her mother told her. You

don't want to look like a native, do you? Mentally, she
consulted her calendar. The twelfth. Should be on the twenty-
fifth. That meant five days off work. If she could make sure
of ten men a day until—that meant she wouldn't notice the
drop in money.
"You finished?"
"I was finished back at Bobbin Head."
"Why don't you say something? I could be making a dollar!
What do you want for five bucks, bed and breakfast?" She
shook him off like a helpless puppy. [Pp. 112–13]

The grotesque comedy of such passages (and they are
numerous) does not disguise the sharpness of the author's
irony (*Home Beautiful* is a best-selling interior decorating
magazine). What the Great White Father offers the men is
merely a slightly more tolerable (because they are drunk)
form of imprisonment. The apparent reversal of roles (the
men are now the employers) is totally illusory: in the
mangroves the workers are as much the prisoners of lust as
they are the prisoners of industry across the river. The Great
White Father tries to explain this to them; that his garden
of pleasures is no real alternative; merely a frantic effort to
fill a void, dependent upon the transitory good will of one
man. When he dies it is revealed that for years he has been
subsidizing the beer supplies. This has been his major success
as a self-appointed and recognized leader. But the men do
not want to know about illusions. Leeringly and beerily they
unwittingly aid the company's efforts to "reduce them to the
status of a lower species". Puroil's ultimate aim ("to make
them animals—then ruling them is easier", p. 201) comes
closer to fruition in the Home Beautiful than in the refinery.
  Adrian Mitchell, in a brief article on Ireland's novels
(*Meanjin* 34, no. 2, 1975), justly drew attention to a passage
set very carefully at the exact centre of the *Industrial Prisoner:*

THE COMFORT OF INDIFFERENCE None of the
various grades of prisoners was aware of it, but while the
hours and years of their detention passed, the captive moon
swung round the tiny earth, the tides slid in and out
obediently and the piece of galaxy in which our solar system
nestled comfortably swung slowly in the nothingness that
enveloped all existence and this nothingness tugged gently at

all that had substance; prying loose, looking for weakness, drawing all things to it.

And perhaps, although it may not be considered in good taste to mention the fact, we might remember that the tiny earth which entertains us as guests, or lice, upon its surface while its present chemical state endures somewhere between the unbearable heat of the past and the unbearable cold of the future—this nice little home of ours is dying under us. We are now clever enough to measure by just how much our day is lengthening, and just when we shall draw the moon in to us as a ring of rocks and dust, and when we shall fall unnoticed into the sun. And cheerfully set out this information for children to understand, in books with coloured pictures showing the future final disaster. Just like a fairytale.

We don't know when we came here, or where we came from; we're having a free ride through space and call it life. And we are now aware that the earth is indifferent to us. She is not complimented when we set aside areas of natural beauty for ourselves, nor concerned when we wreck our surroundings. Her fate is sealed. We may as well plunder, exploit, bomb, bulldoze, alter, shift, drain, kill—anything— for all she cares. [Pp. 191–92]

But it would be a mistake to feel the novel endorses the fatalism of this view. There is too much anger contained in its accounts of the prisoners' lives, too much vituperative energy directed at greed, selfishness, and incompetence, for it too to succumb to the comfort of indifference. Right at the beginning, on that first day, we learn that "somewhere beyond the refinery's dome of dust and gas the sun shone splendidly golden" (p. 3). At other points we learn of an earlier refinery manager, Gentleman Joe, who knew and cared for all his workers; who called them by their proper names and visited them if they were ill. The Samurai recognizes the need for hospitals where people do not work just for wages: "Where they're dedicated. Like St Joe's" (p. 219). And he struggles for a "shining idea", "just beyond his grasp", for "a key that could open up this present attempt at civilization so that the whole vast machinery might suddenly get to its feet and work". But the key eludes him. "Perhaps next time he would grasp it and see it face to face" (p. 220). He dreams of "taking a little further the dim feelings of every Australian. Obstinate, irrational, vengeful. National." Of channelling the emotions of his "politically backward countrymen", of "training for a mighty engagement" (pp. 311–12). But the final destruction of the refinery is not the result of the Samurai's vision or of political machinations. Just another combination of spite, hatred, and incompetence. The Samurai is merely an observer.

Ireland suggests, then, that this is a world in which men can dream of change, in which we can know of "splendidly golden" suns elsewhere, but in which we must also recognize the harshest and more common truths. The artist in the novel, the Colonel, puts together "a hundredweight of welding scrap" and enters it in a sculpture competition. Title: "Unknown Industrial Prisoner". It wins first prize. Art imitates nature and nature imitates art.

Almost at the end of the *Industrial Prisoner* the unnamed narrator mentions "the true function of man" and suggests that this may merely be "to be himself, just as he happens to be, and his whole duty simply to live. But how can that be?" (p. 375). This is a question to which the novel has frequently turned, especially through the meditations of the Great White Father and the Samurai. What lies beyond the seemingly meaningless and repetitive patterns of existence? Certainly the models of savagery, fraud, and futility we have been shown, the images of industry and machinery out of control, all suggest a world of random disharmony, a world where virtue is as irrelevant as it is unknown. The narrator further refers to his "galaxy of painted slides", his "bleak ratio of illuminations" (the ironical pun is intended), drawing our attention at the close to the apparently pointless hurly-burly of his kaleidoscopic intent. For though the refinery has been largely destroyed by the end of the novel, none of the prisoners is free. And over in the west, beyond "the great empty stomach of Australia", "more foreigners were messing about with the lives of people for whom they had no responsibility" (p. 379). The narrator despairs. He no longer possesses even his "benign lump of faith". He sets off down the path to Puroil and bumps into the Volga Boatman.

> I didn't want to have to stop and try to explain—how could I?—so I tried to slip past him. He didn't intend to get in

the way but he dodged towards me. I went the other way.
So did he. . . .

   The Boatman and I were concentrated absolutely on where
we wanted to go. We had no mind left over to escape each
other. Back and forth we went from side to side, left right
left right in perfect time, getting no farther forward; each,
for the sake of a tiny inconvenience, wishing the other had
never existed. [Pp. 378–79]

On this absurd image of trivial and endless futility (it could
be a scene from Samuel Beckett) the novel ends.

   Or does it? "Back and forth . . . from side to side, left
right left right . . . getting no farther forward" suggests again
that political framework to which I drew attention at the
beginning of this discussion. The constant tussle between left
and right, between oppressed and oppressor, "each, for the
sake of a tiny inconvenience, wishing the other had never
existed"; this tussle palls into insignificance in the face of
the totally debilitating inhumanity these lefts and rights have
created. Their traditional antipathy has failed to halt the
monstrous creation that is the Puroil refinery. Perhaps it has
actually created it. Certainly the refinery is the measure of
our society, of their failure. Ireland's position, I suspect, is
that of the radical conservative (not unlike Solzhenitsyn). His
novel becomes a polemic for a united effort against human
exploitation and injustice. Conventional political positions go
by the board: "the staff policies and Union policies appropriate to an old-style shearing shed" (p. 180) which
characterize Puroil are castigated alike. In a society where
freedom is illusory for all, you may as well blow everything
up and start again. The vigor with which Ireland invests
his descriptions of plant crashes and fires conjures up
something of the anarchist—the most radical of all conservative positions. In this sense the novel really does only
begin where it seems to end. It is essentially a tract for our
times. An attempt to interpret the direction in which our
world is moving; to force us all to rethink our fundamental
position. To rethink, especially, our concept of what it is the
novel can achieve.

Michael Wilding's *The Short Story Embassy: A Novel*
(1975)[7] is another recent Australian work that points our

fiction in a new direction. It is organized along similar fragmentary lines to *The Unknown Industrial Prisoner*,[8] with a constantly shifting point of view, so that at times even the question of which character (if any) is writing the work seems irresolvable. Like Ireland again, Wilding is concerned to challenge our preconceptions of the novel form. In fact, *The Short Story Embassy* could be called a pastiche of various forms of writing: prose fiction, verse, biography, confession, letters, catalogues, and criticism. It is derivative in the sense that (like the anatomy again) it includes verbatim extracts from other texts which are relevant to its immediate purpose. Thus brief, encyclopaedic accounts of the life of Thomas Paine (pp. 37–38) interrupt the narrative flow when his name is raised in conversation; as one, in reality, might turn to such sources in a similar situation. When Laszlo, a writer in the novel, mentions his interest in Henry James's *Notebooks*, we are offered a characteristic passage from them in a footnote (p. 76). There are comic tombstone epitaphs (pp. 78–79), ostensibly from the local cemetery, though we later learn that Laszlo collects volumes recording them. The question of the relationship between the reality of the printed word and the reality of life around us is a major preoccupation of the novel, as we shall see. There is also a sixteenth-century elegy written by an unfortunate in the Tower just before his execution (pp. 121–22). Here it is attributed to a similarly named character who mysteriously disappears. In addition, there are echoes of Malcolm Lowry's *Under the Volcano* (the central character there is also a frustrated writer), of *Hamlet* (Laszlo, Polonius-like, hides behind an arras to overhear Wendel and Valda), and of such nostalgic literary props as "Colin Wilson sweaters and Jack Kerouac lumberjack shirts" (p. 21).

All of this suggests a good deal of self-conscious indebtedness used for comic (and serious) effect, and this is indeed the case. The writers at the Embassy are totally immersed in their literary world, so it is appropriate that we too should be. The novel's foster-parents, as it were, are frequently celebrated; most obviously through the use of the names of famous short story writers (and characters) to designate various appropriate parts of the Embassy, the bastion committed to preserve the story from the encroachments of novels and novelists, poetry and poets. Thus we have the Henry James carpet (no doubt very plush, and of complex design), the O. Henry guest suite, the Katherine Mansfield sanitorium, the Borges library, the Chesterton refectory, the Pat Hobby construction room, the Edgar Allan Poe graveyard, the Maugham verandah and the Earlier Brautigan potting shed. This last is the most contemporary and the most important. The American Richard Brautigan's novels are clear models for Wilding's work. *Trout Fishing in America* (1967), *A Confederate General From Big Sur* (1965), and *In Watermelon Sugar* (1964), Brautigan's best-known titles, are loosely episodic, digressive fictions, held together by no particular plot or story-line, closer in form to a series of brief stories and sketches than to the conventional novel. They are peopled not so much by characters or recognizable persons as by attitudes and points of view. In *The Abortion: An Historical Romance 1966* (1971) Brautigan conceives of a public library where authors can deposit unpublished and unpublishable manuscripts. Perhaps it was this work that suggested to Wilding the idea of an embassy for the protection of short stories. (And perhaps, too, his insistence on the *Earlier* Brautigan potting shed is a tongue-in-cheek attempt to draw our attention away from this later and more closely paralleled title.) Certainly the potting shed underlines the nature of his indebtedness: in *The Short Story Embassy* slips and cuttings from other writers are planted together and allowed to grow into a new if partly composite whole. The best analogy, from modern times (though Dryden and Swift and many others provide earlier literary examples) would be the collages of the Italian futurist painters early in this century. There the totality of the work was the sum of its variously and obviously "borrowed" parts together with the individual artist's own arrangement and contributions. Such collages were profoundly original and yet "unoriginal" at the same time. They suggested that art relates directly to art as well as to the "real" world, that a painting can be "about" painting as well as "about" life. They required (and still require) a great deal of skill and knowledge on the part of a viewer attempting to hold all the disparate elements together. Equally obviously, they require a certain ready familiarity with the collage elements; so arguably, they are art of a rather specialized kind: art for artists, art for art (not to be confused with art for art's sake, which doctrine they hold in anathema).

I believe we can argue along similar lines about *The Short Story Embassy*: that it is most fully a novel for novelists or novelists *manqués*. Though only a brief work, it demands of its readers a good deal of expertise, experience, and interest in literature. The very scope of its allusions and references emphasizes this. For it is fundamentally a novel about writing a novel and about reading one. Both implicitly and explicitly it is an account of some of the problems (and some of the delights) inherent in the acts of literary creation and recreation. It further explores ideas of literary prejudice and rivalry, and the nature of the relationship between the short story form and the novel. Its great comic irony lies in the emergence of a *novel* from the embattled pens of the apostles of the *story*.

Three of *The Short Story Embassy*'s characters are creative writers. They form the Embassy staff. Their tasks are to produce, publish, and publicize stories; to oppose dramatists, novelists, and poets; and to ensure that reading matter other than stories gains no more than a temporary visa to enter the Embassy's portals. They are also the guardians of "the state of new writing". The fourth character is Tichborne, an academic critic, intent on discovering the innermost secrets of the inky art. His name is carefully chosen. It is that of a long-landed English Catholic family which achieved fame on two occasions. The first time was through Chidiock Tichborne (1558–86), who became involved in a religiously inspired plot to assassinate the Protestant Queen Elizabeth I. He was hung, drawn, and quartered for his troubles. On the evening before his execution he wrote the famous elegy Wilding includes in the novel. Here, "scratched with a diamond on a window of the tower" (p. 121), the critic Tichborne offers it as his own work before he disappears from the Embassy. This idea of the critic as a parasite, the pretender to property not his own, is picked up again in echoes of Roger Charles Tichborne (1829–54), a much-removed cousin of Chidiock. This equally unhappy man disappeared at sea between South America and England. His grieved and deranged mother advertised widely for his return. Many claimants came forward, most notably, in 1865, one Arthur Orton, "a small butcher at Wagga Wagga, in Queensland", as the eleventh edition of the *Encyclopaedia Brittanica* quaintly puts it (1910–11, vol. 26, p. 932). Lady Tichborne accepted Orton as her son and then died, leaving an immense legal tangle and a bevy of disbelieving, scandalized, and rapacious relatives. Lengthy action ensued. Orton was convicted of perjury and sent to prison, living thereafter on a series of confessions and retractions. The Tichborne Case, as it became known, was one of the great *causes célèbres* of mid-Victorian times. It revived interest in the earlier Tichborne episode, even in Australia, where Marcus Clarke wrote *Chidiock Tichbourne, or the Babington Conspiracy. A Historical Romance of the Days of Queen Elizabeth* during 1874 and 1875. (Wilding's novel was written during his work for a book on Clarke, where he argues that Clarke's short stories have been unjustly neglected because of their innovative nature—just as the writers at the Embassy claim their stories suffer for lack of an informed and sympathetic audience). So our modern Tichborne carries the sins of several generations: a critic among writers, he is a Catholic among Protestants, an imposter climbing up the family tree. His arrival at the Embassy is greeted with guarded hostility by the others (they know he writes reviews). He characterizes himself by his account of how, in the hallway for the first time, he found copies of short story magazines including "that small local product in which I had reviewed Wendel's collection. I wanted to leaf through it to see if there were any annotations or signs of reaction to the review; but the possible embarrassment of being found standing there reading it prevented me" (p. 8). Such discreet vanity is his trademark. He wants to understand, he wants to be liked. Yet the more he seeks the former, the more foolish he appears, and the more dislikeable he becomes. On his first evening we see clearly the limitations of his acquisitive, critical mind. Valda pretends that each night the writers sit by the fire and take it in turns to tell stories. Too much for Tichborne! To be in on the act at the very moment of creation is beyond his wildest critical fantasies. He eagerly presses for a story.

> Tichborne settled himself down into the armchair and Valda curled up on the Henry James carpet. She said: "I was tripping and this cat was looking at me and I was looking at the cat and the cat was looking at this bowl of milk. And suddenly I became the bowl of milk."
>
> "How did you know you were the milk?" Tichborne asked.
>
> "I was there, in the bowl. I could feel the bowl all round me, sort of wrapping round me holding me in place. And then the cat started to lap me up."
>
> Valda wriggled her shoulders up.
>
> "It's tongue was all itchy. You know how cats' tongues are all prickly and spikey. Well, it was lapping me up and it was all itchy."
>
> "And then you became the cat?"
>
> "No, I was the milk."
>
> "But if the cat lapped the milk up, then you'd become the cat because it was swallowing you."
>
> "No, it doesn't happen that way; you can't change your substance."
>
> "But you'd already changed your substance into the milk." Tichborne persisted.
>
> "No, I'd just become the milk, that's different."
>
> "Oh my god," groaned Wendel.
>
> "What was it like being in two places being in the bowl and in the stomach of the cat?"
>
> "I wasn't in its stomach," Valda said. "I felt its tongue lapping me up but I was still in the bowl."
>
> "But what happened when it had swallowed all the milk?
>
> "I'd gone back into my body by then," she said. [Pp. 15–16]

The painfully methodical nature of Tichborne's interrogation of Valda enacts the point—and places the critic. (It is the writer, notice, who sits on the magic Henry James carpet.) Unable to respond to the imaginativeness of her *jeu d'esprit*, he crushed its spontaneity with his literal-minded questions, which seek an explanation and an answer beyond the realms of art. Later that night, when this same cat brings him a lizard, he feels "all cold and scaly and anxious and paralyzed" (p. 17). The section in which this occurs is headed "A Short Way with Critics". The subject of Valda's maligned story has thus found an easy method of coping with this dissenter. Indeed, the fact that Tichborne can here transform himself into a lizard ("all cold and scaly"), under the stimulus of fear, nicely underlines the point of the previous story-telling section. For Valda's metamorphosis into a bowl of milk has not only been a pleasant experience (unlike Tichborne's), but one imaginatively and spontaneously conceived. The critic is incapable of experiencing or understanding such freedom. He is the prisoner of his anxieties, the victim of his mental matter-of-factness. As Laszlo says, there is a "premium on inventiveness in a writer" (p. 21).

After this disastrous start to his fact-finding mission, Tichborne is happy to find an axe in the potting shed. When he had been taken there previously by Valda he had noticed only the seedlings. Now, with his instrument of destruction, he sets about chopping the firewood (more evening stories in mind?). At their typewriters, the others are immediately disturbed, as they were earlier by Tichborne's taking them coffee. He has become a disruptive influence in their lives. A desperate and bitter Wendel offers him the task of building a sheltered workshop:

"It's an important project to emotionally cripple and retard writers," Wendel said. "It promises to fulfil a valuable role for new and experimental writers of fiction, a role that the underground poetry press and the theatre workshops have already performed for younger poets and playwrights."

"Where's the underground poetry press?" Tichborne asked.

"It's in the basement of Liberty Hall. We're training moles with gelignite to destroy that. After we've trained the eagles. The problem with the eagles has been to get them to fly through the theatre workshop windows with the tortoises. If there was more open air theatre it would be easier. Like Greece.

"Not," he continued, "that there is any longer a clear line between underground and traditional publishing, or that fiction writers have failed to share in the current healthy publishing boom. Yet the writer of fiction still faces obstacles different from those of the poet and dramatist."

"You can increase those," Laszlo told Tichborne.

"It is widely observed in the trade that collections of stories don't sell; neither do stories look attractive in the roneoed

'underground' form available to poets. The number of magazines publishing stories has declined and the editors can't represent all the new writing being attempted. Novels, of course, are expensive to produce and are therefore risky. All these factors make it difficult for the younger writer of fiction to find an audience. This new project provides at a modest price an additional outlet for fiction writers and one that can be different from those provided by literary periodicals and commercial publishers. This project will create a sheltered workshop type situation for the fiction writer." . . .
"And what am I to do?" Tichborne asked.
"You are to create the sheltered workshop. You are to build it up from nothing, from the scorched earth and the grass roots. You are to put writers into crippled and spastic environments. There's ground, there's timber, anything else you need, just ask for it. But we give you total responsibility for the project. Evolve it as you think fit." [Pp. 45–46]

But the critic botches even this job. His devastations continue. He becomes *persona non grata* after being discovered reading the *Daily Poet* in bed. He becomes totally the voyeur of art, fantasizing over Valda:

I used to like to draw her out in conversation; I wanted to hear from her those experiences that are the raw material of our time; attempting suicide, having abortions, being raped, walking the streets, catching venereal disease, participating in multiple sexual situations, lesbianism, fucking dogs. All this, suitably transmuted into art, could make her one of the great writers of our time. Reading her stories, transmuted by her writer's vision, you can forget any suspicion that you are reading pornography. What she has to say would speak for all of us. And she is so beautiful too. I do not feel that Laszlo adequately encourages her talents. In a richer soil, a more fitting climate, she would burgeon and flower. [P. 95]

Wendel at last, after starting to make a coffin ("There are no Epitaphs for Reviewers or Critics. Perhaps they never died. Perhaps they were buried in unconsecrated ground. Along with Publishers" p. 100), drives Tichborne out with tales of venereal disease. The thought of being exposed to "the raw material of our time" is too much for the critic. Only the writers are strong enough for this.
The technique of the comically dramatized dialectic be-

tween writer and critic is the essence of Wilding's art. Between the writers themselves there is a similar tension of ideas and intent. For instance, over the question of the "reality" of fiction. Wendel assures Laszlo that the basis of "fictional creation" precludes "simple identification" of a character with an actual person (p. 9). Yet the latter feels he is being parodied and ridiculed in the others' stories. He especially fears the stories of Valda, his lady, for they are often about sex, about encounters of which he has no knowledge. He suspects they are based upon her experiences before they met, and he is consumed with jealousy. The "fiction" of these stories seems stronger and more persuasive than the "reality" of their present relationship. The distinction between art and nature is uncomfortably blurred. Laszlo indeed has another theory: that nature can imitate art, that his stories predict the future. He has been writing stories about V.D. Suddenly a "V.D. plague" surrounds the Embassy (like the unmentionable literary quarterly, it is rumoured to have come from Melbourne). Laszlo is terrified. As a writer he seems to have assumed a god-like stature: has he *caused* the outbreak? He dares not write a single further word.

In any event, the Embassy is routed; whether by V.D. or critics or the writers themselves is totally unclear. Yet this seeming confusion at the end of *The Short Story Embassy* dramatizes clearly enough what I take to be one of Wilding's principal contentions: that out of the seemingly chaotic formlessness of the Embassy, with its petty jealousies, phobias, and rivalries; and out of the seeming formlessness of *The Short Story Embassy*, a novel does actually emerge. The tussles of creativity and criticism, of fiction and reality, which are the principal motivating forces behind its action, are resolved dramatically and thematically in terms of the work in which they are shaped and embodied. Thus Laszlo is forced to admit on the last page that the critic Tichborne has been the catalyst for much of the action we have read about and which has somehow fallen into the shape of a novel. The apparent enemy of creativity has become its agent. So too the defenders of short stories have moved beyond the limitations of their form. Their brief and regular accounts of ideas and happenings at the Embassy make, at the very least, a novella. Even the argument over art versus nature is seen as part of the art itself. In this concern to examine and then balance the rival claims of various branches of literary activity, Wilding reminds us of earlier attempts to resolve a battle of books. Indeed, *The Short Story Embassy* displays a comic intensity and a breadth of literary experience not so far removed from Swift's classic pamphlet. And, as with Swift, Wilding's eclecticism is the measure of his achievement.

Frank Moorhouse's *The Electrical Experience*[9] is also concerned with form and with the relationship between what is being said and the manner in which it is being presented. Indeed, a question other critics have raised is whether or not the book can even be considered as a novel. It is subtitled *A Discontinuous Narrative* (as were Moorhouse's two earlier books, *Futility and Other Animals* [1969] and *The Americans, Baby* [1972]. The biographical note in the 1969 book says that the author "writes short stories and does not intend to write a conventional novel" (perhaps implying already, however, that his narratives could be regarded as an *unconventional* novel?). In *The Americans* a note refers to *The Electrical Experience* (then being written) as a "documentary-narrative", while the second book itself is fully sub-titled *a discontinuous narrative of stories and fragments*. I do not propose to enter into a debate concerning the respective claims that the novel, the short story, the discontinuous narrative, the fragment, or the documentary may hold to Moorhouse's work. I see *The Electrical Experience* as a coherent and innovative fiction; a striking and imaginative attempt to come to terms with some of the problems of form and subject which we have already seen to have been the concern of Ireland and Wilding.

In particular, *The Electrical Experience* is one of the most startlingly presented fictions I know. Its differentness is obvious as early as the title-page, which is printed negatively, using black paper with white letters (so that the words *The Electrical Experience* stand out as if they were, in fact, electrically lit). Numerous other pages, containing what are called the "Fragments", are similarly printed. Their appearance is suggestive of light being shed on darkness, an appropriate and ironical image, for they are largely snippets from the mind of T. George McDowell, soft-drink manufacturer, dogmatist, and Rotarian from the New South Wales south coast. The "Narratives", on the other hand, as their conventional black ink on white paper suggests, contain the major actions and descriptions of the book. We also find a number of pages devoted to photographic illustrations. Taken from the period during which most of the narrative is set, the 1920s and 1930s, they show the bottling of soft drinks, cars, big-game fishermen (McDowell meets Zane Grey on a fishing trip) and the president of the United States addressing the 1923 Rotary Convention (which McDowell attended). These photographs and the Fragments occupy a smaller portion of *The Electrical Experience* than the Narratives, but they serve to underline the latter's inherent limitations. It is a mistake to regard them as subsidiary or even as supplementary to the remaining narrative. Clearly they are part of it and cannot be divorced from it; any more than we can begin to consider the text as residing in the Narratives alone. An inkling of this lies in the fact that the Narratives give us no description of McDowell's appearance —this is provided by the photographs. Similarly, our concept of his anecdotal, practical, and factual mind is spelt out in the accumulation of the Fragments. His mind is indeed composed of fragments—of handy hints, home-spun philosophy, and disconnected facts.

The "discontinuous narrative" is further evident and defined by other typographical devices. Thus each of the fourteen Narratives has its own title page where the typography attempts to prepare us for, and comment on, that which is to follow. The heavy face of the first section, titled "A Black, Black Birth" is appropriate to the title and by its portentousness underlines the title's irony (Terri's family attempts to explain her apparent deviance by the fact that bush-fires ringed the town, turning the sky black, on the day she was born). The Hollywood style typography titling the third Narrative, "George McDowell Changes Names", underlines the American influence on George's life (he becomes

T. George McDowell, and has visited the United States seventeen times by the end of the book). Narrative 12, "Gwenth McDowell's Statement Concerning her Sister, Teresa McDowell, June 1969", is itself printed entirely in a typewriter face, with unjustified lines and with apparent errors typed out with hyphens, though still readable. These devices devastatingly characterize the dangerously self-right-eous and unimaginative Gwenth. She alters "animal sex" to "biology" (p. 158) and calls herself an "educationalist" rather than a "teacher" (p. 159). In Narrative 13, too, Moorhouse has two measurements of line justification, so that the short-lined sections of the page can be seen as providing a direct insight into McDowell's mind (rather like a Joycean stream of consciousness narrative) while the rest of the page indicates and narrates his engagement with Becker and others. It is particularly appropriate that McDowell's last appearance in the book should be depicted in this way, for he has always been a man without true friends, one who has stood apart; as his true self now stands apart on the page. The final Narrative, "Filming the Hatted Australian", is of a different kind from the previous thirteen. Its own white-on-black title page suggests its separateness from the others and yet also its relationship to them as a whole. For a "A Coincidental Narrative", as it is sub-titled, offers a more explicit attempt to impose a retrospective judgement on McDowell's gener-ation than anything we have seen before. McDowell himself enters it only indirectly, through old Fred's recollection of him as "fair, a fair man, but as hard as nails" (p. 193). He has become part of the past, part of the memory of the south coast, like one of the forgotten or misremembered names he has attempted to recall for Becker in the previous section.

Moorhouse's concern for these literally discontinuous aspects of his narrative is picked up in other ways as well. Quite different styles of writing are adopted for different sections. In "George McDowell Does the Job" (dealing with, among other things, the conception of Terri), McDowell's attempts to exercise "self-control" over his sexual feelings are described in prose that is itself unnaturally strained and unspontaneous: "He observed that the limitations and restrictions on the matter of sexual indulgence, placed by Thelma in their marriage, sometimes aroused him, her unwillingness, he had perhaps that sort of personality which was, which savoured, well, the restraint she imposed, the limitations on when, and her refusals" (p. 16). Like McDowell's own sexuality, the sentence is a poor, awkward and repressed thing, straining to make itself understood. Equally, the entire eighth Narrative, "The Secret of Endurance", recounting McDowell's meeting with Zane Grey, lives up to its name. It is all one sentence, breathlessly and brokenly narrated, reflecting the lack of ease, the awkwardness and naïve enthusiasm of T. George in the presence of the great man (the phrase "Zee Gee said" is constantly repeated).

Throughout much of the book there is also a flux in the point of view, from narrator to character and back again, so that on many occasions we are unaware of the author, as it were, of particular comments and asides. This lack of authority in much of the book, this absence of an omniscient narrator, adds to the fragmentary, discontinuous nature of our knowledge of characters and events. Unlike Stewart, the director in the "Coincidental Narrative", Moorhouse can offer no assured or convincing viewpoint from which to survey the world he has created. Our knowledge, our view, our judgement—all of these are constantly being challenged or modified. One might also point to uncertainty as a major theme and device in the book. It is uncertainty about the value of his own nature and achievement that drives McDowell down the desperate road of good fellowship and progress.

From this point of view it is interesting to consider the time sequence of the fourteen Narratives. The central events related in each one take place in a particular year, which is sometimes mentioned, and which can other times be calculated from such information as ages and anniversaries. Narrative 8, "The Secret of Endurance", the only Narrative whose date is historically verifiable (Zane Grey's famous visit to Australia), is also the only one that cannot be more or less dated from internal evidence. The intention seems to be to challenge us once again when we feel to be on safe ground. The dates are as follows: 1, 1969; 2, 1938; 3, 1938; 4, 1929;

5, 1939; 6, 1936; 7, 1924; 8, 1936; 9, 1930; 10, 1939; 11, 1969; 12, 1969; 13, 1969; 14, 1973 (?). This sort of discontinuity in the time sequence of the basic events of the narrative underlines the structural and stylistic discontinuities I have already described. It is further emphasized when we realize that a number of the Narratives pertain to events from various years. Thus Narrative 11, as its title suggests, though set in 1969 recalls a number of important events from 1923. Similarly, Narrative 5 flashes back over something like thirty years, pausing here and there at times we could not begin to date. It is clear that our knowledge of people, places and events in this book (as in Moorhouse's earlier works) is obtained discontinuously and fleetingly, with no apparent guidance or patterning from the author. As in a crowd, we notice some faces and forget others. We are reminded of similarities and dissimilarities. We learn through the accretion of detail, which we sometimes misplace, and which may or may not be true. Our knowledge, for example, of the policeman's widow is scattered briefly throughout the book. We learn neither her name nor that of her husband—yet we do know that she drove an Essex car. Narratives 1, 2, 5, and 13 suggest that McDowell knew her only for a short time (perhaps they slept together only once) but that his relationship with her had a profound effect upon him, for her memory frequently appears in his mind—despite (or because of) his efforts to suppress his adultery with her. This fragmentation of presentation, in which the reader can, if he so wishes, assemble the parts to form a less discontinuous whole, is the principal and most characteristic structure in the book. We learn, for instance, of James Tutman and of Terri McDowell in a manner similar to that by which we learn of the widow. We get to know their parts, that is, but not their whole, just as Becker has to assemble knowledge of both George and Terri from fragments provided by themselves and by each other.

Moorhouse's presentation of his "discontinuous narrative" is thus highly complex and sophisticated, implying a concept of the nature of experience (fleeting, random, disconnected, unlinear) as well as an attempt to come to terms with the question of how to structure fiction when life itself has no

structure. T. George McDowell certainly believes in structure and purpose, even if he finds these difficult topics to
discuss. When confronted with Dr Trenbow's Big Questions
he stakes his soul on little answers: "if you've followed the
rules inherent in your craft, the answers will be obvious"
(p. 82). McDowell's craft, the manufacture of aerated drinks,
is a small-town craft, doomed like the town itself to fall
beneath the strength of the encroaching city. The advent of
electricity becomes the symbol of this change. It stands for
Progress, but also for destruction. It destroys Tutman's ice
business (his customers buy refrigerators, despite his warning
that they may be gassed in their sleep) and it destroys him.
T. George McDowell, in attempting to embrace and exploit
such mechanical and technical change, also becomes its
victim. He believes so firmly in objects and objective facts,
in the importance of a "life plan", in cleanliness and tidiness,
in control, success, progress (an "implacable law"), hard
work—in all the bourgeois ethics apotheosized by Rotary—
that he forgets to leave room in his mind for anything else.
Once he begins to forget the facts, as he does in Narrative
13 (waspishly titled "The Enterprising Spirit of the Anglo-
Saxon Race"), he ceases to be a full-time human being. He
has put all his eggs into one basket (or all his soft-drink
into one bottle) and then he has dropped it. The book does
not ask us morally to judge this, simply to observe it; to note
that T. George McDowell's "electrical experience" is anything but electrifying; to observe that his attempts to see life
as progressive and ordered, as continuous, are denied by the
very way in which they are presented to us.

My argument in this chapter has been that if the Australian
novel is to remain an alive and alert text of our society it
must recognize that the social models on which it has been
traditionally based are no longer tenable. The ideology that
sustained the earlier novel—a buoyant commitment to
originality, individuality, and the virtues of unpremeditated
experience—has collapsed. The newness of the novel form
in its first two hundred years was one of its greatest strengths.
Its ability to order and "explain" experience give it a
particular force at a time and a place when such order and

explanation was not only possible but necessary and desirable. This is no longer so. We have ceased to hold an affirmative view of the future. We fail to see progress as a positive good. Our world, like these books of Ireland, Wilding, and Moorhouse, is composed of fragments, held together only by the energy with which we can invest our experiences of them. All three writers recognize these fundamental changes. Their work I have discussed here reflects a willingness to move beyond accepted forms and themes. It is an attempt to arrive at an art form that can enact and comment upon that sense of transitory stasis which is our notion of order. From this point of view they are among the most modern exponents of contemporary Australian fiction.[10]

NOTES

1 Bettina Knapp, *French Novelists Speak Out* (New York: Whiston, 1976), p. 1.
2 Maurice Nadeau, *The French Novel Since the War* (London: Methuen, 1967), pp. 191, 192.
3. Ibid., p. 185.
4. Ibid., p. 187. This and the preceding quotation are from Robbe-Grillet's book on the problems facing contemporary novelists, translated as *Towards a New Novel* (1965).
5. David Ireland, *The Unknown Industrial Prisoner* (Sydney: Angus & Robertson, 1971). All page references are to this edition.
6. Alexander Solzhenitsyn, *One Day in the Life of Ivan Denisovich* (Harmondsworth Mddx.: Penguin, 1963, translation by Ralph Parker), p. 7.
7. Michael Wilding, *The Short Story Embassy: A Novel* (Sydney: Wild and Woolley, 1975). All page references are to this edition.
8. Wilding in fact established himself as a short story writer before turning to novels. Parts of *The Short Story Embassy*, and of his later novel *Scenic Drive* (1976), actually appeared in magazines and elsewhere as integral units before the novel was published.
9. Frank Moorhouse, *The Electrical Experience: A Discontinuous Narrative of Stories and Fragments* (Sydney: Angus & Robertson, 1974). All page references are to this edition.
10. It remains to be seen if Australian literary criticism can be similarly responsive to the necessity of innovation. In France the "new novel" and the "new criticism" have gone side by side, with practitioners frequently working in both fields. The most relevant work here, D. R. Burns's *The Directions of Australian Fiction,*

1920–1974 (1975), totally ignores *The Unknown Industrial Prisoner* and fails even to mention Michael Wilding. Moorhouse is always referred to as "Moorehouse". Bernard Bergonzi, in *The Situation of the Novel* (1970), suggests that if the novel becomes genuinely responsive to the demands of our modern world, "then many of our critical procedures for discussing it will need revision; perhaps, even, we shall do well to think of another name for it" (Penguin ed., 1972, p. 42).

DATE D

WITHDRAWN

PR9609.6 .S74   c.1
                                100106   000
Studies in the new Australi

3   568 1
GOSHEN COLLEGE GOOD LIBRARY